CARGO CULT

CARGO CULT

Strange Stories of Desire from
Melanesia and Beyond

Lamont Lindstrom

SOUTH SEA BOOKS
CENTER FOR PACIFIC ISLANDS STUDIES
SCHOOL OF HAWAIIAN, ASIAN, AND PACIFIC STUDIES
UNIVERSITY OF HAWAII

UNIVERSITY OF HAWAII PRESS
HONOLULU

98 97 96 95 94 93 5 4 3 2 1

"Cargo Cult" [song] copyright Cargo Cult [band]
(Touch and Go Records)

Library of Congress Cataloging-in-Publication Data
Lindstrom, Lamont, 1953–
    Cargo cult : strange stories of desire from Melanesia
and beyond / Lamont Lindstrom.
       p.   cm. — (South Sea books)
    Includes bibliographical references and index.
    ISBN 0-8248-1526-2. — ISBN 0-8248-1563-7 (pbk.)
    1. Cargo cults. I. Title. II. Series.
GN472.75.L56   1993
306'.014—dc20   93-5399
                                         CIP

Cartography by Manoa Mapworks Inc.
Honolulu, Hawaii

Designed by Paula Newcomb

For Nora Rika

Contents

ILLUSTRATIONS

EDITOR'S NOTE

MONTY LINDSTROM's *Cargo Cult* is the fourth title in the *South Sea Books* series published by the Center for Pacific Islands Studies, University of Hawaii, in association with the University of Hawaii Press. The series is designed for the general reader with interests in the Pacific Islands and their peoples.

Appropriately, beginning with the accounts of the first European explorers in the sixteenth century, the world's largest ocean has spawned a vast literature. The writings of early traders, colonial administrators, and missionaries followed those of the explorers. Novelists, poets, journalists, adventure and travel writers, and various combinations thereof, were usually among the last upon the scene.

The very hugeness of the Pacific, the number and diversity of its seemingly countless islands, and the vast distances that separated them from Europe and America all combined to make the Pacific a very special place in Western thought. The Pacific provided ample room for fantasy, and its literature is rife with myths, misconceptions, and the works of fertile imaginations. One of the earliest and most popular and prevailing of myths, one that is encouraged by the visitor industry, is the notion of Pacific as paradise—the aquatic continent of abundance, leisure, endless summer, and hula girls.

Lindstrom's concern is with the term *cargo cult*—an umbrella that shelters a great diversity of phenomena and has become surrounded by a mythology all its own. The term enjoys a wide currency that cuts across the entire range of Pacific literature, has jumped beyond the boundaries of the region, and has become a magnet collecting writers of every conceivable type.

The term is recent, appearing first in the pages of *Pacific Islands Monthly* in 1945. Although coined by others, it was quickly taken over by anthropologists, who gave it both popularity and scientific respectability. Lindstrom suggests that it has become "anthropology's monster" and, like Frankenstein's creation, is often embarrassing and out of control.

Lindstrom accomplishes what most writers wish to accomplish. He tells a good story—the story of *cargo cult*—analyzes its intellectual history, and entertains. He writes well and with humor, at times joshing his anthropological colleagues. At the same time, he is serious and could not be otherwise. The notion of cargo cult has engaged anthropologists and has played a significant role in the theory of their discipline.

Perhaps as an unintended contribution to Pacific studies, Lindstrom's work inevitably points to the importance of *Pacific Islands Monthly*. Like many other issues both before and since, the early debate about the origin and nature of cargo cults appeared in the pages of that news magazine. Throughout its history, *Pacific Islands Monthly* has chronicled Pacific history, helped shape regional opinion, and in the process, influenced the course of island history. Founded in 1930, it has over six decades of history, and as Lindstrom's work makes clear, there is need for a writing of that history.

Lindstrom is an American anthropologist who has conducted extensive field research on Tanna Island in Vanuatu, and, understandably, he gives special attention to one of the most well known of all the so-called cargo cults, the John Frum movement, which has its roots on that island. Fortuitously, the timing of his work could not have been better. Dr. Joël Bonnemaison's *Isle of Resilience: People and Place in Tanna* will appear as the next volume in the South Sea Books series. Working from the perspective of a French cultural geographer, Bonnemaison provides other dimensions for a consideration of Tanna's intriguing history, and his work both complements and enhances the value of the volume at hand.

ROBERT C. KISTE

PREFACE

THIS BOOK TRACES the genealogy of the term *cargo cult*. This is a term that has enjoyed considerable currency within academic anthropology and has also spread far beyond that discipline. I wrote most of this story during 1990–1991, when I was a Rockefeller Fellow in the Humanities, hosted by the University of Hawaii Center for Pacific Islands Studies. I thought at first that I was writing an overview of contemporary social movements in the South Pacific. But a short retrospective on cargo cults (ten pages at most) ran away with itself and turned itself into a book.

The deeper and deeper I trailed into cargo cult's history—its origins, and its life and times—the stranger its story became. The history of a single academic term may seem an outlandishly trivial pursuit, but the cargo-cult story is neither petty nor insignificant. This story recapitulates, in summary form, three generations of anthropological theory and Pacific Studies. Moreover, the term's genealogy exposes a heritage of powerful motifs and themes that constitute certain fundamental understandings of Pacific Islanders, along with essential truths we hold about ourselves.

I thank the Rockefeller Foundation for the Humanities and Dr Robert Kiste, director of the Center for Pacific Islands Studies, and his staff for their generous support and assistance during my tenure as a fellow at the center. I would also like to thank Cluny Macpherson, Karen Peacock and the staff of the Hawaiian/Pacific Collection of the University of Hawaii Hamilton Library, the University of Tulsa's Research Office, Karen Brison, James Carrier, Cynthia Frazer, Steve Leavitt, Tod Sloan, Peter Stromberg, and Geoffrey White for advice, encouragement, and support during the completion of the book.

This is a genealogy of texts. A thickly cluttered but also far-flung narrative archive recounts various chapters of the cargo-cult story, and I am indebted to many colleagues and friends who helped me hunt down some of the more esoteric but often the most interesting cargo-cult texts. I thank Pauline Aucoin, Ron Brunton, Ken Calvert, H. E. (Lynn) Clark, Michael Cohn, Charles de Burlo, Robert Foster, R. J. Giddings, Jessica Glicken, Renée Heyum, Jim Hobbs, Kingsley Jackson, Martha Kaplan, W. Kelly, P. F. Kluge, David Lempert, Nancy Lutz, Ron May, Hank Nelson, Hildy Richelson, Michael Smith, Annette Weiner, Terence Wesley-Smith, and others who paused, at least briefly, to listen to cargo-cult stories. Finally, I thank Vi Nakamura and Dale Phelps for their assistance with manuscript preparation.

1 WHAT HAPPENED TO CARGO CULTS?

In April 1984, the *Los Angeles Times* published a human interest piece headlined "They Wanted to Buy Lyndon Johnson" (Wallace, Wallechinsky, and Wallace 1984). The Wallaces, that household of trivia virtuosos, told the story of a strange group of Pacific Islanders living on New Hanover, Papua New Guinea, who raised $1,000 "to send to President Johnson to persuade him to come and be their munificent leader." This is cargo cult.

> Cargo cults develop when primitive societies are exposed to the overpowering material wealth of the outside industrialized world. Not knowing where the foreigners' plentiful supplies come from, the natives believe they were sent from the spirit world. They build makeshift piers and airstrips and perform magical rites to summon the well-stocked foreign ships and planes . . . the faithful still expect the Americans to arrive soon, bringing with them lots of chocolate, radios and motorcycles. (1984)

The *Los Angeles Times* juxtaposed two photographs in its report. The lead photograph shows a group of "natives of New Hanover" dancing with feathers, face paint, and drums. (These dancers, in fact, appear to come from the New Guinea highlands, several hundred miles distant across the Bismarck Sea from New Hanover.) Nevertheless, the dancers' eyes seem to stare downwards at a second photograph below, a headshot of President Johnson in suit and tie.

This book explores this strange concatenation. How is it that a term like *cargo cult*—a label for a type of South Pacific social movement that anthropology cultivated and developed (although, as we

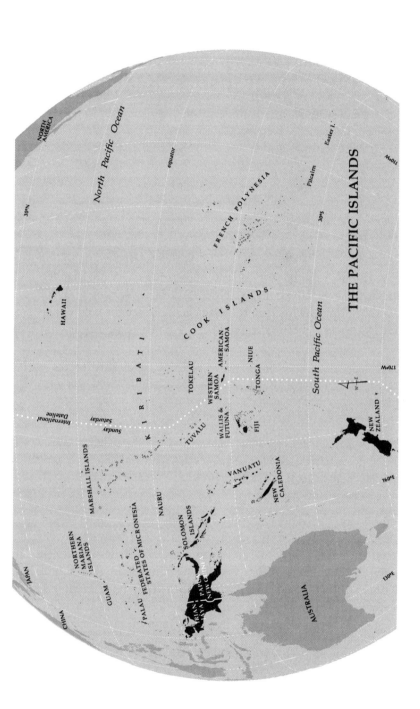

will see, did not invent [chapter 2])—finds itself associated with a president of the United States? One can almost imagine a sort of louche party game. Connect up a scrap of anthropological jargon with the assorted presidents: The "munificent" Johnson and his Great Society, cargo cult. Ethnocentrism and Eisenhower. Polygyny and Kennedy. Slash-and-Burn and Nixon. Joking Relationship and Ford. Extended Family and Carter. Paleolithic and Reagan. Uterine and Bush. Redistribution and Clinton. Here it is, though, already in print in the *Los Angeles Times.* Cargo cult is one of anthropology's most successful conceptual offspring. Like "culture," "worldview," or "ethnicity," its usage has spread beyond our discipline. Other communities nowadays find the term as alluring as anthropologists used to.

But isn't this mere trivia? So what if cargo cult is now another one of the five thousand tidbits of information one needs to know in order to be culturally literate? What does it mean when an idea like cargo cult penetrates the domain of the trivial? An analysis of the appearance of games of Trivial Pursuit in the midst of a politics of American multiculturalism awaits to be undertaken (although the Wallace family, significantly, knows enough to title its trivia columns "Significa"). We might at least begin with the suspicion that what seems the most trivial, what is curiously entertaining, or what goes almost without saying in actuality implicates the most fundamental, primary understandings and assertions of American culture.

Cargo cult is fascinatingly trivial. Who can help being absorbed by stories of Pacific Islanders earnestly scanning the horizons for fleets of great white cargo ships bringing them chocolate, radios, and motorcycles? We can gleefully imagine LBJ, decked out in loincloth and feathers, accepting the delirious adulation of his cultic devotees. Anthropologist Peter Lawrence's account of the Yali movement of northern New Guinea, *Road Belong Cargo* ("The Cargo Road" or "Cargo Way" in Tok Pisin, Papua New Guinea's Pidgin English), comes with a dust jacket promise that " 'cargo cult' in its various forms is one of the most fascinating phenomena to emerge from the meeting of modern industrial and nonliterate societies" (Lawrence 1964, back cover). This book, a classic of the cargo-cult genre, is the only anthropological monograph of any substance to have been translated into Tok Pisin. Philosopher Ian Jarvie, who seized upon accounts of the cargo cult to advocate Karl Popper's philosophy of science, also celebrated cargo cult's allure as "one of the most fascinating problems in social anthropology" (Jarvie 1964, back cover). The introduction to an early bibliography of cargo cults and other nativistic movements, contributed by Pacific historian H. E. Maude, likewise proclaimed cargo cult to be "one of the most interesting by-products of culture contact" (1952, i).

This cargo fascination has levied significant costs and repercussions. Within academia, cargo cult has shaped the theory and practice of anthropological, religious, and Pacific studies. There is a very sizable and still ballooning literature on the phenomenon. Cargo cult has infected anthropological theory and Melanesian studies alike (Kelly and Kaplan 1990, 129). Roy Wagner, for example, once employed the term critically to unsettle one of anthropology's primary theoretical assumptions: "Anthropology should perhaps be called a 'culture cult' for the Melanesian 'kago' is very much the interpretive counterpart of our word 'culture' " (1981, 31).

Ethnographically, of all the stories that anthropologists have spun about the island peoples of Melanesia, tales of cargo cult are among the most captivating. A cluster of images of Melanesian society— big-men, reciprocity, and especially cargo cult—are powerful constructions that tint our appreciation of the region. Tongan anthropologist Epeli Hau'ofa complained of these fixations: "After decades of anthropological field research in Melanesia we have come up only with pictures of people who fight, compete, trade, pay bride-prices, engage in rituals, invent cargo cults, copulate and sorcerise each other. . . . We know little about their systems of morality, specifically their ideas of the good and the bad, and their philosophies; though we sometimes get around to these, wearing dark glasses, through our fascination with cargo cults" (1975, 286). And, true enough, thanks in large part to such anthropological fascination, Melanesia now betrays a cargo-cult culture (see chapter 3): "Cargo cults and Melanesia have virtually become synonymous" (Loeliger and Trompf 1985, xi; Trompf 1991, 188–189).

Islanders themselves have had to shoulder some of anthropology's

Ritual gate on Tanna's cargo road. (Lindstrom)

fascination with cargo cult insofar as cargo has become a powerful and commonplace way of talking about Melanesia. The term now stretches out from introductory anthropology texts, through other academic and journalistic communities, to reach back into the Pacific itself. Notions of cargo cults color the ways in which we understand contemporary religious and political events in Melanesia. But such notions also dispose Islanders' own perceptions and presentations of themselves (see chapter 5). Nowadays, for example, many Melanesian political movements must take care to deny explicitly that they are any sort of cargo cult. For example, the organization on New Hanover that purportedly still awaits the coming of Lyndon B. Johnson with chocolate and motorcycles prudently designates itself today as the Tutukuval Isukal Association. On the other hand, Islanders may also occasionally take pride in their famous and authentic cargo heritage. Lawrence's *Road Belong*

Cargo, for example, is today a sacred text in parts of New Guinea, having come to serve as the Old Testament of the Yali movement (Trompf 1984, 35).

And beyond anthropologists and Islanders, others have been enchanted by cargo as well. The fascinating lights of cargo cult have flared so splendidly that the term has burned its way into the universe of trivia. Even in its early days, cargo cult pulled philosophers, historians, and librarians into its flames. Nowadays it fascinates readers of the *Los Angeles Times,* and its audience still continues to expand (see chapter 6).

But what is the source of such bewitchment? I trace in this book a history, or genealogy, of the term, seeking the logic behind its success. I suggest, in the end, that cargo cult has won through and qualified as genuine trivia in popular culture because it makes sense and carries emotional weight, given certain ways we have of understanding desire itself (chapter 6). This weight is what accords the term its essential charge so that its usage affects both the native other (those Islanders from New Hanover) and also ourselves (the munificent President Johnson). The resonance of cargo cult with certain truths about our desire has propelled the term beyond anthropology into all sorts of academic and popular discourses. If, on New Hanover, "the faithful still expect the Americans to arrive soon," in Los Angeles those Americans still expect people—including themselves—to be expectant.

Who Are the Cargo Cultists?

The *road belong cargo* leads to strange ends. It terminates in an uneasy suspicion that Melanesians are not the only cargoists about. Why has the cargo-cult story proved so popular? Why is the literature on cults so huge? Why did Ian Jarvie choose the cargo cult as his entry into a philosophy of social science? (Why not select theories of kinship or politics instead?) Why do newspapers and magazines return again and again to the cargo cult as a stock curiosity and trivial wonder?

Beyond the expression's catchy alliterative symmetry, an obvious answer is that the term and the concept together have served European colonial interests. This is a conspiratorial theory of the cargo cult. European colonialists once upon a time conjured up and talked about cargo cult as a device by which both to excuse and to justify their domination of the colonized. The conspiracy thesis draws upon Edward Said's (1978) notion of "Orientalism." The cargo cult does not exist per se; rather it appears in the dirty mirror of the European self—a cultic other as a reflection of the imperial self. The standard motifs of cargo-cult writing, too, can be read as European bad conscience. Stock reports that cultists claim that Europeans have highjacked ancestral cargo, for example (see chapter 2), reflect a repressed guilty European understanding of real colonial economic inequalities.

Pem Buck, in a reading of "cargo-cult discourse" that draws on Mondher Kilani's (1983) earlier critique, argued that

> cargo-cult discourse is a component of the discussion of Papua New Guineans by their administrators, missionaries, and anthropologists, and was carried on against the backdrop of the organization of labor for capitalist production. It cannot, then, be seen as a contextless production of social scientific truth. . . . Cargo-cult discourse, like Said's Orientalism, has provided a set of filters which force the user to see a wide variety of phenomena in an identical light. Europeans have imagined cargo elements where they do not exist, exaggerated them where they do, and categorized all Papua New Guinean activity in terms of cargo, thus creating "cargo cults" as an object of analysis. (1989, 158; see Kilani 1983, 10, 14; Lattas 1992)

Prewar resistance to colonial domination was at one time labeled *madness* (chapter 2). This image justified administrative "disciplinary surveillance and the invasion of privacy and social organization" (Buck 1989, 164). In the postwar era, on the other hand, when colonial administrations in Melanesia had to account for themselves in terms of economic development, talk of the cargo cult replaced earlier themes of native lunacy: "Cargo-cult mythology among Europeans helped to mediate and explain their own role in the failure of development. It laid the blame on the anomic, self-defeating, irrational activities of cultists, which were said to prevent a hard-working, entrepreneurial approach to development. . . . Papua New Guineans, through foolishness, psychological problems, or misunderstanding of the new economic system, have created their own underdevelopment" (Buck 1989, 163–164; see also Kilani 1983, 174; Rimaldi 1971, 275).

The notoriety of cargo cults was certainly magnified insofar as a cultic discourse served to excuse colonial domination. Administrators and anthropologists alike have applied the term promiscuously, as Kilani pointed out: "The label cargo cult thus continues to be favored by government for designating social movements that escape its control" (1983, 30, my translation). But, even if one takes the blackest view of anthropologists—subalterns of the world system whose ideological constructs mask political and economic relations of dependency—it seems to me that a conspiratorial theory can only partly explain why cargo cult has become at once so fashionable and so trivial.

An initial countering observation is that talk of cargo cult continues today, even though most of the Melanesian colonies are now independent. The Papua New Guinea newspaper *Post-Courier* in Port Moresby, for example, regularly serves up cargo cults to its readers. Buck pointed out, however, that the expression retains its political functions for local elites in the new Pacific states, since "the pejorative use of the term 'cargo cult' explains to them their own privileged position vis-a-vis . . . the independent Papua New Guinea government, since cargo-cult discourse demonstrates that cargo-cult irrationality is the source of other Papua New Guineans' poverty" (1989, 168).

The conspiracist, however, is perhaps harder pressed to explain cargo cult's popularity in circles far distant from postcolonial Melanesia. As we will see, the label turns up in a variety of high and low discourses; and these cargo stories indict not just the Melanesian native but an astonishing roll-call of people worldwide for being cargo cultists: feckless Australians, incredulous Californian scientists, reckless businessmen, poor blacks, careless consumers, Hollywood-crazed Japanese businessmen, hungry Eastern Europeans, and more.

Kilani alluded to a deeper cultural rationale that may feed our fascination with cargo cults:

> In the understanding of cargo cults, which excels in presenting these as a particular example of a relation between means (irrational) and ends (more or less rational) and in pretending that the search for material goods constitutes the basic interest in "cargo," this manner of reasoning imposes on specifically Melanesian cultural significations the central myth of capitalist culture—that of commodity fetishism as the universal mode of thought and action. (1983, 87, my translation)

Could it be, then, that we are entranced by cargo cults because we are, at heart, commodity fetishists? That cargo cults are so titillating and seductive because we imagine the natives to be exercised by our own secret desires? We want cargo but we know also, at heart, that the moral connections that dominant capitalist rhetoric narrates between hard work and material success are fraudulent and ultimately illusory. Our commodities are equally supernaturally alienated as Melanesian cargo. Our selves are as calibrated in terms of wealth as we imagine the Melanesian other to be. Are we guilty of this awareness, an awareness that denies our dominant Western culture's tissues of truth? Do we take pleasure in tales of cargo cults that crave sudden luxury and abundance without labor and struggle, just as we take a sort of illicit pleasure in bingo, lotteries, television game shows, counterfeit giveaways, birthday presents, rights of inheritance, grocery coupons, sweepstakes, and instant credit (see Trompf 1990, 60–64)?

The desiring commodity fetishist, here, is overdrawn—but no more so than the conspiratorial neocolonialist. Both desire and interest must lie behind the triumphant advance and circulation of the cargo cult within anthropology and beyond. We enjoy contemplating and discoursing upon cargo cults not merely because such a category serves a global political structure of interest, but also because it fulfills a cultural organization of desire. The cargo story is one of endless yearning. This, at heart, is a commonplace story of love (see chapter 6). We relish talking about cargo cults because we can imagine ourselves as cargo cultists. Besides, the fact that *we* are the real cargo cultists is no longer latent or suppressed. Nowadays, so we say, we find that the cargo cult more and more is erupting in the West.

Road Construction Belong Cargo

The history of science undertakes to explicate the origins and growth of scientific theory and method. It would, no doubt, be ludicrous and grandiose for me to claim to be doing the same. This book is a study of a single descriptive term and of its reverberations within anthropology and beyond. My interests in cargo cult are closer to a more recent theoretical endeavor that attempts to unpack some of the tacit assumptions, and the political consequences, built into the language—the academic discourse—of anthropology, and of the other humanistic and scientific disciplines. Under the influence of poststructuralist theory and literary deconstructionism, anthropologists have been motivated to listen more critically to the language we use to describe the world. This includes paying attention to the key metaphors of our discourse (eg, "culture," "worldview," "evolution," and the like), to the genre demands of an ethnographic style of writing, and to the plots or story lines that anthropological texts must assume (Clifford and Marcus 1986; Geertz 1988).

Donna Haraway, for example, describing the variety of ways in which Western science has envisioned primate species, argued: "Scientific practice may be considered a kind of story-telling practice—a rule-governed, constrained, historically changing craft of narrating the history of nature. Scientific practice and scientific theories produce and are embedded in particular kinds of stories" (1989, 4). The problem is to deconstruct—to take a close look at these stories to see how they shape our understandings of the world. In a recent burst of theoretical endocannibalism, anthropology has witnessed deconstructions not only of Haraway's primates but also of other of its constituting metaphors, including the primitive (Torgovnick 1990) and primitive society (Kuper 1988). This progressive digestion of the discipline's theoretical apparatuses and descriptive language is gravitating downwards into middle-range theory and concept. I think it similarly instructive to listen hard to stories of the cargo cult.

I believe, though, that we must do more than simply deconstruct cargo cult into its component elements and generic stipulations. It is also important to know something about a concept's history, about the social conditions in which it emerged, and about the academic and personal interests and desires that it serves. Michel Foucault suggested this sort of "genealogical" analysis, that asks "how series of discourse are formed, through, in spite of, or with the aid of . . . systems of constraint: what were the specific norms for each, and what were their conditions of appearance, growth, and variation" (1972, 232). Even if we shrewdly deconstruct our descriptive language to show that a troublesome term or concept is built of awkwardly fitting pieces, unsound, and even dangerous, we still do not know how that concept surfaced in our discourse, nor do we understand the desires and interests that such a term serves. These desires may keep a term alive and current in everyday discourse, despite the fact that we have efficiently deconstructed it to demonstrate its failings. Even though *cargo cult* may be surgically autopsied, the corpse still lives on.

Nancy McDowell, for example, adeptly revealed cargo cult's failings as a descriptive label. She argued that "cargo cults do not exist, or at least their symptoms vanish when we start to doubt that we can arbitrarily extract a few features from context and label them as an institution" (1988, 121). Her model, here, is Claude Lévi-Strauss's celebrated disintegration of the anthropological category "totemism." Lévi-Strauss argued that anthropology's common sense notions of totemism were wrong. Totemism once seemed solid and real, like cargo cult, but it did so only because we arbitrarily chose to recognize some features of social reality while ignoring others. If we moved to assume a different analytic perspective, totemism disappeared. And cargo cult evaporates, too, if looked at with different eyes. John Kelly and Martha Kaplan seconded McDowell's erasure of the descriptive category: "The cargo cult was an image of ritual against history, a response from the culture of the 'other' to the historical practice of the colonizers; but anthropologists now seek vehicles for study of the culture and history of both colonizers and colonized. As the image of the cargo cult goes the way of the totem, it is being replaced by historically specific studies of ritual as a powerful vehicle of change in structure and history" (1990, 136).

We need to be careful, though, of being unduly hopeful for cargo cult's demise. Let's remind ourselves what happened to the totem. Lévi-Strauss got rid of it by universalizing the term. Totemism is nothing but the general properties of the human brain at work, busy categorizing and creating dualistic structures. Lévi-Strauss promised to dispose of the totem, but instead he managed only to make us all totemistic. He merely swept totem under the subconscious carpet. I argue in chapter 3 that deconstruction of cargo cult has the same repercussions. The cargo cult per se may disappear, but in its place arises the specter of a generalized Melanesian cargo-cult culture. And cargo cult, of course, does not actually disappear. Although anthropologists may now be theoretically more circumspect and less promiscuous in its use, the term merely moves over into other, more popular arenas of discourse (see chapters 5 and 6).

We need to understand why cargo cult is ethnographically wrong, but also why it is right. Why have we invested so much in the term? Why, despite its scholarly and political flaws, does it still appeal? To follow the genealogy of cargo, we need to scout through the archive of cargo-cult stories. This book is concerned, therefore, with texts—with narratives both scientific and fictional about the cargo cult. I do not, and cannot, say anything about the reality of Melanesia. Cargo cult—or something like this under another name—may actually exist on Melanesian islands. Or it may not. People may really be standing on the mountaintops searching the skies for cargo planes. Lyndon Johnson's $1,000 may still be waiting for him in the Bank of Papua New Guinea. Or perhaps it is not. My concern here is solely with the stories we tell about cargo cult, not with their historical and ethnographic accuracy.

Garry Trompf asked the question "What happened to cargo cults?" (1984). He was speaking of the real thing, and his answer was that they still occur in Melanesia, although with less frequency than before. Many long-lived cults, such as the John Frum movement of Tanna, Vanuatu (see chapter 4), have transformed themselves into political parties active within the national arena, or have institutionalized themselves into independent churches. Other groups have withdrawn into themselves, cultivating only local and isolationist interests, although, Trompf noted, the possibility of cargo "restimulation" is a recurrent one (1984, 31).

I, too, ask "What happened to cargo cults?" but my concern is with discourse rather than with ethnographic reality. We might label this discourse "cargoism." Actually, cargoist writers have already invented the term "cargoism," applying it to the sort of mentality that they suspect lies behind island preoccupations with cargo cult. I borrow the term to refer to the distinctive genre, or style, of writing that manifests itself within the bounteous archive of cargo-cult texts, also applying it to the sort of mentality that I suspect lies behind our own preoccupations with cargo cult. The allure of cargo cult radiates not just from Melanesia's ethnographic reality and the facts of cargo cults themselves, but also from the stylistics of the discourse that we have produced around them. Narratives about cargo, like the *Los Angeles Times'* reportage, evoke again and again the same plot with the same leitmotifs. Cargoism exists as a now solid genre of writing for describing Melanesian society.

To pursue the genealogy of cargoism, I dip in and out of a gushing stream of cargoist texts that begins in 1945. In chapter 4, I compare the abundant tales of one well-known cargo cult—Tanna's John Frum movement—narrated by an assortment of different writers. My data are these cargo stories, and I cite, quote, and paraphrase extensively throughout this book. In so doing, I unavoidably distort or fail to take into account the fullness of what a particular cargo-cult writer said, or I cite an earlier work rather than some subsequent text in which an author has revised a cargoist account. I would apologize for this but for the fact that, as Foucault noted, authors do not really exist: "the author is not an indefinite source of significations which fill a work; the author does not precede the works, he is a certain functional principle by which in our culture, one limits, excludes, and chooses" (1979, 159). Cargoism exists no matter who is hard at work producing its texts. If some of my selec-tions from the cargo archive occasionally seem to mock, I intend no disrespect. Since no one in particular authors cargoism, no one in particular is to blame. Instead, cargoism lives through us all; our fascination is what turns cargo into a story. We relish the term's triviality. And, as its heirs, let's get to the bottom of cargo cult's genealogy. How did it all begin?

2 The Birth of Cargo Cult

Cargo cult has enjoyed a durable notoriety within anthropology and beyond. One might posit several explanations for why the term achieved a sudden popularity, supplanting several alternative labels for Melanesian social movements. Perhaps not the least of these is the term's alliterative symmetry and its whimsy. Something deeper than terminological fancy, though, sustains cargo cult's appeal and, to uncover this, we must investigate the term's genealogy. Where did cargo cult come from? And why has it spread?

Mr Bird Flares Up

As an analytic category within social science, cargo cult is young. In effect, the term is a relic of the war in the Pacific. It spun out from the global economic and political disjunctions that the war brought about. The first time cargo cult occurred in print to label Melanesian social movements was in a short article that appeared in the November 1945 issue of the colonial news magazine *Pacific Islands Monthly (PIM)*. This article, contributed by Norris Mervyn Bird, was entitled "Is There Danger of a Post-war Flare-up Among New Guinea Natives?" Mr Bird, whom *PIM* describes as "an old Territories resident," lived before the war in Rabaul (H. E. Clark, pers comm, 1991). Here, at the moment of cargo cult's birth in print, we find ourselves stuck deep into a discourse of dangerous flare-ups, of natives and planters, and of crumbling colonialist certainties.

Mr Bird was worried:

> Stemming directly from religious teaching of equality, and its resulting sense of injustice, is what is generally known as "Vailala Madness," or "Cargo Cult." Various explanations of the "Madness"

15

have been advanced, but the late F. E. Williams, anthropologist to the Papuan Government, after extensive study, gave as his conclusion that the main cause was "ill-digested" religious teaching. This "Madness" is not confined to any one area, but is found among tribes whose dialects and customs differ widely. In all cases the "Madness" takes the same form: A native, infected with the disorder, states that he has been visited by a relative long dead, who stated that a great number of ships loaded with "cargo" had been sent by the ancestor of the native for the benefit of the natives of a particular village or area. But the white man, being very cunning, knows how to intercept these ships and takes the "cargo" for his own use. . . . We have seen grave harm to the native population arising from the "Vailala Madness," where livestock has been destroyed, and gardens neglected in the expectation of the magic cargo arriving. The natives infected by the "Madness" sank into indolence and apathy regarding common hygiene, with dire effect on the health of the community. How much more dangerous, then, will the "Madness" be when a military aspect is superimposed on the religious? Imagine the position, with some thousands of natives armed and trained in the use of modern weapons. . . . It is folly to say: "It cannot happen here, to us." It CAN, and may, happen here, to us. It is ridiculous to think that the discipline instilled with the military training would make such an uprising impossible. . . . Those of us who witnessed the "strike" in Rabaul in 1928 do not wish to see another such—certainly not with thousands of natives armed with modern weapons. What would the result be if the "Vailala Madness" took hold of the regiments of black soldiers now being trained in New Guinea? By his very nature the New Guinea native is peculiarly susceptible to these "cults." . . .The very fact that he is being trained as a soldier, and is expected to fight alongside the white man, and the fact that he is accepted as an equal in barracks by the whites, but is not accepted as equal by society in general, will aggravate the condition and render him still more susceptible to these cults. . . . His discipline and training will be discarded at a moment's notice and he will emerge, as he is, a primitive savage with all a primitive savage's instincts. The New Guinea native is not unreliable. He is worse—he is unpredictable. The result of an organized uprising of these armed savages could be the massacre of Europeans in these islands, together with a host of natives. Is New Guinea to be for ever the "happy hunting-ground" of politicians who wish to try out some crack-brained scheme, some murderously dangerous "experiment"? . . .The New Guinea citizen, having watched the growth of the "Vailala Madness," while being power-less to prevent it, now stands gagged and bound by the Canberra politician and watches the growth of a new "Madness" that may be destined to wipe out his home, his wife, his children, and himself. (Bird 1945, 69–70)

Mr Bird's warning targets both missionaries and colonial admin-istrators. The birth of the term cargo cult, here, is strategic. It emerges in the midst of an ongoing, tricornered struggle among expatriate planters and businessmen, Christian missionaries, and colonial administrators, many of whom had the habit of cloaking their interests behind a rhetoric of doing what's best for the native. Mr Bird's honest racism no doubt reflected the disturbed times. The Pacific War unsettled the expatriate community in Melanesia. It interrupted for several years its internal dissensions and competition to control Islanders and secure access to their labor, lands, and hearts. Planters, administrators, and missionaries had all speedily retreated in the face of the Japanese advance into New Guinea. The Japanese rounded up most of the stragglers. Mr Bird had joined a hastily organized defense force, the New Guinea Volunteer Rifles, along with other Australian planters, traders, miners, and officials. During 1942 and 1943, he and the rest of the Volunteer Rifles retreated from positions in Salamaua and Wau as the Japanese moved into Morobe District (Bird 1947).

In 1942, administration of what remained of Australia's two Melanesian colonies, Papua and New Guinea, passed into the hands of the Australian military. The military administration (ANGAU: Australian New Guinea Administrative Unit) employed Islanders principally to serve its own needs for labor corps and native infantry recruits. The demands of remnant expatriates for plantation hands, of missionaries for congregations, and of the superseded colonial administration for native subjects all became secondary. Sometime during 1943–1944, Norris Bird became a warrant officer in ANGAU, serving as the patrol officer of the North Markham district near Lae. As the Japanese withdrew westward, he and other officers traveled from village to village seeking stragglers. Neville Robinson published a translation of Bird's original Tok Pisin address to villagers which began:

> All listen to this. In the good times all boys could make contracts with their own Masters. They received blankets, shirts, tinned meat, rice, biscuits—a good ration—and at the end of their contract received their money and could go home. In those good times there were schools and there were things in plenty. . . . The Kiap [colonial officer] has come so if there are any Japanese in your land let me know and soldiers will come and kill them. When there are no more Japs in your place the soldiers will go looking for the Japs in other places. It won't be long now. (Robinson 1981, 203)

Three months after the August 1945 surrender of the Japanese, Mr Bird rejoined the old battle for control of the native in the pages of *Pacific Islands Monthly*. With the withdrawal of ANGAU and the restoration of a civilian administration in October, the colony and its natives once again were up for grabs. But the postwar world could be dangerous. Things had changed. *Pacific Islands Monthly*'s editors, introducing Mr Bird's piece, complained: "In the years before the Jap invasion, the primitive natives of New Guinea were making a slow and painful progress towards higher standards of life. But it was a difficult process beset by problems. . . . War conditions have accentuated these problems a hundredfold. Natives now, after contact with tens of thousands of careless white soldiers, are more difficult to handle than ever before" (Bird 1945, 69).

Mr Bird's initial target was the missionaries. These do-gooders had unwisely filled Islanders' heads with visions of Christian equality, and with what result? The unpredictable savages may go crazed, "infected with the disorder" called "Vailala Madness" or "Cargo Cult." *Madness,* as we will see, was the most common prewar label for Melanesian social movements, until it was superseded by cargo cult in 1945.

Mr Bird's accusation of missionary bumbling was not new. Missionaries had encountered such charges before the war as well. In

1935, for example, *Pacific Islands Monthly* published a piece entitled "A Plea for Better Regulation of Mission Activities in New Guinea" by Gordon Thomas. In this, Thomas explicitly related missionization to "unrest or open violence among the native people": "Reports have repeatedly been received of 'fanaticism' amongst natives. Aitape, Morobe, Buka and Namatanai districts have all suffered from waves of mistaken enthusiasm; and in each one there has been a connecting link with religious teachings" (1935, 25–26). Islanders misunderstand both the subtleties of Biblical metaphor and of mission sectarian politics. As a consequence, they expected the millennium to come too soon.

The missionaries quickly fought back in the pages of succeeding issues of *Pacific Islands Monthly*. They had encountered Mr Bird's type before. In January 1946, Anglican missionary S. R. M. Gill denied that either the missionaries or military servicemen were responsible for sparking cargo cults. He countered with the suggestion that Islanders who were most susceptible to cults were those who had been dragooned into military or plantation labor service, rather than those who volunteered to join the Papua and New Guinea native infantry brigades.

> It seems that they have so got into the habit of working only at the Administrator's command, that a kind of slave mentality has been developed—the mentality which only reacts to coercion. In this respect, labour boys, and occasionally impressed village boys, differ greatly from [the native Police and members of the Papuan Infantry Brigade]: perhaps it is because these latter have been under white leaders, and with white comrades in arms, who shared with them, in actual warfare, all that came in the way of hardship, toil, and suffering. (Gill 1946, 52)

Five months later, American Lutheran missionary R. Inselmann more bluntly charged the planter community with responsiblity for cargo cults. He submitted a letter of protest to the magazine which published it under the headline " 'Cargo Cult' Not Caused by Missions":

The primitive natives of New Guinea, under mission supervision, were making rapid progress toward higher standards of life, until their contact with un-Christian whiteman's culture gave rise to the "cargo cult." . . . Not the missions, but whitemen who could not be trusted by the native, gave rise to the "cargo cult." Here is a specific instance: Before Pearl Harbour, natives of Madang were promised protection in the case of an enemy invasion. However, after the first bombardment of Madang by the Japanese, all of the Civil Administration departed, including the officer who had promised protection! We don't dispute the Administration's right to flee before the enemy, but what did the broken promise do to the natives? . . . Mr. Bird refers to native police who deserted in 1942 and carried out systematic murder and rape of the native population in their path. These natives, according to my best recollection, were contract labourers from the goldfields who were abandoned by the whiteman when he was evacuated. . . . Mr. Bird sees danger in the future from flare-ups among New Guinea natives. I see that same danger if un-Christian whitemen continue their injustice in the jungles of New Guinea. (Inselmann 1946, 44)

The *Pacific Islands Monthly,* which inclined toward the planters' faction in this dispute, was obviously a little embarrassed by printing this missionary abuse. It appended a small defense of the honor of the Australian expatriate and administrative communities to Reverend Inselmann's attack.

Mr Bird returned to the debate a month later in July 1946 in a letter to the editor which was headlined "The 'Cargo-Cult'." In this, he suggested, as an aside, that certain unfortunate wartime incidents of runaway whites were best forgotten, and then brought up his side's ultimate discursive weapon: the sister question.

Mr. Inselmann's reference to the Administration officials "fleeing from the enemy," is a gross injustice to a particularly fine body of men. Such isolated and painful incidents as there were are much better forgotten at this distance. . . . My views on the acceptance of primitive natives into a civilised society are well known, but as Mr. Inselmann has raised the subject, in his letter, I challenge him with one question: Is he prepared to accept, as an equal in civilised society, the New Guinea native in his present state of development?

Would, in fact, Mr. Inselmann be prepared to allow the average New Guinea native to marry his daughter or his sister? I have asked other would-be reformers this question and the stock answers are:

• Having neither sisters nor daughters the question does not apply. But would have no objection to these savages marrying other people's sisters or daughters.

• Would not try to influence the women either way, but would rely on their good taste and innate decency to prevent their making a decision that they may later regret.

• A long and pointless dissertation on the equality of man in the sight of God.

• Ditto on the inadvisability of mixing the races (i.e., the "colour line" with reservations supported by quotations from the Bible). (Bird 1946, 45)

Mr Bird's employment of cargo cult is low usage. The term's origins are, at the least, mean and tactical. In this discourse, cargo cult pairs strategically with the question "but would you let one marry your sister/daughter?" Breakouts of cargo cults and miscegenation are both direly predicted if comfortable structures of colonial inequality are permitted to decay.

The debate continued that November with *Pacific Islands Monthly*'s publication of an English summary of a paper by missionary Georg Höltker. A longer German version of this appeared the same year (1946), in an issue of the European missionary journal *Neue Zeitschrift für Missionswissenschaft/Nouvelle Revue de Science Missionaire*. In the article, Höltker, who had worked in New Guinea, reviewed a variety of Melanesian social movements. The German title of the piece is "Schwarmgeister in Neuguinea wahrend des Letzten Krieges." *Pacific Islands Monthly* translated this as "How the 'Cargo-Cult' Is Born: The Scientific Angle on an Old Subject" —the magazine, here, replacing the German *schwarmgeister* 'ancestor cult', 'ghost enthusiasm' with the newly fashionable (but still armored with quotation marks) "Cargo-Cult." The editors introduced their condensation of Höltker's analysis as being a kind of service to their curious readers: "The semi-religious, native uprisings and disturbances which sometimes occur in Melanesia and go by such names as Cargo-cult, Vailala-madness, etc., have been reported from time to time in the "PIM" and various Islands residents have attempted to explain their cause and origin" (Höltker 1946, 16). Höltker categorized four main types of "religious fanatism," of which "religious madness, Cargo-cult, Chiliasm, prophetism, Native King movement, etc." is the final variety. "These Cargo-cult movements can be compared to that weed called horsetail (equisetum) which is almost impossible to eradicate. It is cursed by all farmers. The roots penetrate the fertile soil to a depth of 15 feet and more" (Höltker 1946, 16). Höltker went on to provide a capsule summary of the cargo cult, the lineaments of which had already become standardized in the emergent cargoist descriptive discourse.

> This movement is usually set going by the ecstatic dream of a native "prophet." He claims that some ancestors appeared to him and commanded him to announce the coming of the "golden age." Everyone is supposed to trust his promises as an essential condition of accumulating wealth without much effort. All natives, he promises, will be like their white masters, dressed in European clothes, living in concrete palaces, etc. . . . All white men, missionaries and government officials will be expelled. Strong sexual tendencies, convulsions, hallucinations and fits are the usual outward signs of being obsessed by the spirit of an ancestor. (Höltker 1946, 69–70)

Höltker took a broad view of the causes of cargo cults, blaming various aspects of the interaction between Islanders and Europeans, and also the "psycho-physiological" character of individual cult prophets. He was suspicious of subversive Japanese interference, and concluded with doubts about any social therapeutics that might innoculate against cult outbreaks. Höltker suspected that it was impossible to prevent deeply rooted cargo cults from sprouting like weeds, or fully eradicate them when they did, but at least they might be kept under control so that they would not spread inordinately.

> A new factor in these movements during the war was the arrival of the Japanese. With their innate shrewdness, the Japs were prepared to use the Movements to their advantage, and Jap newspapers even

before the war were deeply interested in such religious movments [sic]. When the Japanese arrived in New Guinea they identified themselves with the ancestors of the natives. Remarkable is the following address given by a Japanese officer at the occupation of Karkar Island by their forces: "Here I am, you have heard of me often before," he said.

Many times I tried to come to you, but I could not. Now I am here. You see, we Nipponese soldiers do work. We are different from the Europeans. They let you work and do not pay you. Europeans never sit down with you at the same table—we do. Such is European; we are not such. We do work—we ourselves —we do work hard. We can give you a good time soon. You want a motor car, you'll get it; you want a horse, a pinnace, a good house, a plane—you'll get it. But you must work with us; help us down the European. And then we'll help you.

The Japs distributed looted goods lavishly and tried to get the co-operation of the natives in warfare. . . . European settlers in the Pacific should realise the grave problem involved in such new native movements. Although they cannot completely be eradicated, sufficient attention should be given to them to keep them under firm control. (Höltker 1946, 70)

The debate in *Pacific Islands Monthly* moved on through 1947 with the publication of several letters, "Of Pinnaces and Cargo-Cult and Government's Wasted Funds" in April; "Disturbed Natives: Recent Events on Rai Coast of New Guinea" in July; and "Of Missionaries and Cargo Cult" in September. The sniping between the missionary and plantation communities—each accusing the other of causing cults by allowing natives to get out of hand or by setting bad examples—faded away in the 1950s. By this time, immediate postwar worries about collapsing colonial power structures had died down. Notably, a conservative government, in both Canberra and Port Moresby, was back firmly in control.

Pacific Islands Monthly's coverage of cults shifted from a focus on their origins—and who ought to be blamed for such—to a focus on their freakiness. Cults, like natives themselves in their primitive state, were basically unpredictable and inexplicable. Their continuing eruption, in fact, was proof positive that still savage Melanesians required administration, education, and a firm, European guiding hand (see Kilani 1983). Something of this paternalism emerges in the titles that *PIM* bestowed upon its cultic reportage: "Restless Sepik Natives: Adherents of 'Cargo Cult' " (February 1948*b*); "They Still Believe in Cargo Cult" (May 1950); "Cargo Cult? Bainings Natives Killed by New Britain Patrol" (July 1955); "Many 'Still Believe' in Cargo Cult: The Cargo Cult Won't Die Quietly in the Pacific" (February 1958); "Their Cargo-Cult Wasn't Anti-European" (November 1959); and "Americans, Cargo Cult and the Future: Complicated Aftermath of the New Guinea Buka Troubles" (July 1962). The natives, restless and complicated, need administration. The future still looks colonial.

In actuality, in these debates, the missionaries were small-fry. The tart but habitual polemics with the men of the cloth over who should be blamed for cargo cults were a sideshow. Mr Bird had a more formidable opponent that he targeted with the perils of cargo cult. This was the new Australian Labor Party government in Canberra, elected in 1944, that had succeeded a previous wartime political coalition administration in Canberra and looked capable of seriously undermining the niceties of the prewar colonial order. The Labor Party Minister for External Territories, Eddie Ward, had already in 1944 stirred the pot by releasing initial plans for the return of the colonies to civilian administration. This transfer of power finally eventuated in late October 1945, a month before *Pacific Islands Monthly* published Mr Bird's remonstration.

Even before the civilian administration was in place, the Labor Party government on 15 October 1945 canceled all wartime native labor contracts. Thousands of Islanders, many of whom had been impressed for extended terms against their will by the ANGAU military government, poured off plantations, from hotels and stores, and out the back doors of European residences and flooded the roads back home to their villages (Griffin, Nelson, and Firth 1979, 102–103). Mr Bird was also perturbed by the prospect that the New Guinea Infantry Brigade, a wartime defense force manned by trained and armed Islanders, might be maintained in the postwar era. The Australian military had armed both settlers and Islanders, and there may have been past rivalry between Mr Bird's New Guinea Volunteer Rifles and the Papua and New Guinea Infantry Brigades which, toward the war's end, had been combined into the Pacific Islands Regiment. Of the two, Mr Bird clearly preferred armed settlers to armed natives.

The Labor Party government's "crack-brained," "murderously dangerous" political experiments (Bird 1945, 70) made the blood of old territorial hands run cold. In reaction, a discourse of cargo cult appears. Mr Bird conjured up the cargo cult as the awful result of Labor Party politicians unsettling the bowels of the old colonial order. The story runs along not unfamiliar lines: risky Christian ideology . . . reckless Labor government policies . . . restless natives . . . murdered sisters and/or black brothers-in-law . . . danger . . . Madness . . . the cargo cult. The "madness," brilliantly, is located ambiguously in both native and Labor Party politician.

Natives with rifles, and especially unemployed natives left to their own devices back in their villages, may both be infected with the cultic disease. The expatriate's solution is to make natives do an honest day's work on the plantation. Such employment is uplifting, civilizing even, and has the further advantage of keeping young, male Islanders under close surveillance. The connections this narrative draws between unemployment and the cargo cult are apparent in a November 1959 *Pacific Islands Monthly* article reporting on cult activity on Goodenough Island (see also Rimoldi 1971, 120). This island had been closed to labor recruiting for some time, an administrative measure designed to ameliorate a noted local population decline. *Pacific Islands Monthly* concluded from this that "boredom and frustration have evidently fostered the Cargo Cult outbreak on the island." Because Islanders were unable to sign labor contracts, "trouble could follow in the shape of Cargo Cult or subversion" (*PIM* 1959, 137).

The term cargo cult was hatched in print as a discursive grenade in a contest over whether the prewar colonial status quo should be revived or reformed. The months following the surrender of the Japanese can be counted a liminal period throughout much of the globe. Old political and economic structures had been scrubbed away by the war, and the shape that new ones should take was in debate. The Australian Labor government's plans to offer Islanders a new deal, reflecting changes in the Pacific colonial order that the war had engendered also worldwide, sparked in New Guinea a reactionary discourse of the cargo cult.

But where did Mr Bird find so useful and bewitching a term? This is difficult to know exactly. There is a troublesome blank in the written record from early 1942 up to cargo cult's sudden appearance in 1945. The Japanese invasion and the collapse of the civilian administration in New Guinea interrupted Australian colonial publications and reports. Cargo cult presumably emerged and gained currency among the resident colonial and military communities during the war years, as perhaps among Mr Bird's New Guinea Volunteer Rifles. Before this, it may also have circulated, orally, within expatriate conversations of the late 1930s (see Hermann 1992, 67).

Before cargo cult appeared and, ultimately, vanquished its terminological competition, colonial administrators, missionaries, and settlers used a variety of other expressions to describe what they later would call cargo cults. The most popular and widespread of such terms was "Vailala Madness." This label dates back to government anthropologist F. E. Williams' several descriptions of a social movement that the colonials first noted in the neighborhood of Vailala village during the latter part of 1919. Williams' report, *The Vailala Madness and the Destruction of Native Ceremonies in the Gulf Division,* appeared in 1923 as Anthropology Report no. 4, published by the administration of the Territory of Papua.

Williams did not invent the label "Vailala Madness." By the time he arrived in 1922 to study the movement at first hand, a number of official descriptions of Vailala Madness already existed. From these accounts, particularly those by G. H. Murray, the acting resident magistrate at Kerema, Williams borrowed a sketch of the early history of the movement and also the name "Vailala Madness" (see Kohn 1988, 30). This, apparently, had been concocted by Murray or some other member of the administrative community who, no doubt, was also in conversation with London Missionary Society missionaries living in the area.

Williams did pause, briefly, to contemplate the utility of his adopted label. He takes note of several Motu, Pidgin English, and local language alternatives, including:

1 The Gulf *Kavakava* (ie, The Gulf Madness)
2 The Orokolo *Kavakava*
3 Head-he-go-round ("The usual Pidgin-English expression")
4 *Kwarana giroa* and *kwarana dika* (the Motuan equivalents)
5 *Haro heraripi* ("an Elema expression, meaning literally 'Head-he-go-round' ")
6 *Iki haveve* (" 'Belly-don't-know'; this is the usual name throughout all the coastal villages in the Gulf Division")
7 *Abo abo* ("giddy or crazy"). (Williams 1923, 2–3)

In the end, though, rather than one of these indigenous possibilities, Williams chose to retain the colonial label that was already part of the official record and certainly was a more snappy expression: "The name Vailala Madness seems the most distinctive and suitable" (Williams 1923, 2).

Vailala Madness filled a colonialist semantic gap. Through the 1920s and 1930s, as Australian authority broadened and officials detected more such events here and there around Papua and New Guinea, the label Vailala Madness was overgeneralized and applied freely to social movements located miles away from the Gulf Division. Williams, thus, served successfully as midwife of an expression that gained a certain amount of currency within the expatriate community, and also within early twentieth century anthropological discourse. He was less lucky, parenthetically, with another term that he himself invented to describe dancing individuals who went into trance during Vailala Madness events. Playing off the Madness motif, Williams devised the word "automaniac" to describe Islanders in trance states. No one else, however, adopted his neologism (see Schwimmer 1977, 38).

By 1945, Vailala Madness' currency was such that Mr Bird used it synonymously to frame his introduction of the term cargo cult: "Stemming directly from religious teaching of equality, and its resulting sense of injustice, is what is generally known as 'Vailala

Madness' or 'Cargo Cult' " (Bird 1945, 69). But there were a number of other alternative phrases and labels that missionaries, colonial officers, and the like were using to describe Melanesian social movements. As noted, *schwarmgeister* had some currency within the German mission community in New Guinea. Other labels appear in the Australian colonial administration's annual reports that occasionally took note of social movements in their yearly summaries of the high points of native affairs and district administration.

For example, the Territory of New Guinea's annual report for 1933/34 labels a case from Kieta, Bougainville, as "outbreaks of a quasi-religious nature," "a disturbance," "the trouble," a "movement," and "local agitation" (Territory of New Guinea 1935, 22). The 1934/35 report uses the expressions "native 'religious' outbreaks," "phenomenon," and "the movement" (Territory of New Guinea 1936, 19–21). The 1935/36 report cites "native religious outbreaks," "outbreaks of a quasi-religious nature," and "serious manifestations" (Territory of New Guinea 1937, 21–23). And the 1937/38 report speaks of "an incident," "the movement," and "quasi-religious meetings" (Territory of New Guinea 1939, 30). On the south side of the island, the Territory of Papua's annual report for 1940/41 describes a "native disturbance" in Mekeo District as a "stupid business" (Territory of Papua 1942, 21).

The word cargo appears in a number of these accounts, although the term cargo cult itself does not yet exist in the discourse. For example, the 1937/38 annual report's description of an "incident" in the Namatanai subdistrict of New Ireland notes that one "disciple" of the cult's leader, an Islander "who, it is said, is something of a religious maniac," said that he had been visited by spirits and "saw and heard many things and one of them was that a shipment of cargo for distribution among those who believed in the teachings of the first-mentioned native had already left Rome and would be delivered in villages by the ancestral dead" (Territory of New Guinea 1939, 30). Similarly, the description of the "native religious outbreak" on Buka records the prophecies of Sanop who "announced that the ship should definitely arrive on Good Friday, but that only people who were without food and pigs would share in the cargoes" (Territory of New Guinea 1937, 29).

The word cargo also occurs in a bastardized Pidgin phrase in missionary Emil Hanneman's 1945 MA thesis written in the University of Chicago's Department of Anthropology: "All the natives desired was the *ast* [*sic*, ie, *as*] *blong kargo* [ie, *kago*] or the secret of the white people's commodities" (Hanneman 1945, 72). Hanneman, however, used the term "quasi-religious movement" which, along with Vailala Madness, was the dominant descriptive label for cult events within the colonial community of the day. The Catholic missionary Patrick O'Reilly, who described movements of the early 1930s on Buka Island, likewise did not use cargo cult, although both these words appear together in one of his sentences: "The intensive cult of the dead ought further to hasten the arrival of these happy steamers filled with cargo" (1937, 147, my translation). Although O'Reilly declared that cargo was the "fundamental leit-motiv" (1937, 155) of the movements, he labeled them variously as "collective movements" (144) and "agitations" (146), and he published his account under the title "Sorcery in the Solomon Islands" (see also O'Reilly and Sedes 1949, 193–200).

Further evidence that cargo cult was not yet recognized as a label in the prewar period comes from *Pacific Islands Monthly*. A piece published in the November 1941 issue about the events in Mekeo is entitled " 'Mekeo Madness': Queer Religious Hysteria in Papua" (*PIM* 1941*b*, 50). This label clearly plays off *Vailala Madness*. In addition to "Mekeo Madness" and "Queer Religious Hysteria," the article also describes the events as an "epidemic of craziness," a "frenzy," a "movement," and speaks of "religious enthusiasts" who "spread lying reports." Another report on Mekeo, several months earlier in the March issue, was headlined "Crazy Natives: Strange Outbreak in Gulf Division of Papua" (*PIM* 1941*a*, 18). To label the event, the text of the article also makes use of "religious hysteria," "outbreak," and "hysterical frenzy." It concludes with an editorial observation, subtitled "Vailala Madness," that "this kind of religious frenzy has been noted on other occasions among natives of the Gulf division; it is usually called 'Vailala Madness'. Quite a little thing—an unusual phenomenon, a girl's dream, an old man's senile imagining—will start a kind of hysteria which will overwhelm a whole community and drive it to the wildest excesses" (*PIM* 1941*a*, 18).

The patrol reports of itinerating ANGAU officers active during the war also do not contain the term cargo cult (see Hermann 1992, 71 fn 20). A 1943 ANGAU account of Islanders in the Ramo district who constructed radio stations out of bamboo, and marched about and drilled with wooden rifles, calls these events a "movement." A 1944 report describes an "outbreak" near the Markham River as a "preternatural cult." By 1947, however, the term cargo cult had made its way into civil administrative patrol reports. Officer D. S. Grove began his account of a 1947 patrol near Kainantu in the New Guinea highlands by noting that "Reports reached the patrol that villagers of Tirai had adopted the Cargo Cult" (reprinted in Berndt 1952/53, 226–234; see also Ruhen 1963, 205–208).

It is unlikely that cargo cult sprang autogenously into existence in November 1945 at the top of Mr Bird's opinion piece. Bird himself suggested that the term was "generally known" (1945, 69). Whatever cargo cult's exact age and currency within oral colonial discourse may have been, the time between its sudden appearance in print and its widespread adoption was remarkably short. Before 1945, the term is nowhere in print. After 1945, it very quickly advances into a variety of colonial, popular, and academic communities. Moreover, a discursive playfulness with the expression soon begins. By February 1948, the *Pacific Islands Monthly* had combined Vailala Madness and cargo cult to coin the noun "cargomania" (*PIM* 1948*b*, 62).

Additional evidence for the emergence of cargo cult in late 1945 consists of the variations and instabilities in the manner in which the term gets written and used during the latter part of the 1940s. These variations only die down in the 1950s, when the form cargo cult is more-or-less standardized. At the moment of the expression's initial use, it appears in quotation marks (Bird 1945, 69)—and these marks have continued to disappear and reappear around the term. *Pacific Islands Monthly* first omits quotation marks in September 1947. They come back in February 1948 but then are gone again in May 1950. By the late 1950s and 1960s, *Pacific Islands Monthly* generally omits the quotation marks. Peter Worsley's influential overview of 1957, however, puts marks around *Cargo,* but not around *Cult.* In the main, in the 1960s and 1970s, the quotation marks disappear (eg, see Burridge 1960; Cochrane 1970; Lawrence 1964; Steinbauer 1979; Wilson 1973). As we will see, though, quotation marks make a comeback in the 1980s. There is also initial instability of capitalization. The term appears variously as Cargo Cult, Cargo cult, and cargo cult. There is parallel variation in the appearance of a hyphen between cargo and cult. Bird's initial comment does not include one, but his letter published in the July 1946 issue of *Pacific Islands Monthly* does (Bird 1946, 45). Sometimes terminological variation occurs in the same article, with quotation marks, hyphens, and capitalization coming and going from line to line (eg, see *PIM* 1950, 85; *PIM* 1951).

The most interesting instability of early usage involves pluralization. Was it the cargo cult, or cargo cults? This vacillation is clearly tied to European representations of "the native"—or was it "the natives"? These were contradictory moods in the European purview of Islanders. On the one hand, natives were diverse, although this plurality often operated at the level of "tribes" (or other equivalent groupings, such as "hordes," "bands," "islands"), rather than serving to distinguish among individuals. Some native tribes, for example, were known to make better workers than others. Some were treacherous while others were peaceable. The women of some made more presentable mistresses. Some groups made better native catechists or businessmen, and so on.

On the other hand, the native was singular insofar as all natives, in the end, were alike in their essentials; all found themselves with the same lack of civilization, at the same lowly level of social evolution; all fell into the same racial category vis-à-vis the likewise singular "whiteman"; and all, it seemed, were susceptible to the cargo cult. Because all natives were the same, all cargo cults were the same—and vice versa.

Mr Bird's original singular form, "The Cargo Cult," also reflected the earlier, equally singular "Vailala Madness." Like Vailala Madness, the cargo cult is a sort of infectious disease that strikes various native groups here and there about the land, but then can spread pandemically from the point of infection if not kept under "firm control" (Höltker 1946, 70). This disorder is marked by a number of fixed and clear-cut symptoms that typify the disease, including prophets, expectations of cargo and world reversal, strange ritual behavior, and bizarre physiological states. In this representative mood, the singular cargo cult is, in its essentials, the same everywhere in Melanesia.

The singular form of the expression dominated cargoist discourse in the 1950s. Anthropologist Cyril Belshaw, for example, offered an "analysis of cargo cult" in a 1951 note he published in the colonial journal *South Pacific*, although this was titled "Cargo Cults" (1951a, 167). Maahs used the singular in his 1956 PhD dissertation, "A Sociological Interpretation of the Cargo Cult," filed with the University of Pittsburgh. The *Pacific Islands Monthly* continued its use of the singular form into the 1960s (eg, *PIM* 1962, 27).

However, the alternative reading of Islanders (or of island groups) as diverse and variable soon motivated a pluralization of the term. Morphologically, also, cargo cults is an easier move than Vailala Madnesses. It appears that anthropologists were primarily responsible for the pluralization of the term—not surprisingly so, in that native variation and diversity is anthropology's bread and butter. The first signs of cargo cults in the plural appear, in 1947, at the University of Sydney in D'Arcy Ryan's BA honors thesis, "The Influence of the Missions on Native Culture in Melanesia." In this, Ryan wrote: "When the native [note the singularity] discovered, as he was bound to eventually, that this new knowledge did not improve his position as spectacularly as he had hoped, he experienced a certain disillusionment with mission-training in general. He began to experiment with other forms of European "magic," and this situation reached its climax in the cargo cults" (1947, 57).

Here, in 1947, is cargo cults already full-blown: naked of quotation marks, lowercased, hyphenless, and plural. Of the three most influential cargo-cult studies of the 1950s and early 1960s (Worsley's *The Trumpet Shall Sound: A Study of "Cargo" Cults in Melanesia*, 1957; Burridge's *Mambu: A Study of Melanesian Cargo Movements and Their Social and Ideological Background*, 1960; and Lawrence's *Road Belong Cargo: A Study of the Cargo Movement in the Southern Madang District, New Guinea*, 1964) only Lawrence still occasionally used the singular.

Although the more anthropological "cargo cults" eventually displaced the more journalistic "the cargo cult," a conspicuous singularity lives on within anthropological descriptions and interpretations of these events. The multiplicity of such events could now at least be remarked in the descriptive label cargo cults. Yet, in the end, such events are essentially alike (see Burridge 1993, 276). They are all cults; they are all about cargo of some sort; and they are all local, Melanesian examples of a universal religious institution, the millenarian movement.

An interpretive singularity is also evident in the rather limited stock of descriptive motifs that anthropologists and others possess to write about these events. Cargoism in general, as a genre of writing, is tightly contained. Observers working within the genre are motivated to notice similar aspects of cargo events, and they draw upon a common language to recount these events (see Kilani 1983; Buck 1989). A singular genealogy of cargoism as a genre, from Williams' 1920s account of the Vailala Madness, to Mr Bird's 1940s fears of native flare-ups, to the *Los Angeles Times'* 1980s reportage on the latter days of the Johnson cult on New Hanover, is obvious.

The Anthropologists Move In

If colonial administrators and settlers coupled to beget the cargo cult, anthropologists were its adoptive parents. In the 1920s, government anthropologist Williams borrowed both the term Vailala Madness and his initial descriptions of it from his administrative colleagues. In the 1940s, anthropologists again stepped in to adopt a new terminology from the colonialist community. Cargo cult's successful migration into the social sciences has had several consequences.

First, the expression became vastly more popular. It escaped from cramped colonialist conversation and writing, and the grainy, insular pages of *PIM,* to circulate internationally through the media of anthropological conferences, books, and journals. It spread through English-speaking academe. It infiltrated Germany ("Cargo-Kulte"); it invaded France ("culte du cargo"); it overran Poland ("Kulty cargo") (Kowalak 1982).

Second, anthropology's fosterage lent the term scientific cachet.

Cargo cult broke through and prospered. It left behind the dyspeptic Mr Bird and his colonial milieu. It became a proper scientific descriptive and analytic category. True, it always carries along a circus aura of sport and faint mockery. Its roots in a politics of ridicule cannot be fully erased. The term is never entirely decorous and tasteful. Still, it is an honest scientific vocable and it has made its way into the world of journal article and book titles, indexical key words, and comparative religion and anthropology texts.

If cargo cult gained from anthropology, anthropologists profited from cargo cult. In the postwar era, the discipline was turning its attention away from the colonial management of native peoples, and the recording of rapidly dying cultures, to issues of social change, modernization, and development and its effects. One such reaction to modernization was the millenarian movement. But what to call this in Melanesia? Although hardly a neutral term, cargo cult was academically and politically far more presentable an expression than its prewar counterpart, "Vailala Madness."

The label "cult," of course, reflected prewar hesitations to recognize what Islanders were doing as serious religion. Careful not to offend Christian sensibilities, colonial reports embraced the word "quasi" and also quotation marks to minimize the religiosity of Melanesian movements, for example, "native 'religious' outbreaks" (Territory of New Guinea 1936, 19), "outbreaks of a quasi-religious nature" (1937, 21). The postwar adoption of "cult" maintained the distance between genuine religion on the one hand (either Christianity or precolonial belief systems), and faddish, spurious cargoism on the other. Furthermore, given cult's more sinister connotations, a fragrance of Vailala Madness might still be scented. Still, cargo cult was obviously a terminological improvement. In an era of colonial housekeeping and new deals for subject peoples, the impolite and impolitic Vailala Madness was hurriedly swept under the carpet. Cargo cults had arrived.

Several writers have identified Lucy Mair as the anthropological mother of the cargo cult. Palle Christiansen, for example, in his overview *The Melanesian Cargo Cult: Millenarianism as a Factor in Cultural Change,* noted: "The expression cargo cult, which presumably originated, and was used to begin with, only among settlers, officials or missionaries, apparently does not date back very far in the literature on the subject, where it appears for the first time in the 1940's. . . . The first anthropologist to use this term was, as far [as] can be established, Lucy Mair in her 'Australia in New Guinea' from 1948" (1969, 19; see also Kilani 1983, 24; Hermann 1992, 66). Trompf has also credited Mair as "evidently the first anthropologist to use the term cargo cult, in 1952 [sic]" (1991, 206, n 6). As we have seen, however, Mair was not the first to use the term, nor even the first anthropologist to do so. That honor goes to Inselmann (1946, 44) and Hölkter (1946, 16, 70) responding to Bird in the pages of *PIM*. Both can be counted anthropologists as well as missionaries. Close on their heels is D'Arcy Ryan's use of the term in his 1947 BA thesis.

Still, Lucy Mair was involved in the early days of the expression, and in its anthropological adoption. There is a conversational nexus here, mediated by Lucy Mair, that extends from Australian colonial and military circles straight into Sydney University's Department of Anthropology, and from there into the wider anthropological community. Mair definitely is the first writer to index the term: "Cargo cult" appears on page 235 in the index to her book *Australia in New Guinea*. She played up the label in a section of the book she subtitled "Native Reactions to White Rule": "A notable feature of the reaction of the peoples of New Guinea to white rule is the occurrence at different times in almost every part of the Australian territories of a manifestation which used to be known as the 'Vailala madness', but is now more commonly described as the 'cargo cult' " (1948, 64).

Mair, who before the war was a lecturer in Colonial Administration at the London School of Economics, had been invited to Australia by ANGAU, the wartime military government of Papua and New Guinea. She arrived in January 1945, to present a series of lectures at the Army School of Civil Affairs in Canberra. Her students were military personnel in training to be administrative officers in New Guinea (Mair 1948, v). While at the school, she conceived the idea of writing a book about Australia's administration of its two New Guinea colonies. To do so, she turned to the colonial archives and also interviewed colonial administrators. Mair introduced *Aus-*

tralia in New Guinea as "based primarily on the study of documents, and on many conversations with persons having an intimate knowledge of New Guinea, gained in the administrative service and in other ways. I was privileged, however, to supplement these sources by a visit of some ten weeks to Papua during the period of changeover from military to civil administration [in October 1945]" (1948, v).

Somewhere in her conversations with administrators and old territorial hands, Mair overheard the expression "cargo cult." She alluded to these conversations in the "Native Reactions" section of her book: "the idea that the movements themselves are mere nonsense, and can be stamped out by being treated as such, is a fallacy, as the younger officers of the District Services are well aware. In their view the motive force of the cargo cult is a feeling of hopeless envy of the European with his immensely higher material standards" (1948, 67). We can presume, then, that by late 1945 cargo cult was current within higher ANGAU administrative circles (Kingsley Jackson, pers comm, 1992).

Also lecturing with Mair at the Army School of Civil Affairs was Australian anthropologist H. Ian Hogbin, on leave from the University of Sydney. Hogbin had spent the first years of the war in the Solomon Islands as a member of the British Solomon Islands Defense Force (Beckett 1989, 25–27). By the end of 1943, he was a lieutenant-colonel in the Australian Imperial Force, working for the Army Directorate of Research. He spent some time in New Guinea, attached to ANGAU, but also trained army officers back in Australia at the School of Civil Affairs alongside Lucy Mair. Hogbin was an anthropologist with some fifteen years' research experience in the Solomon Islands and New Guinea, and Mair understandably drew upon his expertise. Hogbin also provided the photographs she used to illustrate *Australia in New Guinea.*

We can guess that the two anthropologists occasionally discussed the cargo cult. Hogbin, though, does not use the expression in his *Oceania* article on native councils and courts that he published in 1944. And in his 1951 book *Transformation Scene,* which draws on research he undertook while in army employment, he indexed the term only as a cross-reference: "Cargo cult, see Religious cults, new" (1951, 320). Although Hogbin was not a notable booster of the label in his own work, cargo cult begins appearing in anthropological theses written by students at the University of Sydney, to which Hogbin returned after the war. As remarked above, the first pluralization of the expression occurs in D'Arcy Ryan's 1947 BA thesis. The label appears again in a 1950 Sydney University BA thesis on culture contact by Phyllis Robinson (1950, 73, 86–88); and also in a 1951 MA thesis by June E. Watkins, "Messianic Movements: A Comparative Study of Some Religious Cults among the Melanesians, Maoris and North American Indians" (although, here, the expression is both in and out of quotes, and both singular and plural). In this thesis, Watkins announced that her concern "will be with the Cargo Cults of Australian New Guinea" (1951, 2). One can trace, then, a conversational trail along which cargo cult diffused into anthropology. This begins in the settler community of Papua New Guinea, percolates about Australia's Army School of Civil Affairs, is picked up by anthropologists Mair and Hogbin, and then filters into the University of Sydney and, from there, into anthropology at large. Obviously, this is not the only diffusionary pathway the term takes. Other anthropologists, such as missionaries Höltker and Inselmann for example, adopted cargo cult directly from the pages of *Pacific Islands Monthly*.

The military-anthropology trail (if we can call it that), however, is an interesting one. It darkens further the tricky wartime ancestry of cargo cult. Beyond civil administrative fears of cultists as mad subversives, military administrators were nervous about Japanese provocateurs and native betrayal and treachery. Enemy meddling was specifically blamed for several cults in New Guinea. In Vanuatu, also, the American military sent an intelligence party down to Tanna to investigate whether a Japanese spy had instigated that island's John Frum movement (see chapter 4).

The adoption of cargo cult by anthropologists at the University of Sydney and elsewhere, as noted, helped effect the dissemination as well as the pluralization of the expression. This terminological dilation, in part, followed an overenthusiastic use of an alluring new term. Watkins' 1951 Sydney University MA thesis is an early example of this. People went back into the literature to relabel as a cargo cult all those Vailala Madnesses, quasi-religious cults, and native frenzies that had occurred before 1945. Although the term did not exist until after the war, commentators working within cargoist discourse have found cargo cults as old as the 1830s. Ex post facto labelings of cargo cults, such as this one published by Peter Lawrence in the *Encyclopedia of Religion,* are not uncommon: "Western scholars first learned about cargo phenomena in 1857 through the publication of the Mansren myth of the Koreri in the Biak-Numfoor area of Irian Jaya, probably the oldest cargo movement in the whole region, although there were manifestations in Samoa in the 1830s and in Fiji in the 1880s" (1987, 74).

By 1952, just seven years after the first print appearance of cargo cult, the literature on the topic was extensive enough that a South Pacific Commission librarian compiled a *Bibliography of Cargo Cults and Other Nativisitic Movements in the South Pacific* (Leeson 1952). This literature was newly bloated with relabeled prewar native madnesses, movements, frenzies, and uprisings, many of which were now to be known as cargo cults.

The term also made it into the 1972 *Supplement to the Oxford English Dictionary* with examples of usage, the first being from a June 1949 *Sydney Morning Herald* article: "The fantastic 'cargo cult' among New Guinea natives has become a serious problem for Australian administrators. . . . Natives influenced by it believe that the spirits of their ancestors will arrive shortly in ships and aeroplanes carrying cargoes of food, tobacco, axes, and other goods" (Burchfield 1972, 440). The cargo cult also penetrated philosophy of science when I. C. Jarvie, in his 1961 PhD dissertation (published in 1964), nailed his critique of social scientific methodology onto the cargo-cult literature.

Within anthropology, of course, from the 1950s to the 1980s, cargo cult became the orthodox term for Melanesian social movements. As noted, the stock characterization of cargo cults was equally standardized with obligatory descriptive motifs. These motifs appear clearly in the entry for "Cargo Cult" from *A Dictionary of Anthropology* (1972). This is worth quoting at length. The entry dates the origins of the term to 1935 without, however, providing any evidence for its claim:

> Millenary movement among native peoples believing that the imminent arrival of spirits from the dead [sic], bringing quantities of the Europeans' goods for the loyal believers, would precede the coming of the millennium. The term originated in the Australian Mandate territory of New Guinea in 1935. Modern cargo cults are found chiefly in New Guinea and Melanesia, e.g., the Solomon Is.: those places, in fact, where the people have recently and suddenly emerged from a primitive way of life, and missed all the gradual steps in developing their civilizations. They generally take the following form: a leader tells his followers to expect great shipments of modern luxury goods, clothing, guns and food. In anticipation they build an airstrip or great warehouse; although the goods should have come to them long ago the British (or whatever the colonial power) have diverted them for their own use. Therefore the cargo cults are generally anti-government and disruptive, and cause much concern with the authorities. They have developed since World War II, and since then become increasingly more common. They are often quite illogical and the leaders frequently urge the destruction of money. (Davies 1972, 44–45)

Here is cargo cult at its crudest: imminent arrival of spirits, Europeans' goods for loyal believers, millennium, primitive, missed out on civilization, modern luxury goods, airstrip or warehouse, antigovernment, disruptive, illogical. These motifs, as here encyclopedically enumerated, have become the fixed distinctive features of the cargo cult.

Yet, given the term's gauche ancestry and the somewhat awkward semantic connotations of both cargo and cult, anthropology's use of the expression has never been a completely happy one. Recently, use of the term, within anthropology at least, has begun to decay. All of a sudden, the quotation marks are back. The history of cargo cult's anthropological usage might be summed up as "from quotes, to no quotes, back to quotes."

Almost from the beginning, though, there was an uneasy search for more neutral alternatives. Lawrence (1964) and others, for example, substituted "cargo movement." Rimoldi on Buka chose to write of "the Welfare" in that the "cargo cult label was not appropriate to the [Hahalis] Welfare Society" (1971, 1). Similarly, Allen used the Pidgin English word *kago,* to check cargo cult's more troublesome baggage (1976, 254). Others wrote of crisis cults, nativistic movements, messianic movements, prophet movements, adjustment movements, protonationalist movements, micronationalist movements, local protest movements, self-help development movements, regional separatist movements, and Holy Spirit movements (see eg, May 1982; Whiteman 1984, 58), and the list of alternatives to *cargo cult* continues to lengthen.

Beyond scouting about for a different, possibly more neutral descriptive terminology, a second strategy used to surmount the cargo cult is simply to dissolve it away. Cargo cults do not exist. Rather, they are an observer's effect: a *trompe l'oeil* which results from a bent way of looking at Melanesian sociability and politicking. The following chapter explores this deconstructive cargo-cult meltdown.

But if anthropologists today are busy distancing themselves from the cargo cult with prophylactic quotation marks and other means, other communities have seized upon the label. Nowadays, let's be honest, cargo cult is more than a little embarrassing. Anthropology tiptoes around the term. But it is far too late to eradicate *cargo cult,* even if anthropology were willing. Anthropologists have lost control of their adopted vocable. The label has gone wild. It cannot be effaced. It has escaped the bounds of anthropological discourse and now turns up in a surprising range of texts. We will later have to follow the wayward term into its new discursive haunts.

3 CARGO-CULT CULTURE

Cargo cult for anthropologists has always been a little prickly. Except, perhaps, in the first flush of excited postwar usage, the adopted term, a problem child, has not grown easy to embrace. Yes, the expression proved winsome and hardworking, but could one really overlook its rather dubious ancestry? More important, was it accurate? Cargo cult has vexed ethnographers who trust in the possibility of factually representing Pacific Islands cultures. Is it really European cargo that Melanesians truly desire? Is it always correct to describe what Melanesians are doing as a cult?

Anthropologists soon began to fudge their use of the label. First "cargo" was fiddled and redefined. "Cult," too, was a nuisance in that it was often an inaccurate and misleading label. It was embarrassingly obvious that both cult and cargo required intensive cultural contextualization. Calling Melanesians cargo cultists only remained possible by nativizing (or "Melanesianizing") the term.

Anthropology's evolving use of cargo cult, thus, has demanded more and more efforts to contextualize the label. The task has been to clothe cargo cult with enough cultural information that the expression is at least minimally presentable to go about in public. There are some Melanesians who we might still agree to call cargo cultists, but this labeling nowadays is only made possible by an accompanying, backgrounding ethnographic text that it is neither really cargo nor really a cult which people are up to, rather something more Melanesian.

Recently, anthropological unease with cargo cult has culminated in a thoroughgoing deconstruction of the term by Kilani (1983), McDowell (1988), Buck (1989), Kaplan (1990), and others. Such deconstruction, which completes the ultimate logic of cultural contextualization, concludes that cargo cults do not exist. The term is

41

an observer's category that misleads in two directions. It bundles together phenomena that may actually be very different; and it artificially isolates aspects of general symbolic and behavioral systems. Cargo cult is a burden upon understanding. The term should be dissolved away, melted down into Melanesian culture itself.

Dropping cargo cult into the purgative acid baths of deconstructionism is useful in several ways. The term's disintegration helps break down arguably bogus boundaries that separate cargo cults from Christian religious conversions, business endeavors, and politicking in Melanesia. Deconstruction also recasts what once was called "cult" in a far more favorable light. No longer can we simplistically portray such events as a sort of diseased reaction to European contact. Instead, we must interpret them as normal Melanesian cultural ingenuity and creativity.

Yet, deconstruction of cargo cult has an alarming consequence, because it takes to the limit an implication inherent in earlier attempts to contextualize cargo cult by nativizing the term. Melting down cargo and cult into ordinary Melanesian cultural practice establishes an awful equation between cargo cult and Melanesian culture. Cargo cult sinks down and disappears into the fundamental structures of Melanesian cognition and sociability; but in so doing it contaminates and consumes these. What used to be Melanesian culture becomes cargo cult writ large. Island business is cargo; politics is cargo; religion is cargo. Everything is now cargo. Melanesian cognition converts into "cargo thinking"; Melanesian religion into a "technology"; and the Melanesian psyche into "cargo sentiment."

This cargo cult equals culture equation results from the inescapable circumstance that every deconstruction is a reconstruction of something else. The term never really disappears. It reemerges as a subtext that continues to inform—and infest—ethnography. If cargo cult *truly* could be eradicated and forgotten, then its deconstruction might permit us to look at Melanesian culture with a different eye. But cargo cult is here to stay. Despite our best efforts to liquidate the label and silence its misemployment, the empty shell of its presence continues to tinge Melanesian ethnographic discourse. Attempts to drain the expression of its meaning by converting cargo cult into ordinary Melanesian culture, paradoxically, have worked to transform Melanesian culture into cargo cult.

Nativizing Cargo

In the early days of cargo cult, cargo meant cargo. Recall Lucy Mair's military school opinion that "the motive force of the cargo cult is a feeling of hopeless envy of the European with his immensely higher material standards—the same feeling that may later be the core of an independence movement. There is no way to meet it except the slow one of increasing the native's economic opportunities and giving him a reasonably devised education" (1948, 67).

Mair repeated some of the popular cargo stories of the day. Cargo ships from Australia lie off Papua New Guinea's capital, Port Moresby, waiting for the tide to change. They do so to give Europeans on board time to remove Islander names from the ancestral cargo's bills of lading. Or, a cult prophet named Batari from Talasea, New Britain, spies an off-loaded crate marked "battery" that he fails to receive. Truth dawns that the whites are filching his cargo.

Those whites living at the remoter limits of extensive shipping networks were certainly often themselves nervously eager about the arrival of their cargo. Cultic themes of anticipation and waiting for cargo that may never arrive have striking parallels in the European experience. Isolated missionaries, planters, and traders commonly searched the horizon anxiously for their tardy shipments of tinned food, flour, mail, and the like to arrive. At the same time that John Frum movement supporters on Tanna Island were fervently awaiting their mythic cargo, for example, the resident Australian Presbyterian missionary was writing this letter home:

We have received no cargo since early April. Some goods, ordered as long ago as last September, have still not arrived. And once again this month we are in the dark as to our chances of getting supplies. The Morinda missed us and went on to Vila. The Polynesian is due tomorrow but seldom has cargo for us. Is our cargo in Vila waiting some small boat to bring it down sometime? Or is it, as last time, still on the wharf at Sydney? (Armstrong 1952, 8–9)

People's recent wartime experiences also sustained the common sense definition of cargo. The Allies and the Japanese both imported impressive amounts of military supplies into the Pacific, and both employed Islanders to move this cargo about (see White and Lindstrom 1989). Westerners themselves marveled at these military hoards. What, then, must the native have thought?

> The war not only deprived the natives of some of their material possessions; it opened their eyes wider than ever to the pitiful inferiority of their possessions compared with those of the Europeans. Although the exact effect of witnessing all the expenditure and wastage of war was unknown, it seems certain that the sight of hundreds of ships unloading cargo of unbelievable quantity, hundreds of gleaming new aircraft, and thousands upon thousands of troops, including American Negroes, deepened the already existing consciousness of the discrepancy between white plenty and brown poverty. (Souter 1964, 238)

It was a pretty obvious conclusion that the natives wanted Western merchandise.

In the pre-1945 days before cargo cult, cargo was an element in descriptions of the various Madnesses and quasi-religious native movements. Descriptive summaries of such movements occasionally listed the sorts of cargo expected: "food of all kinds, axes, horses, dogs and many other things, including firearms" (Territory of New Guinea 1935, 29); "cases of meat, tobacco, loin cloths, rice, lamps, and rifles" (1936, 27); "motor cars and aeroplanes . . . rifles" (1937, 29). What the terminological triumph of *cargo cult* achieved, though, was to foreground these lists and desires for cargo as the defining feature of such events. Earlier descriptions, as one might surmise from the term Vailala Madness, had highlighted other elements as well (eg, trancing and other seemingly mad behavior, the abandonment or revival of traditional practices, destruction of gardens, predictions of world reversal, anticolonialism, the formation of potentially dangerous crowds, and so on). Although Williams, for example, reported native desires for European goods in his initial 1923 description of the Vailala Madness, his 1934 retrospective on that movement omitted this cargo element (Mair 1948, 65). After 1945, such omission was no longer possible. Should a particular event or movement not manifest a demand for cargo, excuses now had to be made to explain why these particular cultists were *not* desirous of cargo.

The new label, with its focus on cargo, influenced the postwar policies of colonial governments. Since the natives were now recognized to entertain unrealistic demands for cargo, and since these demands, as Mair pointed out, might inflate into untimely movements for independence, the administrative response had to lie in increasing both economic and educational opportunities for latent cultists. In other words, these natives must learn that their ancestors are not in the business of making or shipping cargo. Rather, cargo is the property of hardworking white men who profit from two thousand years of civilized, technological advance.

Along these lines, the Australians in Papua New Guinea continued a practice begun during World War II, and rounded up a few of the more presentable cult leaders and prophets, flew them to Port Moresby, and occasionally to the Australian cities, and toured them through offices, factories, stores and the like (see, for example, Lawrence 1964, 168–169 on New Guinea prophet Yali sightseeing at government expense in Port Moresby).

The postwar Australian administration also launched in 1950 a small monthly magazine written for a local audience of educated Islanders. Most of the first year's issues of the *Papua and New Guinea Villager* contained a diverting column entitled "How You Get It." (F. E. Williams, who died in a wartime plane crash in 1943, had produced an earlier government publication, *The Papuan Villager,* between 1929 and 1941 [Kohn 1988, 28].) This news sheet undertook to explain, in what passed for simple but authoritative English, the true industrial origins of a series of cargo items: money, tinned fish, soap, blankets, matches, and so on. Needless to say, no ancestors were involved.

Leave it to anthropology, though, to undermine popular certainties. By the middle 1950s, anthropologists had begun to spread about a new interpretation: *Cargo did not really mean cargo.* This undermining was launched on pleas to "understand" the natives. In May 1950, *Pacific Islands Monthly* published a cargo report that began: "It is impossible to understand how the New Guinea natives can go on clinging to this mad cargo-cult idea. The arrival of their ancestors' 'cargo' has had to be postponed so often now that one would think that even they would wake up (*PIM* 1950, 85).

Eight years later, however, the opaque native cultist started to clarify. *Pacific Islands Monthly* interviewed anthropologist Peter Lawrence on cargo cults, as the "latest to kick the ball around." Lawrence exhorted: "It is essential to understand how these people think of us and our way of life, because if you are going to change their ways of thinking and their way of living, you must know what you are up against. It is questionable whether any administration in any dependent territory like this has really been able to achieve this, but it is up to every European in this territory to try to understand the native" (*PIM* 1958, 59). Colonial administrations everywhere perhaps have a tough time getting the native right, but anthropologists would do their best to explain why the "Cargo Cult won't die quietly" (*PIM* 1958, 59). Anthropologist Lawrence had his interpretive work cut out for him, though. *Pacific Islands Monthly,* to conclude its article, next quoted Dr John Gunther, the assistant administrator of Papua and New Guinea: "To put the aspirations of the NG [New Guinea] people very simply, they are: To have the cargo that we Europeans have got" (*PIM* 1958, 59).

Gunther's assured common sense, here, perhaps confirms Lawrence's assessment of colonial administrators. By this time anthropologists had already exercised their theories of culture to complicate cargo. The discipline had for some years been in the business of making sense of queer native customs and beliefs in terms of the practical utility of these customs, or the sudden meaningfulness of these beliefs when situated within foreign yet systematic cultural frameworks. Colonial administrators should pay attention. Cargo, for Melanesians, did not mean what it did in Australia. To grasp the significance of cargo, and of desires and cults of cargo, one must first locate cargo within Melanesian culture. This, after all, is what anthropology was all about. Anthropologist Raymond Firth summed it up: Cargo desire "can be looked on, pityingly, as mere delusion. . . . But the anthropological analysis goes deeper" (1951, 112–113). Anthropology's nativization of cargo made cargo into a symbol. True, *kago* meant European goods in Melanesian Pidgin English, but cargo—as symbol—really stood for something more complicated. Nativization of cargo also converted Mair's "envy" into loftier emotions. The emotional fodder of cargo cults was not, or not just, an avaricious desire for wealth, but deeper cravings for equality, independence, salvation, identity, moral regeneration, and so on.

William Stanner, in an essay published in 1958, denied that cargo was cargo. Rather cargo was a "factitious motif."

> There is a sense in which cargo is but a figment, an obsessive thing of the mind. A great many Melanesians are familiar enough with the actual kinds of goods which are idealized as cargo, but the idea is none the less a rather wild work of the imagination. As it is used by the Melanesians, it evidently conveys no sense whatever of either the vast miscellany of utility functions or the provenance and source of the goods of desire. The natives make from an aggregate, which really has only the accidental unity of shipment or destination or juxtaposition, a meaningful unity. (1958, 2–3)

Besides, if cargo really was cargo, cultists should worry more about its distribution when it arrives (Stanner 1958, 24). Kenelm Burridge pursued this point in *Mambu*, published in 1960: "What would happen if, by some strange chance, the cargo arrived while the rites were in train? All Kanaka [ie, Islander] communities have very carefully particularized ways in which wealth should be redistributed: kin and political relationships are intimately associated. Yet nowhere in the available literature is there any indication of how the cargo would be distributed were it to arrive" (1960, 42). Capitalization served Burridge's discrimination of European cargo from Melanesian Cargo: "To save confusion, therefore, 'cargo' is used here to refer to manufactured goods, and Cargo, with a capital

C, when what is meant is the whole complex of meanings, symbols, and activities to be found in a Cargo cult" (1960, 26).

Pacific Islands Monthly confessed it was baffled by natives who refused to swear off mad cults despite repeated failures of any cargo to arrive. Anthropology's answer was that cargo is not Cargo; and desire for Cargo is not envy of cargo. It does not much matter to cultists that cargo ships and planes never actually arrive to off-load money, tinned fish, soap, matches, blankets, and other European goods. This sort of "small *c*" cargo is only a symbol, a "factitious motif." People's attention and hopes are fixed elsewhere.

But if Cargo is not cargo, what is it? Anthropologists and others have proposed several answers to this question according to their various interests and understandings of Melanesians and Melanesian culture. Grossly, one can tease apart sociological, psychological, and spiritual interpretations of Cargo's symbolic loading. These readings of Cargo, however, all share a number of important assumptions. Cultists feel a lack or an absence in themselves or in their society. This sense of anxious inadequacy ensues from Melanesian encounters with Europeans and European culture. Cargo, thus, is an object of desire. It stands for whatever will address the shortcomings that natives presently experience. The "inordinate significance" of Cargo, as Stanner understood this, was "really one of things of the future, not of the present . . . the *motif* of a hoped-for new way of life" (1958, 3).

The anthropological interpretation of Cargo as a symbol opened up the ways that cults and cultists could be understood. Cargo, now detached from a literal reading as razor blades, matches, and bush knives, could stand for a miscellany of desired future states that would redress equally varied present-day experienced gaps and lacks. Cargo could be political and economic equality with Europeans; it could be a revitalized traditional system of exchange; it could be a newly harmonized sense of self; it could be spiritual salvation and an apprehension of Jesus; it could be powerful wisdom.

A brief sampling of all the things that anthropologists and others have read into Cargo might begin with Peter Lawrence's writings about cults near Madang in Papua New Guinea. Lawrence retained the literal interpretation of Cargo as cargo, but also transformed this into a symbol of something else by evoking the Melanesian point of view. According to Lawrence, cultists desire European material goods because of the meanings they understand these goods to have. Natives have "the desire for the material culture of the European, and hence for economic and social equality with him" (1954, 1–3). "For them the cargo has become the symbol of the political power of the Europeans, and this power they feel they must combat" (1954, 20).

Jean Guiart (1951b) and Peter Worsley (1957) also developed the reading that Cargo stood for European power, and desire for cargo symbolized protonationalist aspirations of equality and political independence: "Melanesians by no means rejected European culture *in toto:* they wanted the White man's power and riches, but they did not want the perpetuation of his rule. The myth of a Cargo, rightly theirs, but usurped by the Whites, expressed their political mood neatly" (Worsley 1957, 44; see also Harris 1974, 151–152). The recurring failure of predicted arrivals of European goods was inconsequential since desire for Cargo actually expressed a political mood. As long as Islanders suffered under colonial systems of political and economic domination, cults would attract followers who desired freedom and equality.

Burridge, in *Mambu,* offered an alternative interpretation of Cargo. Cargo is a "myth-dream": "a body of notions . . . which find expression in myths, dreams, popular stories, and anecdotes" (1960, 27). A myth-dream, for Burridge, is a sort of unarticulated aspiration or mute desire. Even though cultists may express volubly their fondness for shotguns, trucks, Levi-Strauss jeans, and other sorts of cargo, we must understand such expression actually to be their inarticulate desire for Cargo.

> It is clear that if cargo means manufactured goods, Cargo embraces a set of acute moral problems; that Cargo movements are not due simply to a misunderstanding concerning the origin of manufactured goods, but that they are embedded in, and arise from, a complex total situation. . . . The most significant theme in the Cargo seems to be moral regeneration: the creation of a new man, the creation of new unities, the creation of a new society. (Burridge 1960, 246–247)

A desire for material goods bespeaks deeper, more inchoate desires for psychic and social regeneration. More than a symbolic protonationalist craving, Cargo represents a thoroughgoing moral revitalization: "Access to cargo has become the symbol of manhood" (1960, 259).

A variety of missionaries (eg, Strelen 1977; Steinbauer 1979) have produced yet another interpretation of Cargo—one, obviously, that Christianizes Burridge's myth-dream. "Cargo is the symbol for the expectation of salvation and it has to be treated seriously for that reason" (Steinbauer 1979, 158). Missionaries, here, make the best of a bad thing. Typically, they are distrustful of Melanesian cultists who often reject Christianity wholesale, or who reinterpret its teachings out beyond the bounds of orthodoxy. However, at least cults evince flashes of desire, maybe even hope. Could it be the Holy Ghost, and not the devil after all? Whichever, the trick is to seize the main chance and bend that desire to Christian ends: "Stressing the wholeness of life we shall recognize cargo cults as legitimate endeavours to improve life. From this point of view they are justified and consistent with their purpose. Frequently however dubious and untrue elements are added when they are active. . . . The encounter with Christ as the renewer of human thinking lies still largely in the future. Here is the great opportunity for the mission" (Steinbauer 1979, 160).

As we shall see, however, rather than Christianity absorbing and redirecting cargo cultism, in some ways cargoism as a discourse has digested Christianity. The sometimes explosive "Holy Spirit" movements that erupted here and there around Melanesia in the 1980s and 1990s have not escaped the heritage of cargoism in Melanesia. Cargoism as a discourse cannot be ignored or silenced. It continues to tinge interpretations of all conspicuous Melanesian desire, whether this desire is political, economic, or spiritual. The meaning of today's Holy Spirit movements, like the meaning of contemporary politics and business endeavors in the region, is now trapped in a slippery oscillation. Are these religious movements a wondrous Melanesian Christian revival, or are they just cargo cult all over again in different guise? (See chapter 5.)

The various readings of Cargo as protonationalism, as personal and social revitalization, or as salvation are not necessarily exclusive. Proponents of one may accept all the others as well—although, as one might expect, there has been a certain amount of competition between anthropological and Christian interpretation. Beyond cargo cults themselves, each may contend to explain the other's readings in its own terms. Anthropology's version of cargoism, for example, can incorporate Christianity as a sort of higher-order millenarian movement. If Mr Bird blamed missionaries for *causing* cargo cults, anthropologists have sometimes implied that Christianity *is* a cargo cult (see eg, Schwartz 1973, 170). And not just in Melanesia either. Worsley, who knew his mild Marxist interpretation of Cargo would annoy, mischievously headed many of the chapters of *The Trumpet Shall Sound,* his survey of cargo cults, with epigraphs from the Old and New Testaments.

This quick summary of Cargo readings is not exhaustive of the many things Cargo has been taken to be. The next chapter surveys in greater detail the variety of ways in which lowercase cargo as matches and soap has been uppercased and elevated into Cargo the symbol, as it explores assorted interpretations of one Melanesian cult, the John Frum movement on Tanna, Vanuatu.

I want here to discern the mechanics of anthropology's transformation of cargo into Cargo. How was this accomplished? How was it justified? And what have been its effects? The translation of cargo into Cargo was animated by good intentions. It countered general European presumptions that cultists were irrational or lunatic. Cargo would displace Vailala Madness; cult, a quasi-religion, would supplant insanity. Anthropology's translation claimed to give the native point of view. It also supported a liberal political agenda. The colonial government must answer the indigenous desire for Cargo with greater educational and economic opportunities for native subjects. In the end, though, anthropology's translation of cargo into Cargo has created a cargo-cult culture for Melanesians.

Lawrence gently chided colonial administrators for being ignorant of native ways of thinking and living. Anthropologists and missionaries, in counterpoint, claimed to know their natives. Anthropologists, particularly, trained themselves to speak from the native point of view. It was this ethnographic knowledge of the native situation that authorized the symbolic reading of cargo. Anthropologists took the English word "cargo," or sometimes the Pidgin English *kago,* and refracted this through a lens of Melanesian culture to discern deeper levels of meaning, that is, Cargo. To grasp the true meaning of "cargo" for cultists, one must understand essential facets of Melanesian life and thought. The engine of translation enters a domain labeled Melanesian culture, but then makes a U-turn and comes back out again: The culturally refracted meanings of English "cargo" also consist of European glosses (eg, protonationalism, myth-dream, salvation). Conceivably, the translation process could have terminated midway. For example, "cargo" could have been translated as something like *nauta* on Tanna in Vanuatu, or as *hakats* on Buka (Rimoldi 1971, 281). Translation, however, traveled through the indigenous countryside, loaded up certain ideas like the importance of wealth in Melanesian society, and then emerged and employed these ideas to argue that cargo (now written Cargo) really meant nationalism, or regeneration, or salvation. Anthropological translation thus accomplished the nativization of cargo desire. This desire is neither mad nor irrational. It is normal and ordinary in Melanesia—or almost so.

The argument begins with a claim that wealth has special meaning for Melanesians—a meaning that colonial administrators and other ignorant Europeans heretofore may have overlooked. Stanner complained that cargo understanding was "hampered by the fact that anthropologists study almost everything about cargo-cults except cargo" (1958, 17). Translation must go to work on cargo, in that "wealth, and power as its means, seem to be among the most persuasive *motifs* of Melanesian life. Wealth, certainly, is among the highest if not the highest of the secular 'values' " (Stanner 1958, 21; see Siikala 1979). European ideas about wealth, the accumulation of goods, envy, and so on all miss the point when it comes to Melanesian desire for cargo. Rather, we need to grasp the native point of view of wealth.

This island metaphysics, as developed and elaborated over nearly a century of Melanesian anthropology, says that Islanders crave wealth in order to give it away for it is in exchange that they constitute both their social relationships and their personhood. Lawrence wrote: "Material wealth, apart from its primary utility, had a secondary and perhaps greater value as the symbol of social relationships. Its existence enabled cooperation between, and its abundance conferred prestige on, both individuals and groups" (1964, 28–29). Burridge also argued along these lines, when sketching in the cultural background in *Mambu:* "Just as a denial of equivalence can be formulated in terms of behaviour relating to food, so is it re-established through activities directly connected with the production of foodstuffs. . . . Moral relationships, therefore, are reflected in the way people behave over food; food is economic wealth; the amount produced and the way in which it is distributed yield political power; and each is geared to equivalence, the primary expression of amity" (1960, 83).

Melanesians, thus, *ordinarily* desire food and other sorts of wealth for nonutilitarian reasons. Transactions of wealth both symbolize and generate relations of equivalence, amity, and power. Desire for cargo is customary and rational in Melanesian cultural terms. In the colonial era, the objects of this desire had merely shifted a little.

> The natives developed an obsession for cargo for two reasons. First, it became an economic necessity: it had obvious advantages over their own goods, which it swiftly replaced as the area was brought under control. Second, it became an index of their self-respect. . . . [T]hey attributed to it the same kind of social importance as they had done to their traditional material culture: they came to regard it as the symbol of their status in the new colonial society. (Lawrence 1964, 232)

Under colonialism, Melanesians encountered new sorts of wealth; and they now had to labor to create moral relationships of equality and amity with Europeans. For this, they wanted Cargo.

Anthropology's translation of cargo into Cargo almost-but-not-quite normalized cargo cults. There still remained the complication of cult. Melanesians may customarily value wealth, but the agitated pursuit of that wealth by cultic behavior, to some, still looked unconventional. Stanner, for example, noted: "Cargo, or wealth, the object of the cults, is endowed with a disproportionately high value, and the conduct of natives towards the object has an exaggerated or excessive quality" (1958, 1). If Cargo desire now seemed culturally normal, the cults themselves still smelled exaggerated, excessive, and bizarre.

Explanation for anomalous cultic excess typically turned to abnormalities in social context. Cults were an extraordinary reaction to circumstances in which Islanders no longer possessed the ability to produce the wealth they needed, and in which Europeans denied the possibility of establishing amicable, equal relationships (see eg, Lawrence 1964, 7). Cults were an abnormal backlash of thwarted normal desire. But just how abnormal were they? Here, too, processes of anthropological translation were soon underway.

Nativizing Cult

Having transformed cargo into Cargo, anthropological translation moved on briskly to convert and open up cult essentially into Melanesian culture itself. Again, the motivations for this undertaking were good ones, and also ones deeply ingrained in the anthropological agenda of converting the bizarre into the familiar, and vice versa. A cultural reading of "cult," in part, may have been impelled by the negative connotations of the word. Although an improvement over "Madness," cult nonetheless presented its own problems.

Anthropological translation, no doubt, was also informed by ideals of liberalism and humanism. Whereas prewar anthropology once took the untranslated cult to be a *reaction* to powerful Europeans—and a typically bizarre and inefficient one at that—the normalized cult posed as an ordinary, even admirable example of Melanesian creativity and cultural imagination (see, eg, Rimoldi 1971, 88). Ironically, the earlier "reactionary" reading of cults, unlike the cultural, at least left a space for an ordinary, noncultic Melanesia. It presumed that Melanesians most of the time are not cultists. They become so only in extraordinary circumstances.

The reactionary reading of cult has several variants, beginning with the practical. This version asserts that Melanesian reactions to European domination ordinarily would have taken a rational, political form. European surveillance and suppression of Melanesian political action, however, were such that opposition to the colonial system had to disguise itself in a religious, cultic garb. As soon as European interference declines, however, people should abandon cults for rational economic cooperatives and political parties. Worsley contributed several subtler interpretations of the reactionary cult. First, cults articulate a resistance to ruling ideologies as well as dominant political groups. Cults thus enact

> an integral part of that stream of thought which refused to accept the rule of a superordinate class, or of a foreign power. . . . This anti-authoritarian attitude is expressed not only in the form of direct political resistance, but also through the rejection of the ideology of the ruling authority. The lower orders rejected the dominant values, beliefs, philosophy, religion, etc., of those they are struggling against, as well as their material economic and political domination. (1957, 225–226)

Second, Melanesian cults function to overcome indigenous social divisions and to "weld previously hostile and separate groups together into a new unity" in opposition to European colonialists (Worsley 1957, 228). The leaders of these novel unities look skyward for the broader sort of political legitimacy that they now require.

> A political leader must avoid identification with any particular section of that society. He must avoid being seen as the representative of any one group, particularly, of course, his own. He must therefore show that he seeks to establish his movement on the basis of a higher loyalty. By projecting his message on to the supernatural plane, he clearly demonstrates that his authority comes from a higher sphere, and that it transcends the narrow province of local gods and spirits associated with particular clans, tribes or villages. He is thus able to build upon existing social foundations, to use the small units of village and clan as elements in his organizational

scheme whilst at the same time transcending the cramping limitations of these units by incorporating them in a wider framework. (Worsley 1957, 237)

Cultic religiosity, here, works as an ideological glue that pastes together sometimes hostile local groups, smoothing over their differences for the coming struggle with the common colonialist enemy. This, for Worsley, answers the question: "Why do the movements take a religious form?" (1957, 236).

Anthropological cargoism, however, soon swerved from reactionary to cultural accountings of cults. The first move was an affirmation that cults are creative rather than reactionary responses to the difficult circumstances of the European presence; the second, the claim that cultic organizing is normal in Melanesia. The answer to Worsley's problem of exaggerated and excessive religiosity in Melanesian politicking now begins to locate cultism deep inside Melanesian culture itself.

Firth, for example, in 1953, protested that Islanders are not blind reactionaries. Cults "are not mere passive responses, the blind stirrings of a people who feel that they are being pushed around. Absurd as they may seem when considered as rational solutions, they are creative attempts of the people to reform their own institutions, to meet *new* demands or withstand *new* pressures" (1953, 815).

Cultural dynamism and creativity, more so than blind reaction, might be supposed to be normal features of the human condition in Melanesia as elsewhere, and it is not surprising that anthropologists began to portray cults as a sort of native, Melanesian mechanism of social innovation and change. "It is in the internal conflicts, not the external crises, that the causes for change are to be found" (Christiansen 1969, 127). Cults are not absurd reactions of people who are pushed around by powerful Europeans; rather, they are dynamic endeavors that are indigenous within Melanesian society, as Stanner declared: "Let us be sure of this. Nothing in the interpenetration of Melanesian life by Europeanism *of itself* entails or need lead to cultistic conduct. The impulse to cult can come only from the 'within' of Melanesian life" (1958, 19).

Lawrence (1954, 1964), especially, helped nativize cult by plumbing that Melanesian "within." The first chapter of his *Road Belong Cargo,* "The Native Cosmic Order," presents summary analyses of Melanesian religion, epistemology, notions of time, and leadership (1964, 9–33; see also Errington 1974 for a comparable cultural reading).

First, Melanesian religion is "above all a technology" (McAuley 1961, 18, quoted by Lawrence 1964, 29). The ancestors control the production and reproduction of the world. People, though, may influence their ancestors by undertaking appropriate ritual action. Melanesians overlook, thus, Western logical distinctions between religion/economy, rational/irrational, and ritual/technology. "The means devised to solve the technical problems of explaining [cargo's] source and exploiting it to the natives' advantage were of exactly the same kind as those used in the case of the traditional material culture. . . . The perpetuation of the traditional concepts of knowledge and work gave the people techniques for translating their desire for cargo into the type of action they believed would produce it" (Lawrence 1964, 235).

Cargo cults are just another expression of traditional Melanesian religious values: "Cargo cults and cargo beliefs are not alien imports into the Melanesian religious system. They are, rather, an integral part of that system, and they give expression to some of the deepest Melanesian religious hopes, beliefs, and aspirations" (Strelen 1977, 59). And cargoist ritual stands at the heart of ancestral Melanesian religiosity: "The 'cargo-cults' have merely resumed, amplified, revalorised and charged with prophetic and millenary power the traditional religious theme that the Cosmos renews itself periodically, or to be more exact that it is symbolically re-created every year" (Eliade 1965, 137).

• The anthropological conclusion: Melanesians *ordinarily* seek economic advantage through ritual action. They pray for wealth.

Second, Melanesian epistemology presumes that knowledge is revealed and the wise are inspired. Melanesians do not believe in individual creativity: "Except in minor matters, they dismissed the principle of human intellectual discovery. . . . The deities lived with men or appeared in dreams, showing them how to plant crops and make artefacts. . . . Even when a man composed a new melody or dance, he had to authenticate it by claiming that it came from a deity rather than out of his own head" (Lawrence 1964, 30). Knowledge, thus, "came into the world ready made and ready to use, and could be augmented not by human intellectual experiment but only by further revelation by new or old deities" (1964, 33). Melanesian social activists must always be prophets, in that they must present and legitimate their designs for new order as ancestral revelations.

Moreover, Melanesian epistemology shapes what we would call creative action. Activist Melanesian leaders, literally, must be dreamers, for it is by dreaming that they authenticate their messages of social renewal. People also make use of other means of inspiration including, notably, trance. Trance, like dreams, is a creative process that justifies, epistemologically, the development and dissemination of new knowledge (see Lindstrom 1990).

Anthropologists have pursued this cultural reading so far as to normalize even the "collective nervous symptoms of a sometimes grotesque and idiotic nature" that Williams first noted of the eponymic Vailala Madness (Williams 1923, 1). Williams was wrong about the roots of the Vailala Madness. "Collective shaking," in fact, is "a vital part of pre-contact tradition" (Trompf 1991, 128). These shaking fits are not madness after all, and Trompf prefers the name Vailala Movement (although "Vailala Madness" sneaks back into his book's index [1991, 206, 283]). An understanding of Melanesian epistemology reveals that the Vailala automaniacs were not having some psychotic episode of nervous hysteria or mental derangement. This was not an excessive emotional reaction to the political and economic stresses of the European presence. Rather, Vailala cultists were simply in a trance state and thus opened to receive ancestrally revealed knowledge. In Melanesia, "the dream and the so-called 'hysteria' thus both serve to validate the prophetic experience" (Stephen 1971, 10; see also Flannery 1984; Guidieri 1988, 179).

• The anthropological conclusion: Melanesians *ordinarily* seek to be inspired, rather than creative. Prophetic dreams, mass hysteria, and trance are normal, not reactionary.

Third, Melanesian notions of episodic time expect social change to be abrupt, disjunctive, and total. "Viewed through time, the cosmic order was essentially changeless. There was no historical tradition" (Lawrence 1964, 32). A local sense of lineal, progressive time does not exist. The present, then, is the past and also the future. Social change, when it occurs, is not progressive. Rather, it is disjunctive. Such disjunctiveness also holds true of cult doctrines. "Each attempt at explanation—each cargo belief or myth—[was] in itself a separate and complete 'history' of the world. It bore no relation to earlier attempts at explanation, which were all in error and had been, as it were, erased" (1964, 241). Given this cosmology, Melanesians who desire social change naturally spend their time scanning the horizon for a sudden advent of the new.

Anthropology has deepened further Lawrence's cultural reading of Melanesian time and change. McDowell, for example, has suggested that Islanders

do not conceive of the past as a series of interconnected events in a cause-and-effect chain. For them there is no gradual, cumulative, evolutionary change; change is always dramatic, total, and complete. . . . This episodic conception of history and change is not restricted to the past but provides a model for change in the future as well: coming change must also be total, drastic, and radical. (1988, 124; see also 1985, 33; Errington 1974, 257; Kahn 1983, 110; Guidieri 1988, 183–185; Kempf 1992)

A cultural order is an autonomous and total "package" (Brunton 1989, 166) that people take or leave all at once. Social change in Melanesia occurs when people rally around a prophet with a new package.

In sum, Melanesians normally change their societies by organizing cults. "What we call 'cult' or 'movement' is nothing less than the ordinary form of ritual and interpretive innovation in Melanesian societies" (Wagner 1979, 164). Or, again, "as a means of generating new moral codes and new meanings, the ecstatic cult is surely the natural and creative concomitant of secular efforts to mould the Melanesian future" (Stephen 1971, 14). Or, once again, "in summary it appears that an analysis of cargo cults as phenomena of social change should not be separated from that of the other forms of change that characterize Melanesian societies. The cults are only an aspect of the social dynamic in Melanesia" (Kilani 1983, 114, my translation).

• The anthropological conclusion: Melanesians *ordinarily* expect and strive to change their lives in a total and disjunctive manner. The cult is a normal institution of social innovation.

Finally, the Melanesian leadership type, the big man, parallels the cult prophet. Melanesian polities favor cults.

> Leadership depended on personal pre-eminence in important activities, but secular skill alone was inadequate. What counted was mastery of ritual by which men could ensure success. The leaders were men who "really knew" and who could direct the activities of others—those who did not "really know"—to the best advantage. It was popular conviction of this ability that enabled the particularly successful leader . . . to lure followers away from his less fortunate rivals. (Lawrence 1964, 31)

Whereas some leaders deal in pigs and traditional lore, others trade in cargo prophecy. "Millenarian leaders, whatever their spiritual preoccupations, must also act as political entrepreneurs if they are to accumulate a following" (Roscoe 1988, 515; see also Errington 1974, 261). Cargo is an especially promising field for enterprising men: "Such individuals might once have bent their talents towards becoming headmen, but now that the office has lapsed the cargo motive supplies an alternative means of achieving social distinction" (Hogbin 1958, 219–220). Cults are just a variety of routine Melanesian politicking that has been colored by the colonial encounter. The apparent reactive novelty of Fiji's Tuka Movement, for example, might actually "be read as an indigenous dynamism. . . . Read in these terms, events once seen as millennial or protonationalist are dissolved back into Fijian ritual-political dynamics of history making" (Kaplan 1990, 10–11). Anthropological labels such as "millennial" or "protonationalist" disguise the fact that cults are just another indigenous political institution.

• The anthropological conclusion: Melanesians *ordinarily* conduct politics along cultic lines. Big men and prophets, as leaders, share similar political interests, characteristics, and strategies.

Anthropology's cultural translation of the native Melanesian cult, which was itself a reaction to an earlier reactionary theory of cargo cult, is a success. Like Cargo that does not mean cargo, now cult does not mean cult. The cult is not—or not just—an aberrant ritualized reaction to a powerful European presence. Anthropology instructs us, rather, that cults are normal, creative Melanesian institutions of cultural dynamism and change. Melanesian economy runs on ritual. Melanesian social planning passes as revelation. Melanesian time is episodic. Melanesian change is sudden. Melanesian leaders are prophetic. Cults are culturally constructive.

This cultural reading, however, extracts a cost. Translation always is a reciprocal operation. Reading cargo and cult in terms of Melanesian culture rephrases that culture in terms of cargo and cult. According to Wagner: "Cargo cult is just a name we give to Melanesian culture when its usually covert interpretations of the world around us emerge into the open" (quoted in Counts 1972, 374). Schwartz agreed: "It would not be far amiss, in fact, to speak of [Melanesian contact culture] as a *cargo culture,* combining postulates of native Christianity and the revised native cosmology that developed in the process of contact" (1976, 170).

The nativization of cargo and cult unavoidably converts Melanesians into normal cargo cultists: "Such a characterization presents itself as a condensed representation of the Melanesian and of his way of life, of which the principal traits are: magico-religious thinking, a mode of action poorly adapted to achieve desired goals, and finally the incapacity to adopt rational behavior that only a civilizing program could curb" (Kilani 1983, 19, my translation). Cargo and cult emerge as standard operating procedure for Melanesians. Thanks to anthropology, Melanesians now are known to be cargo cultists even when they are not actively having a cargo cult.

Cargoism

Anthropology's nativization of Cargo and cult by way of a cultural reading has turned both into "cargoism." According to Lawrence, American anthropologist Thomas Harding coined the word cargoism in 1967 "as a philosophy in its own right" (1987, 80). Harding provided a straightforward definition: "Cargoism is nothing less than the Melanesian world view applied to the task of providing meaningful interpretation of European culture" (1967, 21). Although I have shanghaied and reoriented Harding's word to label our own discourse about the cargo cult, originally, of course, that discourse employed the term to characterize Melanesia's pervasive cargo-cult culture.

Cargo and cult have infiltrated and permeated our knowledge of Melanesia. The cultural reading of cargo and cult has overwhelmed, or at least darkly colored, other possible constructions of Melanesian culture. Everything is now saturated with cargoism: Melanesian philosophy is cargoism; Melanesian worldview is cargoism; Melanesian cognition is cargoism; Melanesian psychology is cargoism. The Melanesian sense of time and space inform an everyday "millenarian praxis" (Biersack 1991).

Cargoism is also called "Cargo Thinking" (with a focus on cognition) or "Cargo Sentiment" (with a focus on emotion and desire) —the ways Melanesians ordinarily think and feel about the world. Cargo thinking and feelings are always there in the background, constantly informing people's behavior. Cults are recurrent, group enactions of cargoism, although "cults are by no means the only behavioral manifestations of cargoism. . . . [C]argoism is far more often expressed in individual and verbal behaviour than in organized collective form. It imparts a definite quality to daily life, in addition to impelling dramatic collective action. As a cognitive system cargoism is pervasive, its behavioural output continuous and varied" (Harding 1967, 21). Here is the culmination of cargoist discourse: The revelation that sporadic cargo cults are only surface manifestations of an underlying, constant, routine, and normal Melanesian cargoism.

Recent deconstructions of cargo cult have condemned the term as distorting. It bundles together social phenomena that actually are very different, or it artificially highlights and isolates certain features from a uniform cultural horizon: "For that is what many anthropologists have been doing: isolating and classifying these phenomena as if they constituted an objective, separate institution, category, or class of events" (McDowell 1988, 121–122). Similarly, Kaplan sought "to dissolve the analytic construct of 'cult', finding it to be more a category of colonial discourse and practice than an analytic window into the complexities of the making of history in colonized societies" (1990, 3–4; see also Kilani 1983, 10; Buck 1989, 158; Scott 1990/91). Dissolving the category cargo cult allows us better to understand "how cargo cults interpenetrate with a people's ideological or cultural construction of change. . . . The beliefs and assumptions that underlie the cargo activity also undergird a variety of other arenas of social action and realms in which cultural meaning is constructed and generated" (McDowell 1988, 122).

Unfortunately for recent deconstructionists, however, cargoism arrived here first at least thirty years ago. Yes, if we "dim our old categories" (McDowell 1988, 122) and quit "drawing arbitrary lines that separate cargo cults from other aspects of sociocultural life and experience" (1988, 127), we might see that, say, Melanesian "religion" is significantly akin to Melanesian "politics" which is analogous to Melanesian "economics." But cargoism already reached this same conclusion by way of a different route. Rather than dissolving cargo cult away, it instead stretched and dilated this into Melanesian culture itself. For cargoism, too, Melanesian religion equals politics equals economics because all these are really cargoism at heart. Despite attempts to deconstruct the term, it may not be possible anymore to excise cargo cult from the equation. This equation has had only one answer for too many years. Melanesian religion plus politics plus economics add up to cargoism.

In 1958, for example, Jan Pouwer was already taking the measure of the breadth of Melanesian cargoism: "Attempts to bridge this gap [between ideal and reality] need not only be embodied in messianic movements; they may also be the background of cooperatives and of nationalistic movements. Certainly all these attempts have at least partly religious components and motives" (1958, 249; see also Firth 1953, 816; Stanner 1958, 24). In years since, many more such equations have been toted up. Melanesian religious, political, and economic action all are computed to be a form of cargo cult. As Harding implied, since Melanesia has a cargo-cult culture, the number of such equations is infinite:

> The non-cult manifestations of cargoism were legion. They were apparent in discussion preceding the House of Assembly elections in 1964 as well as in the decisions of many voters; they were evident in the renewed interest in pagan spirit concepts; in the desire of some people for the local establishment of a "workshop" (factory); in native reaction to information regarding the African origins of mankind. . . . Inasmuch as almost any novel event or information regarding Europeans is apt to be placed immediately in a cargoist context, this list could be greatly extended. (1967, 22)

Many similar cargoist equations could be cited. McDowell provided a sampling of a number of these (1988). Christian conversion is a cargo cult; interest in development is a cargo cult; business activity is a cargo cult; political elections and national independence are cargo cults; and so on. Here are a few examples. Ogan, writing of Bougainville, suggested " 'bisnis' and 'kago' (i.e., material and spiritual riches obtained by supernatural means) were never differentiated in Nasioi minds" (1972, 162; for similar equations, see also Errington 1974; Allen 1976, 307–308; Counts and Counts 1976). Like business, "development" in general "can have cult dimensions" (Clark 1988, 40). So can religious conversion: "the ready acceptance of Christian beliefs may have been closely related to 'cargo-thinking' " (Wetherell and Carr-Gregg 1984, 201). Ogan has also described the relationship between politics and cargo on Bougainville, for example, "cargoist sentiment can be projected on a politician, without any effort on his part" (1974, 128). Throughout Melanesia, "where there is anything in the nature of a political programme or a political plan, it may have in it some elements of symbolic fantasy of the kind associated with 'Cargo Cults', and similar movements" (Firth 1953, 817). Cargoist "thinking" or "sentiment" seeps in everywhere.

The uncomplicated and culturally uninformed reactionary reading of cults, as noted above, at least left space for a noncargoist, noncultist Melanesia. This space disappears in anthropology's more ethnographically sensitive readings that have plumbed Melanesia's cargo-cult culture. A variant approach, which combines something of both reactionary and cultural readings, locates a noncultist space in the precolonial past. Melanesians today may labor under cargo thinking and sentiment, but this bemused cargoism is an effect of their unhappy encounters with world imperialism and capitalism: "Cargo thinking was a product of the forced interaction between two economic systems, the gift economy and the capitalist economy, with their religious support structures" (Buck 1989, 164). Cargo thinking mediated the confrontation between these two systems, and eased the "transition to capitalist production" (1989, 166). We might take such useful cargoism to be a form of reaction, accommodation, and resistance to powerful colonizers, or to be a creative and dynamic process of local history-making (see Kilani 1983, 167; Kaplan 1990). Either way, it radiates from the colonial encounter. Precolonial Melanesians of the past were not tainted by cargo thinking and sentiment.

Not so fast, though. Anthropology's cultural reading has already captured that past as cultic. If Melanesians have a cargo-cult culture today, they had one yesterday too. Ronald Berndt surveyed New Guinea highlands cults of the late 1940s that occurred before direct European contact and determined that "such manifestations in themselves are not directly the result of alien contact, direct or indirect. Explanation must be sought in terms of the indigenous culture" (1954, 269; see also 1952/53). Likewise, Richard Salisbury concluded "contact with Europeans is not a prerequisite for cultism" (1958, 75); and Deryck Scarr suggested that Fiji's Tuka cult is "very likely pre-European": "Any purely reactive explanation of *Tuka* in terms of dispossession or decay does injustice to the Fijian imagination, its fertility and its capacity to play with, interpret and integrate an alien cosmology" (1984, 93). There is no space or time free of cargoism. How could there be? Cargoism is merely Melanesia's cargo-cult culture betrayed in thought, emotion, and deed.

Madness Redux

It is no great step from cargo thinking and cargo sentiment to a cargo psyche. Could it be that Melanesians are cargo cultists not just because of their culture but because of their personality as well? The reactionary reading's Vailala Madness once preserved a space for Melanesian sanity. Vailala Madness is episodic and temporary. Melanesians, although mentally perhaps a little weak, ordinarily are not crazy. Vailala Madness is an unusual disorder "to some extent born of the mental confusion that followed the inrush of new European ideas" (Williams 1934, 372). Besides, some of those outwardly afflicted with the Vailala Madness were faking it (Williams 1923, 8), and merely exhibited "pathomimetic" behaviors (Schwartz 1976, 184–186). These cultic impostors were rascals, not demented.

The real crazies, in Vailala Madness, tended to be some of the prophets and leaders: "among primitive people, a lunatic, epileptic, or super-normal, will inspire fear or respect merely by the strangeness of his conduct; and where the subject trades upon his infirmity he may easily build up a strong influence" (Williams 1923, 36). Some innate psychological trauma or exceptional stress can send these men into ecstatic trance: "the possessor [prophet] indulged in political activity which seemed to be an aggressive outlet for a feeling of guilt. One wonders whether cargo cult leaders in general have been subject to some such personal strains" (Belshaw 1951*b*, 8).

Psychologist B. G. Burton-Bradley cataloged the maladies that cult prophets may suffer: epilepsy, schizophrenia, affective psychosis, hysteria, thyrotoxic psychosis, general paresis, tuberculous spondylitis, obesity, gonorrhea, chronic dermatitis, and narcolepsy (1974, 236). Prophets are particularly prone to grandiose paranoia and require, therefore, both psychiatric treatment and surveillance: "the abnormal prophet must be recognized as such, subjected to psychiatric examination, and treated medically both in his own interest and in that of others. His existence cannot be denied" (Burton-Bradley 1970, 128). A cult's rank and file, on the other hand, more-or-less normal, are only temporarily deranged by the Vailala Madness.

Anthropology's cultural reading of cargo cult, however, trumps reactionary Vailala Madness in that it manages to nativize madness itself (Lattas 1992). Cargoism's madness is normal and routine, not episodic and temporary. The Melanesian personality becomes known to be ordinarily cargoist in temperament. There is a "cargo cult syndrome" (Burton-Bradley 1986, 46). The *Field and Clinical Survey Report of the Mental Health of the Indigenes of the Territory of Papua and New Guinea* lists "Cargo" movements as a "psychological Mechanism Productive of Abnormal Behavior" (Sinclair 1957, 20). The report distinguishes active cult upsurges from background cargo thinking, which is a "continuous process": "The central feature of 'cargo' thinking is its expression of an unrealized need. This is a form of insecurity. The mechanism used to bridge the gap between the need and its fulfillment is a magical one which involves the use of phantasy" (Sinclair 1957, 44). Cargo thinking, here, expresses a constant pathological state of psychological insecurity among Melanesians. "Cargo thinking . . . meets psychological needs. It . . . permeates almost all aspects of social life and embellishes the symptomatology of many forms of psychiatric disorder. The anxiety that gives rise to cult activities has its origins in dissatisfactions and insecurity, and the cargo mechanism has as one of its results the reduction of that anxiety" (Burton-Bradley 1974, 236).

Perhaps such anxious, psychic tension traces back to customary family dynamics in Melanesia: "The psychological residues of relationships with parents, exacerbated often by untimely deaths and the resulting uncertainty about one's own future, stimulate strong feelings of guilt and strong needs for reassurance" (Leavitt 1989,

516). Given this constant undercurrent of anxiety within the Melanesian temperament, "Europeans, as well as their wealth, are highly cathected. They become symbolic representations of ancestors who are in turn imbued with the emotional valences associated with parental figures. From that perspective, failing to receive the cargo becomes a *rejection*" (1989, 464).

Alongside this "pathological anxiety" of rejection (Burton-Bradley 1973, 390), several other conditions have been proposed as the psychological bedrock of cargoistic Melanesians. Perhaps the problem is simply that they are stuck in the juvenile state of cognitive development that Piaget labeled preoperational: "the major question is whether the cognitive capacities of a major proportion of the Indigenes have failed to reach the stage of 'formal operations', or, if rather, that under the stress of the challenge to their cultural orientation the cognitive capacities have undergone regression to earlier developmental stages" (Lidz, Lidz, and Burton-Bradley 1973, 381–382). Cognitive immaturity explains many of the twists in cargo thinking. Melanesians share a child's "artificialism"—the belief that parents have created and control nature, and therefore cargo as well (1973, 382). They assume an "infantile omnipotence" and believe that, through ritual, they may control the world just as a child influences a parent (1973, 382–383). This infantilism leads to an obsessive ritualism: "the origins of this repetition compulsion are probably found in *circular reactions* of the sensori-motor period that Piaget has described, in which the child seeks to achieve an effect by carrying out the movement that preceded the effect—a precursor of cause-and-effect thinking related to operant conditioning" (1973, 383).

This metaphor of the cargo-cult child is a familiar one; and although the figure of childlike native is somewhat more polite than crazy native, it is abnormal rather than developmental psychology that dominates explications of cargo mentality. Some, for example, have suspected that the underlying disorder is schizophrenia: "Very much as the schizophrenic patient had become confused by the contradictory and the egocentric communications of his parents, the Indigene became confused by the contradictory communications of two very different belief systems. . . . He was placed in a bind or

so-called 'double-bind' by the conflicting beliefs and expectations"
(Lidz, Lidz, and Burton-Bradley 1973, 384). Schizoid Melanesians
regress when they are unable to find an ego identity appropriate to
modernity (1973, 384). "The schizophrenic in the ensuing perplex-
ity regresses to earlier types of egocentric cognition in which
animistic and magical beliefs come to the fore, and he again fails to
differentiate what is internal from what is external, and overesti-
mates the efficacy of the thought and wish" (1973, 385).

Psychologists Burton-Bradley and Otto Billig scrutinized, along
these lines, the drawings and doodles made by a cargo leader of
Buka Island's Hahalis Welfare Society, who was locked up in a
Papua New Guinea mental asylum for cutting the head off his six-
teen-year-old nephew to bring on the cargo. They detected that
"the patient's drawings show progressive structural changes that
can be correlated with the spacial structure observed in graphics by
schizophrenic patients" (Billig and Burton-Bradley 1978, 165).
And another "crayon drawing seems to deal with the patient's preoccupation with the cargo cult. The helicopter drops the desired
cargo while the patient expresses his hostility against the whites
by attacking them with the double-tailed snakes" (1978, 162).
(Regarding this close attention and "preoccupation with the cargo
cult" [see chapter 6], one might only counsel "physician, heal thy-
self.")

Melanesian schizophrenia soon leads to paranoia as well. Islanders
misunderstand that colonialist Europeans are actually trying to help
them develop economically and politically, and they blame Europeans for their own failings.

The beliefs become paranoid as the failure to gain the Cargo is no
longer considered his own deficiency, or that of his ancestor spirits,
but due to the cheating European. The hostility toward the white
man engendered by the white man's contempt for the Indigene as
well as his refusal to share the Cargo, is now projected and the
European is regarded as a malevolent person, even at a time when
the European is seeking to guide the Indigene to the skills he
requires to govern himself again and become economically self-suffi-
cient. The projection of blame and the hostility to the European

helps the Indigene regain self-esteem, just as it tends to permit the schizophrenic to retain some self-esteem by projecting onto others his undesirable impulses as well as reasons for his failure in life. (Lidz, Lidz, and Burton-Bradley 1973, 385)

We can perhaps understand how the conspiratorial theory of cargo cult (see chapter 1) easily inverts this sort of blame-the-victim argument about who, exactly, projects what upon whom. Not the psychiatrist, though. Cargo "is no less delusional because a psychiatrist can understand the origins and metaphorical meaning of the idea as well as the functions it serves" (1973, 386).

Theodore Schwartz also fingers paranoia as the cardinal psychocultural condition that "was part of the nexus of causation of cults" (1976, 191). Schwartzian paranoia, however, is no passing effect of acute schizophrenia. Rather, Melanesians manifest an ordinary "paranoid ethos or institutionalized paranoia" which is "part of the cultural context in which such cult occurrences were precipitated and within which they made sense to emotionally and cognitively attuned participants" (1976, 191). Schwartz, initially, proposed the term *paranoid ethos* as descriptive of Melanesian culture rather than individual psychology per se. After living with Melanesians, however, he changed his mind: "I thought it might be possible to dissociate the paranoid concept in its social application from individual psychopathology. But as my experience among various Melanesian groups broadened and eventually included noncultists as well as cultists at various levels of acculturation, I felt that something more than mere analogy was involved" (1973, 356).

Melanesians are normally paranoid after all. "Although the patterns become particularly visible in heightened metastable states of Melanesian cults, such patterns are observable in normal life as well" (1973, 157). A few Islanders suffer the standard paranoia in a grandiose form (Burton-Bradley 1972, 670; 1978, 886), and their cargo interests are so excessive that even most of their neighbors recognize that they are sick. Burton-Bradley offers a diverting series of case studies of extravagant cargo thinking, where individuals have turned to rituals of human sacrifice (1972), cannibalism (1976), and Kung Fu (1978) to persuade ancestors to send along the cargo (see also Pataki-Schweizer 1976). The cannibal cargo cultist killed his own young son, cut out his heart, and ate slices of it raw: "I tried to boil it but was not successful. I had hoped that the steam and the rest of the mixture would go up to God and he would then send me the power in my dreams to do the right things for my people" (Burton-Bradley 1976, 430). Burton-Bradley cautions, given Melanesian cargo mentality, that missionaries ought to ease up a little on the details of Abraham's faith and Christ's passion.

Or perhaps the root cause of cargo mentality is simpler, physiological rather than psychological in origin.

Looking at Papua New Guinea we have to recognize the tropical environment. This contributes to a pattern of health factors which is of particular disadvantage to the developing brain, both *in utero* and in the first months and years of life. . . . Such damage will impair the capacities for concentration, foresight, and judgement. This can lead to more powerful experience of emotion as intensely present with loss of inhibitory control and reduced reality testing. These physiological deprivations can lead to greater vulnerability to dissociation and disorganization of cortical functioning when exposed to additional physical or emotional stress. This is fertile soil for movements which emphasize the affective rather than the cognitive function. (Andrew 1984, 89)

The terminological shift from Vailala Madness to cargo cult in 1945 at first dulled prewar themes of native lunacy and dementia. The new label, which was both more polite and more scientific, outfitted cults for the modern age. Ironically, the cultural reading of cargo cults has returned full circle to Madness. But this Madness no longer is a sudden, temporary insanity. Rather, it is a peculiar but ordinary psychological constitution that compels Melanesians to pursue Cargo by way of cult.

Anthropology, just doing its job, has nativized Cargo, Cult, and even Madness. Its context-sensitive, sometimes empathic cultural readings, in the end, have stained Melanesia with both a cargo-cult culture and psyche. Nowadays, suspicions of cargo cult are always lurking in the background. Any conspicuous Melanesian hope or desire today might be read as cargo; any conspicuous Melanesian social action or organization might be revealed as cult. Those who desire, and those who act, therefore, must always glance back over their shoulders lest cargoist discourse overtake, label, and explain them away.

In chapter 5, I discuss how cargoism as a discourse continues to infect and inflect discussion of a number of notable social organizations and events in Melanesia today. Before this, though, I turn to one long-lived cargo cult from Tanna Island to explore the variety of ways in which cargoism's stories have framed John Frum.

4 STRANGE STORIES OF JOHN FRUM

Anthropologists fostered the cargo cult, but they were by no means the only ones feeding the discourse. Cargoism as a genre of writing comprises several subtypes. Administrators, missionaries, adventurers, journalists, and others also have had reasons to write about Melanesian social movements. Their several interests, not surprisingly, tinted their writing. The cargo cult of a colonial administrator, concerned to oversee and control, differed from that of the anthropologist (concerned, roughly, to understand), the missionary (concerned to combat), or the adventurer and journalist (concerned to instruct, amaze, and entertain).

All these figures and more have written about certain events and conversations that took place on Tanna Island, Vanuatu (an archipelago which, until national independence on 30 July 1980, was the colonial New Hebrides). Tannese words and deeds, in this writing, have come to be known as the "John Frum movement." The name John Frum first appears, on paper, in 1940. The writers who herald John's advent, as text, are British colonial District Agent James M. Nicol, Presbyterian missionary H. M. (Jock) Bell, and local "police boy" Joe Nalpin. Over the last half century, John Frum texts have multiplied and inflated as more and more people have written about the movement. This literature is sizable. The Story of John Frum, could all its chapters and verses be collated, would outweigh a Bible.

The discourse of cargoism makes unlikely heroes. Thanks to five decades of cargoist writing, John Frum is famous. He began diffusely as a "one fellow something" (O'Reilly 1949, 194)—A man? A spirit? A spook?—but quickly triumphed as a star and leading light of the cargo-cult circuit. Written cargoism captured a dim murmuring from obscure and peripheral island conversations, and

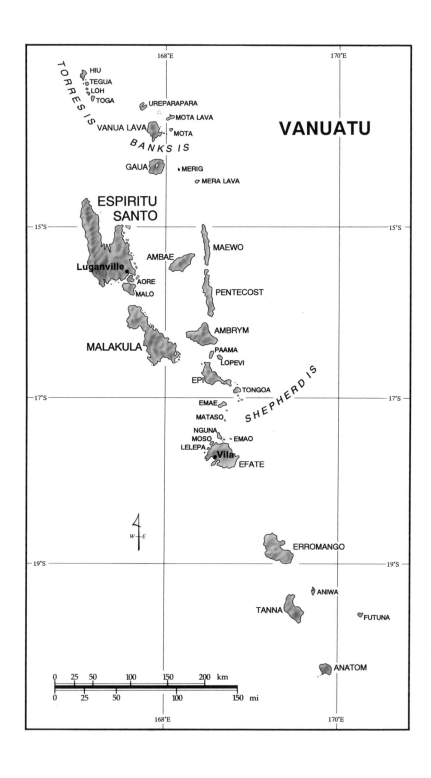

John Frum cargo cult T-shirt, printed by French colonial officials for the elections of 1977. (Collection of Annette Weiner)

broadcast this to the world. John Frum texts have traveled thousands of miles beyond the oral universe of island conversation out of which the hero first emerged.

In the world of cargo cults, "the celebrated John Frum" (Eliade 1965, 136) is a luminary. Nowadays, he is even a classic: "a 'classic example' of cargo cultism in Melanesia" (Trompf 1984, 43). "The Jon Frum Movement has become a touchstone for determination of the characteristics of cargo cults" (Calvert 1978, 212; see Burridge 1993, 282). Moreover, Tanna itself has become known abroad, insofar as the island is known, as the home of John Frum. Its culture is now cargo-cult culture. Paul Theroux wanted most of all to visit Tanna because he "had heard that a cargo cult, the Jon Frum Movement, flourished on the island" (1992, 187). Tanna is "the oddest outside-time island in Vanuatu" (1992, 213). With strange propriety, Tanna's nearest neighbors, Polynesian speakers who live on Futuna, a volcanic plug 70 kilometers away, call the island that they see on their western horizon *gauta*, a word that also means "cargo" (Janet Keller, pers comm, 1992).

This chapter reads through the prolix John Frum literature to delineate varieties of the cargo-cult story. An assortment of writers with different interests and perspectives have produced John Frum texts. The various subgenres of cargoism are most distinct immediately after the war. By the 1960s and 1970s, the several perspectives on John Frum to a large extent have blurred together. The story lines become more uniform. The tone of the writing settles down into either a sort of mock amusement or earnest admiration. There is now a canonical John Frum story line replete with stock motifs.

Although early accounts of the John Frum movement are stylistically distinctive in important ways, from the beginning the various cargoist subgenres borrowed cult stories and interpretation from one another. Cross-fertilization among John Frum stories occurred as various secondary accounts all cited the same, limited primary sources. Blurring also occurred where writers assumed dual perspectives. Some missionaries wrote like anthropologists. Some anthropologists borrowed the point of view of colonial administrators.

The several subtypes of John Frum writing begin (and end) in different years, and cross-fertilization among the several subgenres is affected by the dates of their appearance and disappearance over time. Colonial administrators began writing John Frum reports in 1940 and stopped writing in 1980 upon Vanuatu's independence (although little of this material was published). Missionaries began writing in 1941. Their work, too, mostly disappeared by the mid

1980s when Europeans withdrew from or were forced from pastoral roles on the island. The American military produced a brief spurt of John Frum surveillance in 1943. Anthropologists only discovered John Frum in 1949, but their John Frum texts continue to flow. Adventurers and explorers first described John Frum in 1960, although their accounts are irregular until the 1970s, when they flourish. Newspaper reporters and tourist writers both found John Frum in 1968. Finally, local academics and politicians of soon-to-be independent Vanuatu produced occasional John Frum commentary starting in the late 1970s.

I survey below the John Frum stories of colonial administrators, the military, missionaries, anthropologists, adventurers, reporters, and tourist writers. There are, of course, differences among the contributors to each of these subgenres. Presbyterian writings about John Frum, for example, differ in both tone and amplitude from those of Catholic and Seventh-day Adventist missionaries who were also active on Tanna. I ignore most internal subgenre variation and attempt to tease out the principal themes and motifs of each sort of cargo writing. The availability of texts and the relative prolixity of the different voices in the archive, however, have influenced unavoidably my overviews.

Alongside written John Frum texts, there is also a growing library of John Frum film and video. This opens with David Attenborough's 1960 BBC production *Cargo Cult*. Some years later, Gunther Sachs took his movie camera *In Search of John Frum*. Claude Otzenberger, working for Tele France, filmed *Le Retour du Cargo* in 1979. The BBC screened Nigel Evans' *The Fantastic Invasion* in 1991. John Frum has also starred in a number of other Japanese, European, Australian, and North American television programs. There are conspicuous affinities of style between the adventurist subgenre of cargoism, as discussed later, and John Frum film. I restrict my discussion, however, to written John Frum texts although visual cargoism invites its own critical attention.

Also, for obvious reasons, I avoid producing my own summary account of the John Frum movement. Readers will soon know enough of John as they scan the assorted stories of his movement. I focus first on early interpretive differences among the subgenres.

The concluding portion of the chapter looks, instead, at two John Frum motifs common to all cargoist subgenres.

The ultimate standardization of a common John Frum story line relates, in part, to the success of the term cargo cult itself within anthropology. By the 1970s, with cargo cult now ensconced in dictionaries and encyclopedias, people knew how such movements should operate. John Frum accountings had to present themselves within the descriptive context of cargo cult, as the generally applicable categorical label. John Frum is either a cargo cult, or it has to be excused for differing here and there from the cultic norm. The rich John Frum archive, of course, has also underwritten some of the terminological fortunes of *cargo cult*. John Frum and cargo cult have matured together.

Anthropological writings of John Frum, blurred in with other subgenres, have been a dominant voice. Anthropology's success here has much to do with the claim that it stakes to ethnographic authority (see Clifford 1983). We are the cargo-cult experts. But, more importantly, anthropology's discursive dominance also has much to do with the decreasing political and economic dangers of the cargo cult itself. In the immediate postwar years, cargo cults were a menace. They appeared to threaten political and economic institutions already profoundly undermined by war. Then, the most forceful knowledge of cults consisted of the colonial report. Nowadays, remnant cargo cults have, in the main, diminished into advantageous local tourist attractions, and humble anthropology and other, more popular discourses can guide their public interpretation. The emotional tenor of written cargoism, along these lines, has declined from fear, loathing, and ridicule to a bemused mild curiosity.

Ironically, at the very moment of its discursive triumph, anthropology now denies its own achievement. Having written up John Frum as a cargo cult, anthropology now wishes it could erase those early, overly enthusiastic statements that, in the light of more and more and more anthropological understanding of Tanna, appear painfully crude and inaccurate. Anthropology's recent message is that John Frum is no cargo cult. Once it may have seemed so, but we now know far too much about Tannese culture and mentality to be able to apply the simplistic cargo-cult label with any measure of intellectual or political comfort.

But it is too late. Everyone already knows that John Frum is a cargo cult. The stock motifs of cargoist writing reproduce this knowledge each time Tanna is described. If cargo cult is anthropology's monster, then the discipline's good Dr Frankensteins may find themselves engaged in a mortal pursuit across the globe, from steamy Melanesia to icebound Arctic seas, in a vain attempt to obliterate their own adopted creation. Like the monster, cargo cult has escaped and is on the run.

John Frum for Administrators

British District Agent James Nicol, who had been resident administrator on Tanna since 1916, was the first to write down the name John Frum. He did so during an inquiry he held on 27 November 1940 to investigate the mysterious disappearance of goats from the herds of Seventh-day Adventist converts on the island. This inquiry, which convened at Lenakel, the colonial headquarters on Tanna's west coast, disclosed rumors that men were gathering secretly at night at Iamwatakarik kava-drinking ground near Green Point several miles south of Lenakel. There, the gathered throngs drank infusions of kava *(Piper methysticum)*, the traditional Pacific drug substance, and listened to the words of a shadowy figure who named himself John Frum. The goats were disappearing into earth ovens to feed the hungry crowds (Guiart 1956b, 152; Rice 1974, 251).

Nicol's report of the inquiry, and his subsequent accounts of the movement that he continued to submit to his superiors in Port Vila until 1944, when he was crushed to death by his runaway vehicle, have, like the goats, also disappeared. The "John Frum file" kept in the British District Agency office in Lenakel had vanished by the mid-1970s (Ken Calvert, pers comm). Rumor intimated that some itinerant investigator had helped himself to the file. Cargoists chase strange treasure. Here is ironic mimicry indeed. The cultist pursuit of hidden cargo becomes a paradigm for cargoism's hunt for secret cargo texts.

Journalist Edward Rice, who spent several weeks researching

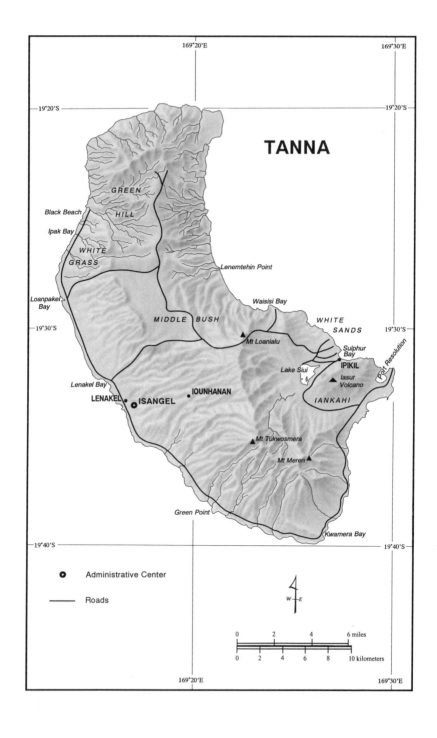

John Frum on Tanna in the early 1970s, described his first encounter with the British district agent then serving on the island. After sharing a beer, Rice mentioned that he would like to see the government files on John Frum. The agent "refuses, saying that they're classified. I offer to steal some great secret American document (bad joke, that, considering Watergate et cetera) in return, but the District Agent says that even if he had the authority he will not give me the John Frum file" (1974, 171). Rice, however, appended a footnote to his piqued encounter with British colonial authority: "The John Frum file. But see the Appendix, page 251" (1974, 248). And here the cargo is! The appendix ("John Frum Cult—Diary of Events") summarizes official British communications about the movement between 1940 and 1957.

Although the sacred files themselves have vanished, we can still find primary British and French administrative John Frum texts reproduced here and there throughout the John Frum archive. Other writers besides Rice have quoted selections of this material, including anthropologist Guiart (1956*b*) and cultural geographer Bonnemaison (1987). Guiart, in fact, offered in another appendix a version of a Nicol "Report on Jonfrum" of 6 June 1941 (1956*b*, 406–409). Subsequent colonial administrators on Tanna continued to provide additional John Frum commentary.

Administrative stories set forth a colonialist argument on John Frum and on cargo cults generally. This perspective, at heart, is that John Frum is foolery or madness inflamed by unwise mission interference with native culture. There is also little doubt in administrative minds that the cult is ultimately subversive of the mission and, eventually, of governmental authority as well.

Nicol, in his administrative report, was the first to point his finger at the missionaries, blaming them for the John Frum troubles: "There is no doubt that although the trouble started against the Missions it would only have been a short time before the authority of the Government would have been challenged" (quoted in Guiart 1956*b*, 409). Nicol's report also inaugurated an emblematic administrative cargoist motif of criminal foolery. Nicol disparaged John Frum enthusiasm as a "racket" and a "hoax" (Guiart 1956*b*, 408).

Sir Harry Luke, who was the Western Pacific high commissioner during the first years of the war, also provided an early John Frum text. Although Luke was based in Fiji, he toured his administrative territories in mid-1941. Luke published his personal diary in 1945. On 15 July 1941, the diary records that he met the "Tanna 'Prophet' Jonfrum and his accomplices, who have now been arrested and brought into Vila" (1945, 203). This particular John Frum was an Islander named Manehevi. Nicol's counter-cult Tannese advisors had incriminated Manehevi as the rascal who was impersonating John Frum, and Nicol arrested him along with several others, and shipped them up to prison in Port Vila that June. Luke believed his encounter with Manehevi noteworthy enough to remark in his diary, and he also included a photograph of Manehevi in the book. His analysis was: "This native has been attempting, by imposing himself on the more ignorant of his fellow-islanders as a sorcerer, to organize an anti-white movement in Tanna, something like Apolosi's on a smaller scale" (1945, 203–204). Because Luke was writing in pre–cargo-cult days, his descriptive prototype for John Frum was an earlier Fijian social movement, led by Apolosi, that began in 1914 (Worsley 1957, 29). Luke's administrative line, here, is that John Frum is simple criminal deception. He signals this duplicity by belittling the word "prophet" with quotation marks. John Frum's message should be taken as neither real prophecy nor real religion. It succeeds only by playing to ignorant Islanders. However, although a fraud, the cult is nonetheless dangerous in that it is anti-white.

Subsequent administrative commentators rehearse the same motifs. Alexander Rentoul, a onetime patrol officer in Papua and New Guinea, replaced Nicol on Tanna for several months when the latter went on leave in 1943. Rentoul sent a letter (" 'John Frum': Origin of New Hebrides Movement") to the editor of *Pacific Islands Monthly*, in January 1949. This letter arrived in the midst of *PIM*'s heated dispute between missionaries and planters over which party was to blame for cargo cults. Rentoul joined Mr Bird and the anti-mission side. Yes, John Frum was anti-white but mostly he was antimission. Disaffected Presbyterian Tannese, some seeking educational opportunities, had earlier fallen away and joined the rival Seventh-day Adventist mission but were inevitably disappointed in that this mission, too, offered only "Pray, pray, pray and sing, sing, sing all the time" (Rentoul 1949, 31).

> The result of all this . . . was that natives in large numbers left both Missions, and rejoined the "heathen" in the various villages, announcing that they had left the John the Baptist Missions, and formed instead the John Broom ("Jon Frum," he pronounced it) movement, the object of which was to sweep (or "broom") the white people off the island of Tanna—Tanna for the Tannese was their slogan. I believe that this movement did originate in this way, and was first prompted by dissatisfaction with the Missions, and that it had no connection with Communism or other outside influence. The Tannese, in my opinion, are not the sort of weak-minded natives likely to be influenced by such teachings, and are quite capable of starting a movement of their own, directed primarily against the Missions, and only indirectly against some of the other whites. (1949, 31)

Rentoul advanced the standard colonialist line: Don't blame the administration. John Frum is the missionaries' fault.

Rentoul's letter also introduced an important motif that is shared by many subsequent varieties of cargoist writing: cargo as mystery. This theme is what climaxed in Rice's quest for the hidden cargo texts. The mystery motif shadows an alternate thematic portrayal of cargo as a fraud. There is a hidden, secret core to cargo whose truth must be revealed. This dark heart, for colonial administrators, is rotten. For many other cargoist storytellers, though, the evaluative polarity reverses and the hidden truth of cargo is sacralized as the good desire for equality and salvation. And for still other cargoists, unfathomable mystery itself stands for cargo's truth. District Agent Rentoul, though, presumed that secrecy was prima facie evidence for flagrant trickery. He relied upon a common ploy to expose John Frum secrets: "I went to some pains to find out the exact meaning of the title, but I met with a wall of silence, until one day I did a favour for one of the heads of the movement and, as a token of gratitude, he gave me the whole story of its origin, which I pass on to you for what it is worth" (1949, 31). The whole John Frum archive is studded with artful investigations and disentangled mysteries of this sort.

Postwar District Agent G. L. Barrow also told a "Story of Jonfrum" in the British colonial administrative journal *Corona*.

> The Jonfrum cult first came to light at the end of 1940 at Green Point in the south-west of the island. By April, 1941, its retrogressive nature was sufficiently clear for Nicol to round up the principal people involved and try to disentangle the story. It transpired that in the hills in the south of the island there lived from time immemorial a devil named Karaperamun. A figure dressed in white robes, with a white covering over his face, had appeared to various people among the rocks by the shore and announced that he was none other than Karaperamun who had now taken the name of Jonfrum. On his instructions a house was built for him at Green Point and from there messengers carried his teaching round the island. The gist of it was that, if all the Tannese were faithful to him, Jonfrum would in due course come to earth and usher in a brave new world on Tanna. Everyone must leave the missions and must drink *kava*. They must get rid of their European money because when Jonfrum came he would bring his own money. They need not worry about gardens or houses and they could kill all their animals because Jonfrum would provide more. There would be dancing and *kava*-drinking to their hearts' content and no one need ever do any more work. The Tannese swallowed it all to such an extent that they even threw their compromising European money into the sea. Jonfrum was finally exposed as a Tannese named Manehevi, a shiftless man of no great intelligence and no fixed abode. His only explanation of the whole thing was "Mi play no more" [I'm only kidding]. (Barrow 1951, 379–380)

Barrow, here, evoked the now stock administrative theme of criminal foolery in his story: "retrogressive nature . . . round up the principal people involved . . . disentangle the story. . . . The Tannese swallowed it all." He also suggested that a drop in copra prices during the late 1930s had created "many idle hands with nothing to do and all day in which to do it" (1951, 379).

Barrow went on to describe the effects of the American wartime occupation of the New Hebrides between 1942 and 1945 during which a new currency (US dollars) and thousands of tons of cargo did indeed flood the archipelago. The Americans began to arrive in March 1942. That previous September, District Agent Nicol had intercepted a letter that native policeman Joe Nalpin sent to his father on Tanna. Nalpin's letter predicted that John Frum would "send his son to America to bring 'The King' ":

> At this point world affairs took a hand in the situation. The origin of the reference to someone coming from America has never been traced. It first appears in Joe Nalpin's letter written three months before Pearl Harbour when knowledge of America was very scanty on Tanna. Then, in the early days of 1942, the American forces arrived in Vila and Santo. Word quickly came back from the exiles that all Jonfrum's prophecies were coming true. (1951, 380)

A thousand Tannese men enthusiastically signed into army and navy native labor corps and sailed north to work at the growing American installations on Efate (see Lindstrom 1989).

In Barrow's account, feckless false prophet Manehevi is merely "shiftless," but letter-writing Joe Nalpin is "a shrewd and slippery gentleman" (1951, 380). A further thematic slide—a move from shiftless playfulness ("I'm only kidding") and slippery shrewdness to rank lunacy—is short and easy within administrative cargoism. The discourse, of course, here recalls prewar stories of Vailala Madness in Papua New Guinea. *Pacific Islands Monthly,* which, as we have seen, principally boosted the colonial administrative and business communities, repeated the stock motif of cultic madness to introduce an overview of the John Frum movement that it published in January 1950. This article, said *PIM,* adds "to our knowledge of this primitive psychological kink" (Priday 1950, 67). District Agent Barrow, similarly, presumed psychological kinks and lunacy to explain the next notable John Frum event that occurred in late 1943.

> Suddenly in October the uneasy calm was shattered. This time the scene was in the extreme north of the island. A certain Neloiag had proclaimed himself as Jonfrum and King of America and was building an aerodrome to receive his brother who was to come from America. He had gathered a bodyguard of toughs armed with clubs and shot-guns, and the police sent to arrest him were unable to do

so. Then, for no apparent reason, he walked into the British Agency and gave himself up. It was obvious that he was quite mad. (Barrow 1951, 380–381)

The logic of an official cargoist discourse of criminal foolery or lunacy led either to the prison house or the asylum. The British and French administration jailed the tricksters it located among cult leaders, while asylum doors clanged shut on the mad: "Neloiag and fifty-five of his followers were sentenced to varying terms of imprisonment and sent to Vila. There Nelioag [sic] was given a medical examination and certified as insane. Ultimately he was transferred to the Lunatic Asylum in Noumea" (1951, 381).

Cult leaders are tricksters and lunatics, but their foolery can only be compelling because their followers are ignorant. A complementary cargo motif of native ignorance led Barrow and other writers of administrative cargoism to appeal for improved native education programs that might temper cultic neuroses. The simple repression of outbreaks of the disease is not enough: "Suppression of an undesirable popular movement by force can never be more than a palliative which gives an opportunity to diagnose and cure the source of the trouble" (Barrow 1951, 382). The cure for John Frum, as for the cargo cult in general, is a quick course in moral and technical education. Befuddled natives must be taught to understand the real world and the way this works.

> If Tanna is to be guarded against such retrogressive movements in the future the first essential is a revival of Christianity for, without a firm faith with absolute standards of right and wrong and higher values than mere physical gratification, there can be neither spiritual stability nor social order. The next need is for education in the broadest sense of the term, training for life as it is in the world today, the inculcation of moral values and technical ability, the diffusion of knowledge to give a proper sense of proportion and responsibility. Finally there is a need for economic and political institutions which will give the Tannese a sense of having some say in their own destiny. (1951, 382)

Barrow, here a cautious reformer, gave the Tannese only *some* say in their own destiny—actually, he gave them only a *sense* of having that partial say. Even so, he believed that his colleagues within the administrative community might view these proposals as radical. Barrow warned, though, that "in the state of the modern world" there is "a militant enemy itching to exploit any dissatisfaction, particularly among subject peoples" (1951, 382). John Frum could be worse. He could be Karl Marx or Joseph Stalin. If nothing is done on Tanna, moreover, "there is no reason to think that the whole story will not begin again" (1951, 382).

Twenty years later, administrative cargoism had not much changed when writer Austin Coates visited Tanna. The British government had commissioned Coates to compile the Western Pacific Islands volume in a series of literary overviews of its remnant colonies. Coates' report rehearses the stock administrative motifs of blaming the missions, hidden cult truths, and Melanesian mental imbalance: "The Presbyterian despotism of Tana [sic] will be recalled, as also . . . the people's mental retreat into a secret world, about which mission and administration knew nothing. . . . The movement was religious and psychic, stemming from the adventist aspect of Christianity . . . which on the Melanesian mind is capable of producing what could be termed a state of mass imbalance" (1970, 275–277). Barrow's appeals for reality training also continue to echo a generation later. Coates, too, complained that, "one senses the secret world, from which the New Hebrideans must somehow be persuaded to disengage themselves" (1970, 278).

Administrative cargoism powerfully influenced later subgenres of cargo discourse. Administrators, along with missionaries, were closest to John Frum action on the ground—at least until the advent of anthropologists who professed a better understanding of the natives and their cargo cult. Administrative writings have become primary texts recycled in a variety of secondary accounts of the John Frum movement. Although the other subgenres of cargoist writing have borrowed some of the colonial administrator's narrative motifs—for example, the rascal or lunatic cult leader, veiled cult truths, anti-white but mostly antimission cult motivations, ignorant natives, and palliative educational schemes—they have rejected or refracted other administrative themes. Other paraphrases of cargoism have their own John Frum stories to tell.

John Frum for the Army

The American military landed near Port Vila in early 1942 to forestall the southerly advance of Japanese forces into the southwest Pacific. By the end of the year, the Americans had established a number of installations around Efate Island and also on Espiritu Santo. On 18 October 1943, James Nicol contacted British Resident Commissioner Richard Blandy in Port Vila to report a potentially dangerous uprising led by the mad John Frum prophet Neloiag, whom he had detained. He requested police support from the capital to arrest as well Neloiag's followers, then hard at work leveling an airfield in north Tanna for American planes. Nicol also asked for American officers who might disabuse cult enthusiasm (Carson and Patten 1943, 6).

A small army sailing vessel, the USS *Echo,* left Port Vila carrying forty-seven members of the New Hebrides Defense Force, eight British native policemen, and five Americans including Assistant Intelligence Officer Captain Donald Carson and Major Samuel Patten who served as observers on the mission for the III Island Command on Efate. The *Echo* arrived at Lenakel on 21 October. The next day, the expedition headed north.

At 0500L/22 the NHDF [New Hebrides Defense Force], Police, Mr. Nicol, observers, Jonfrum, who had been in jail [ie, Neloiag], and about fifty friendly natives from White Sands on the eastern part of the island started for the village of the Jonfrumites. Between 0600 and 0700 everyone got drenched by a heavy rain but soon crossed the western ridge of hills and proceeded north along the high inland plateau. At 1115L we arrived at Green Hill (location and village) and stopped for lunch. About 1200L we resumed the march and at 1230L entered the old village of Ikalau (now called Lemanburasem). The village itself was nearly deserted but just to the west of it we found a cleared area in which one hundred and fifty or two hundred natives were eating their noonday meal. . . . Part of the NHDF then formed a circle facing out along the edges of the cleared area to guard against possible snipers. Mr. Nicol questioned the natives and obtained from some of the men he knew the names of nine of Jonfrum's chief lieutenants (or disciples). . . . Mr. Nicol gave instructions for the rest of Jonfrum's Army to report to Green Hill at daybreak the next day. Major Patten using broken Pidgin English and an interpreter told the natives that the American forces had no connection with Jonfrum and that they did not want an airport built on Tanna because they and the British and French were fighting the Japs in the Solomons. After that the NHDF and Police gave a demonstration of their strength and nearly scared the natives to death by firing about ten rounds apiece from rifles, tommy guns and a Bren gun. As a farewell gesture a small grass hut on the edge of the clearing was set afire. The friendly local natives and NHDF soldiers wanted to burn the whole village but were not allowed to. (Carson and Patten 1943, 1–2)

The *Echo* departed Tanna on 25 October, carrying Neloiag and fifty-five other prisoners back north to Port Vila.

The Tanna Army: John Frum's men drill. (Lindstrom)

Captain Carson and Major Patten submitted a report and a map of the expedition to Headquarters, III Island Command, in Port Vila. This included a section, "Background for Trouble," that repeats colonial administrative stories about John Frum. John Frum, for example, is "John Broom," an "expected reincarnation of St. John the Baptist who is (figuratively) to take a broom and sweep away the white man and bring the Tannese into paradise" (1943, 4). District Agent Nicol is an obvious source of this cargoist paraphrase. Nicol also guided the American expedition into the green heart of Tanna, serving as both cultural and linguistic interpreter of this opening Tannese/American encounter.

The administrative cargo motif of cultic subversion and treachery particularly excited the interest of military intelligence. Carson and Patten's report concludes with a consideration of "Possibility of Axis Influence in Jonfrumism." Other cargoist subgenres later embraced the motif of external subversion (see eg, Coral Tours Melanesie 1971[?], 78). John Frum raconteurs continue to repeat stories of obscure Japanese spies and, in the 1950s and 1960s, of suspect communist puppet masters who pull John Frum's strings (Michener 1951, 220). The administrative position that missionary blunders were to blame for cult outbreaks, however, in the end eclipsed the army's suspicion of possible Japanese provocateurs.

It is not felt that Axis influence is indicated in the Jonfrum movement. In the first place there is nothing that anyone knows about on Tanna that would be of any value to the Axis. Therefore it would not be of any use to stir up native trouble. Second, the present native trouble is only an outbreak of an older movement in opposition to the missions and white people generally. It only become [sic] violent because of an order given by a leader whom even his followers consider as crazy. Third, as far as is known, only three people of Axis sympathy have been on the island for some time. For a time in early 1942 one of the Vichy French Henin brothers (Henri) from New Caledonia was interned on Tanna. However he was later allowed to go to Vial [sic, ie, Vila]. For about four months in early 1940 two Japanese from Vila were employed in the construction of the Roman Catholic Mission. One was the rather old Sighametu. He had a native wife. The other was a man of about forty called Cami [Kami]. They are reported to have said that Japan would aid Germany in the war. They told the natives that if they had a store they would pay more for native copra and charge less for calico than the British and French. According to them it would take a war before they would be allowed to do that. These Japs returned to Vila when they finished the mission and it is not thought they made a lasting impression on the natives. (Carson and Patten 1943, 7–8)

The *American* presence, however, did make a lasting impression on the John Frum archive. The Tannese themselves, returning home from labor corps duty with the US Army and Navy, also speedily incorporated a range of military symbolism into John Frum ritual. John Frum narrative in general likewise turned to military metaphor. Reverend Bell, for example, grumbling about John Frum's success, complained "fifth column activities were just as effective on Tanna as elsewhere" (cited in Guiart 1956*b*, 412). In the John Frum archive, military figures of speech from this point supplemented missionary and administrative metaphoric alternatives (such as "disciples" or "police"): "[Neloiag] really organized his movement. He had about nine lieutenants (or disciples) and an army (or police force) of about forty-five (Carson and Patten 1943, 5). Neloiag now has chief lieutenants (or are they disciples?). John Frum's police, now, become an army.

John Frum for Missionaries

A clutch of missionaries also lived on Tanna during the early years of the John Frum movement, including Presbyterians William Armstrong, H. M. (Jock) Bell, and Charles McLeod; a Spanish-speaking Catholic priest, Roman Martin; and the Seventh-day Adventist Miller. The Presbyterians, particularly, produced a long-running John Frum commentary, much of which they published in their mission journal *Quarterly Jottings from the New Hebrides (QJNH)*. Mission texts offer a counter-reading of certain administrative cargo themes. And like the latter, influential mission cargo motifs also have been much recycled within the John Frum archive.

Presbyterian jottings, in John Frum's early days, not unexpectedly branded the movement as painful heresy. Tannese supporters of John Frum had "fallen" (Bell, cited in Guiart 1956*b*, 413). On Sun-

John Frum leaders raise an American flag, 15 February 1978. (Lindstrom)

day, 11 May 1941, almost all of the mission's congregation, some thirty-five hundred Islanders strong, neglected to come to church. Experienced missionaries recognized sinfulness when they saw it, and early mission cargoism focused on cultic immorality. *QJNH* circulated primarily among a readership of Australian, New Zealand, and Scottish Presbyterians who had since the 1860s filled many a collection plate in support of the New Hebrides mission. Initial missionary texts betray not a little embarrassment at having abruptly lost their entire Tannese flock, three generations in the converting, to some obscure phantom. Still, God moves in mysterious ways and the awkward John Frum movement perhaps presented a new opportunity for increasing overseas financial support for mission endeavors.

The missionary motif of sinfulness reframed parallel administrative narratives of cultic ignorance or idleness. For administrators, the 1930s collapse of world copra prices led to idle island hands that soon manipulated John Frum into being. For missionaries, sinful idleness was more the result, rather than the cause, of the John Frum movement. In May 1941, H. M. Bell itinerated around erstwhile Presbyterian villages: "Throughout the island we encountered slackness, dirty villages, tracks grown up, English schools with only a few attending and in general a very real spiritual apathy" (1941, 8). Because of John Frum, "fewer were attending church, heathen dances were more numerous, laziness became very popular" (1941, 9).

Charles McLeod, who reopened the White Sands mission station after the war, had little doubt about who was behind the "apostasy of 1941" (1947, 8). No cunning Japanese spies, the furtive provocateur, rather, was the devil.

> Satan objects when his dominion is threatened. Night after night the heathens gathered in a determined effort to win back their brothers. Heathen songs are sung all night every night. Heathen dancing and its accompanying wickedness flourishes. There can be no question on Tanna about dancing. Here it is the embodiment of evil . . . so you see that though there are evidences that God's Spirit is working there are also evidences that evil is still in the heart of Man Tanna. (1947, 8)

McLeod remarked the severe government repression of the movement. But since John Frum is Satan, what is mere jail time? He doubted the effectiveness of the government's response: "fourteen men have long sentences ending with banishment from Tanna. In short this means that they will never see their wives, children, homes or their friends again. . . . This serious punishment is an attempt to kill the movement; but I cannot help asking, does history suggest that they will succeed. As a follower of Christ I know that there is but one way to foil Darkness and that is to let in the Light" (1947, 8).

Not surprisingly, the missionaries also disputed the administrative cargoist theme that *they* were to blame for John Frum. When blame is being handed around, the administration and plantation communities ought to bear in mind their own responsibilities in the matter. An exasperated *Pacific Islands Monthly* reported on a speech delivered to the 1948 Presbyterian General Assembly in Wellington, New Zealand, titling its piece "Alleged Anti-Exploitation Movement in Hebrides: Missionary Accuses Planters-Traders—Again!":

> According to Mr. L. W. Murray, New Zealand secretary of the Presbyterian Overseas Mission, there has been a growth of nationalism and a violent reaction against "exploitation" by traders and planters among the natives of the New Hebrides. He . . . spoke of what he called the "Jon Frum movement" in Tanna, which manifested itself as a resurgence of native superstition and heathenism as well as reaction against exploitation. (*PIM* 1948a, 92).

PIM, once again, rushed to defend its colonial readership with an appended editorial note (which is as long as the article being editorialized). This defense is interesting in that here appears the first print usage of the newly minted term cargo cult to describe the John Frum movement. Such labeling, for *PIM,* substituted for explanation (see also *PIM*'s introduction to Priday 1950). John Frum is *not* an anti-European nationalist movement. Rather, it is just another run-of-the-mill cargo cult, the initial journalistic novelty of which had already much palled.

> The old mission howl of "exploitation"—a silly Communist term designed to tickle the ears of the ignorant—is so well known to "PIM" readers that it would be tedious to discuss it further. But what Mr. Murray calls the "Jon Frum movement," and describes as a new feeling of intense nationalism on the part of the New Hebrideans, seems to be nothing more or less than what is known in Papua and New Guinea as "Cargo Cult." There is nothing new

about "Cargo Cult." There have been outbreaks of it, from time to time, during the last 50 years. . . . [A]s Mr. Murray describes it, it would appear that "Jon Frum" is just "Cargo Cult" under a new name. (*PIM* 1948*a*, 92)

PIM's editors proposed again that such a cult is also "the fault of the missions, who break down the native's ancient institutions and disturb his normal life. It probably is a bit of both—that is, the native reaction to the impact of European civilization" (1948*a*, 92). This final theme, neatly, shifts blame from planters, traders, administrators, and even culpable missionaries upward to the diffuse level of Western civilization itself and its impact. The natives, naturally, are susceptible to the disease of cargo cult which, although mysterious and unfortunate, is an inevitable side effect of civilization.

Three months later, Presbyterian Mission Secretary Murray battled back, complaining to *PIM* that he had been misrepresented. Actually, he had said that colonial exploitation was only *one* of the factors that spark native movements (albeit an important one):

this Movement had a number of roots, some of them probably going down below the surface of consciousness. One of those, without doubt, was the measure of exploitation experienced by the native people at the hands of the whites. I made no comment on the extent of that exploitation, and whether it is being practiced at present, or belongs only to the past. Everyone knows that there has been such. You, yourself, in your editorial footnote, acknowledge that it has had a place—and there is no doubt that, however the matter appears to the white people, to many of the natives it has been a reality. (Murray 1949, 61)

Mr Murray was willing for missionaries to shoulder some John Frum blame, but only if they might share this out with other whites. Besides, "if it had not been for the breaking down of the natives' institutions and the disturbing of his normal life, through the influence of Christianity, the lot of the White Man in these Islands, event [*sic*] to-day, would be a very difficult and hazardous one" (1949, 61).

This was the line that missionary cargoism was generally to take.

John Frum was nationalistic: Tanna for the Tannese. Yes, mission Christianity once may have been rigorous, but exploitative planters and administrators were also at fault. Missionary S. J. Cooper, who manned the Presbyterian station at White Sands in the 1950s, for example, explained John Frum in these terms:

> On an island of about 400 square miles, and with only about 8,000 people, it might seem ridiculous to talk of Nationalism. But this movement is Nationalistic. It is also religious. It has welded together things from the old custom days and parts of Christian teaching. . . . It is this mixture which has been so horribly and insidiously confusing to many folk on the edge of the Church—not to mention many who have been "Christian" for years. (Cooper 1958, 8)

Quarterly Jottings editorials likewise featured the motif of cargo as nationalistic:

> Hundreds who had thronged the Church and apparently were happy in their Christian faith withdrew altogether from the Church, became sullen in their attitude toward all white people including the Missionaries, and in some cases became dangerously hostile. The reason? Jon Frum was at work, a mysterious personage who claimed to be the Prophet of Liberation, the divine Leader who would give Tanna truly to the Tannese. . . . Basically it was, and remains, a nationalistic cult, not essentially different from uprisings in many islands in the Pacific nor indeed from struggles for liberty and self determination anywhere. (QJNH 1959, 4; see also Bell 1941, 9; O'Reilly 1949, 207)

Alongside eruptive nationalism, missionary cargoism maneuvered to deflect administrative blame by cultivating other possible John Frum roots besides regretfully harsh mission policy of the recent past. Mission writers, echoing *PIM*, naturalized the cult by shifting blame to civilization at large and its unhappy, although normal, effects upon the simple native. John Frum is, according to this thematic, a natural side effect of evolutionary progress. Presbyterian Mission Hospital nurse Nancy Eveille who lived on Tanna in the 1950s, for example, sounded this line to conclude her account of

National Geographic author and yachtsman Irving Johnson's visit to Tanna in May 1952:

> In May we had a visit from the American-owned sailing ship *Yankee* which caused quite a stir among the Jon Frumers who of course claimed that Jon had sent it from America. When the leaders gathered their wits and realised that there was an American ship in their midst they put on a show for them. On the second day here the Americans went over to take photos of the volcano. . . . On the ash plain they found hundreds of people and piles of gifts. . . . Towards the end someone sidled up to the American leader and gave him a list of things people wanted when John came. At this stage the British District Agent thought things had gone far enough. He asked the American leader to speak to them and tell them as we had previously, that they're on the wrong track—that he had never heard of J.F. in America and no one was going to bring them things for nothing. . . . I suppose you would call this movement the cargo cult of Tanna. An inevitable part of a race becoming civilised. (Eveille 1953, 8)

Along with nationalism and the disruptive effects of modernity, mission writers shared with administrative cargoism a third causal motif that also unloaded blame from mission shoulders. This was the theme of the rascal leader who hoaxes his mentally confused or otherwise ignorant followers. This motif resonated with the complementary mission stories about Satan on the move and Tanna's great fall. Reverend Cooper gave us one example:

> The coming of Jon Frum is at hand. In fact he was to have come last Friday week on the Lenakel side. A big dance was held, and people waited and waited for him to appear. Two lights shone in a big banyan tree and the leaders said it was Jon's eyes and something was going to happen. It did, but not what they expected or wanted. A couple of police boys who had been sent incognito crept up behind and shone a torch on to Jon. They saw a young chap manipulating the lights. It was the same chap as had been recently seeing visions of Jon. The general populace was disgusted at having been led on by such a hoax for so long. (Cooper 1958, 8; see also Bell, quoted in Guiart 1956*b*, 413–414)

Yet, as fast as administrative and mission authorities could expose one John Frum hoax another would surface. It was maddening.

> The present stage of the movement on East Tanna is a little more serious. When, some time ago, the centre of the movement shifted from East to West Tanna, the leaders organised the followers into a small company of soldiers, "Jon Frum's Soldiers." These men cleared an airstrip, built a barracks, and drilled—armed with hand-made wooden muskets with red-painted bayonets. These make-believe soldiers did a grand route march all over the island and frightened people considerably. The Government Agents stepped in and ordered the men back to the villages, the marching to cease, and the "muskets" to be all handed in. . . . During the lengthy discussions, if the leaders were unsure they would send a messenger to a nearby house where the "radio" man made contact with Jon Frum and brought back the right answer. We understand that the radio was also "make-believe." (Cooper 1958, 9; see also Eveille 1953, 8)

Dogged exposure of make-believe John Frum hoaxes, however, proved no antidote to the movement. Cultic hardheadedness was the stubborn result of ignorance and mental confusion. Native irrationality, in fact, was much aggravated by the Pacific War. In that the advent of John Frum predated December 1941, mission writers were unable to peg *all* the blame for the movement on the war. They argued, though, that people's wartime experiences inflamed their cultic enthusiasm. Missionaries shared this motif with administrative writers, along with a perplexed exasperation at John Frum Americophilia.

> Perhaps the fact of war and the presence of thousands of soldiers in the Group had something to do with the turmoil in their minds. The sight of fabulous equipment and apparently inexhaustible stores of money in the hands of these men who seemed so different from what they had known of white men may have had something to do with the belief that from America would come their deliverance and their future prosperity. (QJNH 1959, 4; see also Bell 1941, 10; Australian Presbyterian Board of Missions 1964, 26; Priday 1950, 67)

Missionary scholar Patrick O'Reilly likewise linked John Frum to the psychic upheavals of war: "the planes, the war, the Americans.

This added here and there a bit of madness. From all this was born fundamentally indigenous, although somewhat mysterious, manifestations that are found from time to time in all primitive communities" (1949, 208, my translation). The war assuaged mission cargoist responsibility by adding madness to cultic mystery. Rather than misguided mission policy, missionary versions of the eruption of John Frum blamed instead a combination of rising Third World nationalism in the face of colonial exploitation, the inevitable march of civilization, rascally or evil cult leaders, and wartime mental turmoil.

These cargoist motifs were more than rhetorically significant, in that they guided missionary schemes to counter John Frum. In addition to practical education, the administration's favored cult antidote, the missionaries encouraged local sovereignty. Notably, soon after John Frum's manifestation, the Presbyterian Mission in 1948 transformed itself into the Presbyterian Church of the New Hebrides. New Zealand Overseas Secretary L. Murray explained, "if there should be a surging up of the idea of nationalism in these islands, with a desire by their peoples to govern their own affairs, it might be an advantage that the church should also be under the control of its own people" (*PIM* 1948a, 92).

And, because the missionaries also in part explained John Frum in terms of colonialist economic exploitation, they were motivated to establish a cooperative trading society at the mission station on East Tanna in 1959 (*QJNH* 1959, 4; see also Bell, quoted in Guiart 1956b, 415). This, they hoped, would allow Islanders to circumvent trader monopolies on copra buying and dry-goods sales and also, of course, "be the means of giving the people, and as a result of their own efforts, material benefits which Jon Frum promised, but never gave" (*QJNH* 1959, 4; see also O'Reilly 1949, 208).

Missionary cargoism also introduced one additional motif that other subgenres of cargo writing, particularly the adventurer, subsequently have adopted. This is the theme of cultic decline. Whereas District Agent Barrow predicted recurrent outbreaks of the movement on Tanna as far as the eye could see, mission writers instead continued to announce John Frum's imminent demise. Recidivist cargoism justifies ongoing native administration. Missionaries, however, must explain themselves to their sponsors in terms of numbers of baptisms, pushing back the Darkness, converting the heathen, and so on, and it is not surprising that their cargoism indulged itself in hopeful predictions that the flames of John Frum had about burned themselves out.

The Presbyterian magazine *Encounter*, for example, observed, "In 1964 there are still followers of the Jon Frum movement but its influence appears to be waning" (Australian Presbyterian Board of Missions 1964, 26). Fourteen years later, in 1978, the last European Presbyterian missionary on the island wrote again of cultic decline: "the normal religious practices of the Jon Frum Movement, such as Friday worship before the red painted crosses, the offering of flowers with appropriate gestures, and talk of the return of Jon himself, had seriously declined. . . . [R]itual appears to be once more on the decline" (Calvert 1978, 217). As John Frum marches on into the 1990s, we must take predictions of his demise as a rhetorical move within certain cargoist stories.

Although missionary cargoism's preoccupations with cultic decline, Satan and sin, and colonial exploitation distanced it from administrative texts, both the subgenres share a number of cargoist motifs. John Frum writing, like the term cargo cult itself, originated during the war years. Early John Frum texts of the latter 1940s were influenced by the chief dispute within the European community over who was to blame for cargo cults. Each faction, recall, was concerned to reposition itself vis-à-vis natives in the postwar era (see chapter 2). Administrators and missionaries, who were writing against one another and for a shared wider readership, recycled and reshaped common cultic motifs to present their respective cases as best they might. Administrators blamed missionaries thus occulting their own imperialism; missionaries blamed traders, progress, and the war, and forgot their officious meddling in island life.

A third party, however, was soon to appear on Tanna's shores. This was the dispassionate anthropologist whose cargo writing claimed for itself a scientific neutrality. A transitional figure, here, was Catholic priest Patrick O'Reilly who was also a skilled avocational Pacific historian and anthropologist. O'Reilly published the first detailed summary of the John Frum movement that employed a rhetoric of ethnographic neutrality (1949). O'Reilly began the conclusion to his piece with the words: "Such are the facts. We have done our best to summarize the written documents and verbal information that we have gathered on the unfolding of this affair" (1949, 206, my translation). *PIM,* which published an English summary of O'Reilly, claimed by way of introduction that this "appears to be a clear and unbiased account of the movement" (Priday 1950, 67).

As a francophone Catholic, O'Reilly was not averse to following the administrative line of blaming Presbyterians for unwise mission practice (1949, 207). Echoing anthropologist Peter Lawrence and his stories of the cargo cult in New Guinea, though, O'Reilly concluded with a plea for greater understanding of the native mind:

> One sees the play of events. It remains to ask oneself what these correspond to in the mind of a native. Under what impulsions and influences does he act? What are his motives and his goals? How does he himself understand these events of which we have considered only a facade of "police reports" or "administrative reviews?" By what links are these revolutionary manifestations entangled, in the mind of man Tanna, with his conceptions of goodness, of liberty, and his ideal of the Melanesian? And here, we feel ourselves deprived. With nearly one exception—that of Dr. Armstrong—all our informants whatever their understanding, their knowledge of natives and their psychology, are Europeans who have no relations with the Tannese except through the medium of Bislama—the New Hebrides Pidgin English. No one has ever really lived with them. No one knows their language. No one has ever earned their confidence, other than in administrative dealings. (1949, 206, my translation)

Father O'Reilly pleaded the need for a new genre of ethnographic cargo text to supplement "police reports" and "administrative reviews," not to mention missionary jottings. Not to worry, anthropology's contextualizing pencils were already being sharpened.

John Frum for Anthropologists

In the wider discourse of cargoism, anthropological storytellers cheerfully borrowed from colonial and mission communities the labels Vailala Madness and cargo cult, along with certain stock cargoist motifs. Anthropological stories of John Frum, likewise, are parasitic on previous administrative and mission texts. Like cargo cult itself, anthropologists commandeered the appellation "John Frum movement" from earlier writers. They also swallowed existing themes in the John Frum archive—notably the missionary's motif of reactive protonationalism.

As with the term cargo cult, however, anthropologists soon found themselves contextualizing John Frum. The discipline demands a conspicuous understanding of native belief and behavior by means of situating all this within the horizons of some coherent cultural system. Anthropologists, obeying their scholarly mandate, soon generated a panoply of John Frum understandings and explanations. Where missionaries and administrators were willing to tolerate a darkened and ineffably secret cultist heart, not so anthropology. The latter's discourse prohibits much mystery.

Anthropology's John Frum stories model, in their progressive development, the unfolding of cargo-cult discourse in general. Earlier writers presumed that John Frum was a nativistic reaction to a burdensome European presence, although they took care to explain the shape which that reaction assumed in terms of Tannese cultural structures. Many latter-day anthropology texts, however, exhibit the explanatory double clutch from external to internal cultic engines. They nativize John Frum so that he emerges—like cargo cult—*sui generis* from ingenious and indigenous Tannese culture and/or mentality.

Anthropology's story of John Frum begins in a 1949 issue of the *Journal de la Société des Océanistes.* Jean Poirier included John Frum in a discussion of New Hebridean movements of "mythic liberation." Anthropology, here, appropriates from mission texts, in particular, the cultic motif of John Frum nationalism and "liberation," but it refracts this so that this nationalism is now "mythic," that is, culturally informed.

Poirier classified John Frum along with cargo cults and generalized its defining characteristics: segregation from the traditional and
colonial orders; reconstruction of new social forms; and an aspiration for maximum liberation (1949, 99–101). He noted but did not
entirely accept the administrative motif of Presbyterian blameworthiness.

Rather, more anthropologically, he accented the creativity of native actors in John Frum drama: "one cannot be so sure
[of Presbyterian culpability] (because, in fact, the missions were
often managed by natives)" (1949, 101, my translation). Poirier
introduced here the main anthropological version of the blame
motif. Generous in its reproof, anthropology curses all the houses of
colonialism: missionaries, administrators, traders, planters—the
fault is systematic, not personal. It is the colonial order at large that
must be condemned for the eruption of cargo cults like John Frum.
And one must take account of history as well, including the untoward effects of the Pacific War on island societies.

Anthropology, however, tempers its impartial blame with recognition of the importance of enterprising native action. European
colonials have no monopoly on creative misbehavior. One must
understand native desire for cargo, in this case, and the creative
ways that Islanders work out their desires. John Frum may assume a
political aspect, but "in truth, it is not a real autonomist movement: it is an agitation born of the war in service of ancient themes
which are essentially an immense desire to profit from European
opulence" (Poirier 1949, 102, my translation). A typical anthropologist, Poirier stressed the particularity of John Frum and why the
movement must *not* be assigned to some universal political category
such as "autonomist movement." He contextualized, and thereby
particularized, John Frum in terms of the war (local history) and
ancient themes (local culture). Such contextualization soon would
lead anthropology, as we have seen, to a full-blown nativization of
both cargo and cult.

In the early 1950s, French anthropologist Jean Guiart employed
and elaborated O'Reilly's and Poirier's cultic themes. Unlike his
two predecessors, Guiart undertook field research on Tanna. He
published a series of commentaries on John Frum (1951*a*, 1951*b*,
1952, 1956*a*), culminating in his *chef d'oeuvre, Un Siècle et Demi de*

Contacts Culturels à Tanna, Nouvelles-Hébrides (1956*b*). Published the same year as Margaret Mead's *New Lives for Old,* this was the first detailed, ethnographic account of a postwar Melanesian cargo cult. The only earlier monograph is F. E. Williams' *Vailala Madness* of 1923. Written in French, however, Guiart's book had less impact upon anglophonic anthropology than did succeeding ethnographies of cargo movements in Papua New Guinea.

At the invitation of the French and British colonial governments, Guiart spent six months on Tanna during 1952 (1956*b,* 7–8). Guiart, scientific anthropologist that he was, wrote to provide the colonial administration a measure of native understanding of John Frum.

> One lacks information permitting a sociological analysis of these events; administrative reports, often too succinct, do not furnish the necessary information, which observers who are insufficiently aware do not know how to collect. To study a concise case back to its origins, that is to say to the first cultural contacts between Whites and Melanesians, can thus be understood as an enterprise responding to a real need. (1956*b,* viii, my translation)

Anthropological hired guns, who *do* know how to collect the necessary information, from this point begin appearing on Tanna to enlighten confused administrators and missionaries, and to ventilate the smoke of John Frum mystery.

Guiart constructed an impressive historical and ethnographic context within which to situate and thereby explain John Frum. The first part of his monograph consists of an ethnography of Tannese society; the second a history of a "century and a half" of culture contact; the third a blow-by-blow account of John Frum events; and the fourth a cultural reading of John Frum that nativizes our hero as an ancient Tannese god. This allowed Guiart, first, to situate the "blame" motif within historical events and, second, to supplement blame of the missionaries with anthropology's complementary motif of native creativity. Anthropology thus counterposes its stories of cultural structures and creative action to earlier administrative and missionary themes of native evil, foolery, and madness.

John Frum may be a reaction to external colonialism, but he is a reaction shaped by the imposing, internal forces of Tannese myth and society. Anthropology's John Frum texts, here, move along with the general cargo-cult literature in a shift, beginning in the 1950s, from the issue of cultic blame to an informed, if sometimes ironic, focus upon cultic behavior and excess.

Guiart's reading of Tannese history, however, led him (unlike Poirier) to join Mr Bird and the administrative side and blame the missionaries for John Frum: "blame can be laid on the Presbyterian missionary methods as a result of which the native social organisation has been entirely disrupted" (1951a, 129; see also 1951b, 89). The French and the Presbyterians, however, never did get along very well in the New Hebrides. It perhaps may also be recalled that Guiart was working for the colonial administration. His narrative endorsement of the administrative version of the blame motif, though, was not absolute. Toward the end of his monograph, he slipped expectedly into the anthropological variant of the theme, and blamed colonial relations of political and economic domination in general.

> It is necessary also to say that, whoever they were, the Europeans are only harvesting what they have sown. The extortions of the first traders, the lack of honesty of their successors, the arbitrary administration that followed an authoritative regime installed by the Presbyterian Mission, none of this was done to win hearts. What has one today to offer after one hundred years of mission presence and more than forty years of direct administration? One tumbledown mission hospital, an administrative dispensary of which it is better not to talk, not one cistern in a land where the lack of water is the most pressing daily problem; and in these present circumstances, no hope for economic and social development, even on a modest scale. (1956b, 225, my translation)

John Frum, in this shotgun version of the blame motif, is a native reaction to colonial structures that kindle but then frustrate native desire for development.

Guiart, at this point, rejoined the anthropological subgenre of cargoism. Tannese Cargo is not cargo. Rather, it is a symbol—the desire for development. What Islanders really want is to "rid themselves of the physical presence of the Whites but conserve for themselves White power, riches, and all that is involved in their level of life" (1956*b*, 225, my translation). Neither mission nor administration personalities per se are to blame for cargo cults. The colonial system itself is the problem.

Moreover, John Frum is neither sin, criminal foolery, nor madness. Rather, it is a rational response to culture contact given the available cultural and social resources on the island. One such island resource is myth—myth that serves to found new social unities and inspire collective action.

> The myth of John Frum furnishes a synthesis, a possibility of coordinating sporadic actions; its symbolism permits organization hidden from European curiosity, and provides the means to search for a larger efficacy. Thanks to him the entire island now seeks independence. . . . The myth of John Frum has crystallized a situation that was characterized by a growing disequilibrium between the will to power and independence of a Melanesian people, and the irritating weight of administrative and missionary paternalism. It has permitted, for the moment at least, a fluid solution that may shift at any instant but which marks positive progress in the battle of "Man Tanna" against an authority that weighs upon him. . . . Despite its messianic aspect, the myth of John Frum is only a means, a method of action. (1956*b*, 258–259, my translation; see also Guiart 1952, 175; 1956*a*, 116)

Far from an evil or loony hoax, John Frum instead is positive progress and a useful mode of action (see also Bastin 1980, 76; Brunton 1981; Bonnemaison 1987, 584). Anthropology, here, borrows and retreads the missionary story of John Frum nationalism: the movement, as Guiart put it, is a "forerunner of Melanesian nationalism" (1951*b*).

Guiart defended the cultic logic of John Frum by exposing the cultural rationale that missionaries and administrators overlooked: "Finding itself in an impasse, indigenous society reacts according to its own means, found within the interior of its own structure" (1956*b*, 257, my translation). Cultic reaction to external circumstance is culturally informed. The anthropological theme that cargo is not cargo, nor cult a cult, structures Guiart's text. Tannese "Cargo" is the desire for autonomous development. Tannese "cult" is only a modernized form of indigenous politicking and religion. Guiart investigated, along these lines, how the details of island political competition between Christians and pagans (164) and a series of troublesome land disputes (174) shaped localized John Frum organization and action. He also read John Frum himself as an avatar of the traditional culture hero Karapenmun (227–233): "the patronage of the old god in his new form masks and justifies, better than a real return to traditional paganism, the rupture with a Christian life that was felt to have become useless" (257, my translation). Finally, Guiart remarked internal variation among various sects and factions within the movement (255–256). John Frum, under the anthropological gaze, loses his monolithic unity (see also Brunton 1981, 373; Bonnemaison 1987, 599). In sum, Guiart's text conspicuously and thoroughly understands John Frum.

Guiart's stories, particularly his English summaries of island events (1952, 1956a), rebound and recycle through the subsequent John Frum archive (see eg, Wilson 1973, 322–326; Steinbauer 1979, 85–88). Having himself absorbed and rewritten earlier administrative and mission primary texts, Guiart for twenty years served as John Frum's biographer and mouthpiece. Anthropology's texts, which shine with an ethnographic authority burnished with assertions of fieldwork experience and objective observation, rapidly overshadowed the reports of administrators and the jottings of missionaries.

There is a tension in Guiart's John Frum ethnography, however —a tension that amplifies into two conflicting themes within ensuing anthropological cargoism. On the one hand, Guiart nativized John Frum as indigenous Tannese religio-politics; on the other, he classified the movement as a New Hebridean exemplar of generic protonationalism. This tension, of course, besets cultural anthropology in general which must ride two horses: one races deeper and deeper into the thickets of cultural particularity and difference; the other charges in the opposite direction toward the rarefied, always receding, checkered flag of universal comparability. This latter theme—John Frum as a generic reactive stage along the way to worldwide economic and political modernization—dominates anthropological stories of the 1950s and 1960s. The countering motif—John Frum as a unique and internally Tannese cultural creation—comes into its own during the 1970s and 1980s. This latter-day narrative triumph of John Frum nativism underwrites recent attempts to erase the categorical reality of the cargo cult and to replace this with Melanesian cargo-cult culture.

Anthropology's version of the "universal reaction" motif fit into the discipline's onetime concerns with social change, evolution, and social progress. John Frum was no mere reflexive reaction to the brutalities and disruptions of Western civilization; he was, rather, a mode of resistance that prepared the ground for directional, progressive social change. Anthropologist Ian Hogbin, for example, summarized Guiart's John Frum material in *Social Change* (1958, 212–214), his Josiah Mason Lectures. He compared John Frum and Melanesian cargo cults with a twelfth century religious movement in Normandy, and concluded that "800 years ago Europeans were in many respects as ignorant as the primitive natives today" (1958, 219). The cargo cult, according to this thematic, is a Melanesian instance of a universal type, the millenarian movement. This is classic social evolutionist theory wherein today's Melanesians are equated with yesterday's Europeans insofar as both are located at different levels on the same historical trajectory of human progress. Their present, thus, illustrates our past (see Fabian 1983).

Peter Worsley (1957) also picked up Guiart's John Frum stories in support of his materialist overview of social change. Again, Melanesian cargo cults, including John Frum, are a form of universal millenarian movement. These, religions of divided, disorganized, and downtrodden peoples, "serve as an expression of reaction against what is felt as oppression by another class or nationality. . . . [T]he main effect of the millenarian cult is to overcome these divisions and to weld previously hostile and separate groups together into a new unity" (1957, 227–228). The significance of John Frum, therefore, is that it united the Tannese into a new anti-European solidarity: "The dynamism of the John Frum cult might be the stimulus to the building up of a unified, independent and probably anti-European movement" (1957, 167–168).

The "universal reaction" motif, presuming as it did directional social change, conveniently guaranteed the ability to predict the future. Like missionary cargoism, this sort of anthropology also predicts the eventual decline of John Frum and other cargo cults, although for different reasons. The missionaries await an epiphany of the Holy Spirit; Worsley looks for a progressive shift from irrational religious to rational political nationalism.

> Future nationalist developments will probably be less and less under the aegis of millenarian cult leadership. We have seen how there is an eventual break away from this kind of political expression to that of a simple kind of political party. I believe, therefore, that the activist millenarian movement is typical only of a certain phase in the political and economic development of this region, and that it is destined to disappear or become a minor form of political expression among backward elements. (1957, 255; see also Wilson 1973, 347)

Anthropology foretells, thus, that as the Tannese move forward to the next stage of political evolution, John Frum will retire.

Guiart's other, cultural particularist theme, however, makes him a more cautious cargoist prophet than is Worsley. John Frum may be an exemplar of a typical millenarian stage of political development, but he is also a "veritable mode of understanding" (1956b, 258). According to this second motif, John Frum is more than a standard reaction of the generally oppressed. The movement is nothing less than an expression of Tannese culture and mentality. Who can tell, then, if John Frum will be "replaced by a theme less irrational in appearance" (1956b, 258)?

More recent John Frum writing has also wearied of the "universal reaction" motif. Strumming, instead, Guiart's second thematic string, it travels in the opposite direction to nativize John Frum. Such anthropological particularization, of course, ultimately subverts the general validity of the category cargo cult. John Frum, in this alternative reading, is *not* a cargo cult (see Brunton 1981, 358;

McClancy 1983, 87; Bonnemaison 1987, 613). We now know much too much about him. John Frum no longer fits the definition cargo cult—particularly the more popular, simple forms of this as reactive native cupidity or Third World protonationalism. Joël Bonnemaison wrote: "the John Frum movement appears to us very different from a classic messianic movement of the cargo-cult type, and the interpretive key is to study the ideology and history of the Tannese people rather than a general explication of millenarian movements" (1987, 465, my translation).

Latter-day anthropological John Frum stories dish up a far richer and thicker potage of Tannese culture and history than even Guiart was able to provide. Now thoroughly garbed in a raiment of Tannese context, John Frum appears as a creative, local reaction to internal island problems. Ron Brunton, for example, suggested that "the John Frum movement arose to deal with an internal problem in Tannese society. . . . [T]he movement was a rather sophisticated, and generally successful, attempt by pagans to halt and reverse a process of progressive social disintegration which came about because Tannese Christians refused to participate in traditional marriage exchanges" (1981, 357–358; see also Richardson 1987, 8).

Bonnemaison nativized even further. He applauded Brunton's contextualizing strategy, but worried that Brunton ignored the lush content of John Frum beliefs by focusing too much on their social functions (1987, 613). Bonnemaison demanded instead a "positive" accounting of John Frum.

> As far as one only sees in John Frum prophecies and beliefs a simple cultural dressing of a basic political and economic alienation, otherwise called a "cargo cult," reacting by an imaginary flight from a situation of frustration or real oppression, one risks not going very far in explaining the movement . . . one defines them not by what they are, but by the cargo that they wait for in vain—and which never arrives. . . . This negative view that consists of explaining the other as the opposite of what one believes oneself to be and of only seeing in him a frustrated desire to imitate, never leads very far toward comprehension of a movement as complex and unexpected as that of John Frum. (1987, 613, my translation)

Bonnemaison's "positive" conclusion is that Tannese millenarianism is not a reactive side effect of Western contact, but is itself
traditional. John Frum millenarianism expresses "religious sentiments already there, well before contact with the white world"
(1987, 615). The John Frum dream

> issues from a traditional collective memory that lives in the meta-
> phor of a lost golden age and in the nostalgia of the Great Time and
> the Great Space. Christian eschatology grafted itself onto this pagan
> millenarian sentiment that preceded it, and similarly the different
> versions of John Frumism today appear as many local variants of the
> same syncretic construction, effected by the encounter of Tannese
> and Biblical myths. . . . The myth of a lost unity burns in effect like
> a red fire in the depths of the Tannese collective conscious. John
> Frum millenarianism from this perspective is only one of the local
> variants of this quest (1987, 619, 627, my translation)

The kindling for John Frum fire, thus, is a local reading of Christian themes, but these are bent toward ancestral, indigenous,
already present Tannese desires to establish a utopian island unity.

Here, cargo cult disappears altogether from view, and anthropological stories conjure up in its place cargo-cult culture and cargo-
cult mentality—or, in this case, John Frum culture and John Frum
mentality. "Cargo cult mentality is a perfectly normal attitude of
mind and the basis of an actual outbreak should be blamed on the
particular mitigating circumstances in that area rather than any
abnormality of the people concerned" (Calvert 1978, 212). Anthropological cargoism mutes the motif of cargo madness—but this
returns by the back door of cargo mentality, or what Bonnemaison
called "metaphysical thought" (1987, 627).

> John Frum thought reasons, as we have seen, not in terms of lineal
> causality, but in terms of magico-religious images, of metaphors and
> mystical signs. . . . The march, sometimes detoured, of John Frum
> disciples expresses this ensemble of dreams and contradictions,
> dreams at once Christian and pagan, modern and traditional, where
> the golden age is situated both at the dawn of time and in the last
> hours. For the man of Tanna, should time reunify itself in the reuni-

fied space of his island, it will terminate itself in the extraordinary harmony of its beginning. His history is that of rupture, but his territory is that of an Arcadia: Custom is a millennium. (Bonnemaison 1987, 629, 633, my translation)

Anthropological cargoism, too, thus terminates itself in an extraordinary effort to erase cargo cult. Custom—Melanesian culture itself —not cargo cult becomes the millennium. John Frum is standard Tannese action, not disturbed reaction. And if custom is a millennium, anthropology is its prophet.

This final terminus of anthropological cargoism, however, invites its own theoretical and political dangers, as we have seen in chapter 3. More prosaically, anthropology cannot anymore so simply atone for its past definitional sins. It is impossible to resituate John Frum and erase the embarrassing cargo cult merely by revising anthropological theory, because cargo cult long ago escaped from the arcadian confines of that theory. John Frum wanders stranger detours than anthropology. He lives today in the writings of far more powerful cargoists.

John Frum for Poets

Anthropologists may assert ethnographic authority, but they cannot claim much of a readership. Other cargo subgenres reach larger, more popular audiences. Beginning in the late 1960s, for example, several minor although engaging literary productions written for the nonacademic reader employed the character of John Frum. He features more prominently in journalistic writing that also dates from this era.

Having here entered the realm of John Frum literature in the strict sense, we might briefly shift our focus away from story motif and theme to questions of narrative style and tone. John Frum literature and reportage mostly play out in two main keys. There is dark-toned parody or irony, and writing of this sort may sound a number of halftones located somewhere along the continuum between cruel parody and gentle irony. And there is a brightly lit romantic heroism, although such admiration is commonly flavored with more than a pinch of paternalism.

Parody is the flavor of a piece that appeared in *PIM*'s magazine section in October 1968. This, "narrated by" Don Marsh, is titled "The Surprising Gospels of John Frum: He Who Swept Sin Away." *PIM* introduced Marsh as an Englishman who played music in a "John Frum band and worked behind the counter of a trading post, where he first heard the stories of the cargo cult adherents and decided to put them on paper" (Marsh 1968, 83). Something of Marsh's dry style appears in this excerpt from "The Gospel According to Nako":

"Why have you chosen red for your colour and not purple? You will surely have the Communists complaining." This Freethinker [Marsh] received his enlightenment from my [Nako] own tongue: "John chose red for himself because his brother in Europe wears red every time he gives away his cargo of toys to the very young at Christmas time." I thought I had amazed him and I had. He gasped: "But that other fellow in red is called Santa Claus. He is not a brother to any god—he is a myth. No adult in the British Isles believes in Santa Claus." I knew I had won the discussion. With chiding I replied: "That is the reason you don't get toys anymore— because you have ceased to believe, O ye of little faith. But we Tannese of the true faith still believe and so we shall receive our promised cargo and, what is more, we shall receive it many times a year from John and not just once a year deliveries like Santa Claus makes; and you can't get much cargo in a sled. Santa Claus would be of no use to us because it never snows in the New Hebrides." (Marsh 1968, 85)

In "narrating" his John Frum gospels, Marsh was exercising his poetic license, but such exercise and such license are not always entirely obvious. Parody and, more often, irony of this sort stains journalistic news stories as well as literary accounts of John Frum. The dominant parodic style that overflows both subgenres, in fact, works to blur the line between ostensible John Frum fiction and John Frum fact. Alarmingly, Steinbauer (1979, 87–88) quoted liberally from Marsh's fables in his factual comparative and quantitative overview of Melanesian cargo cults. The brotherhood of John Frum and Santa Claus undoubtedly is Marsh's invention, not the pseudonymous Nako. But, we need ask ourselves, does this matter?

Within the bounds of cargoist writing, a particular motif may not, in fact, be true, but this by no means implies that it is discursively faulty as a cargoist theme.

The more liberal minded might condemn a parodic or ironic cargoist accent to be a pernicious form of native abuse. This other sort of writer accentuates, instead, John Frum's heroism in a style no doubt greatly informed by the radical chic of the latter 1960s. In these other stories, John Frum, by no means Santa Claus, is rather a sort of Tannese Che Guevara—his followers the Black Panthers or the African National Congress of Vanuatu. Tanna the Third World has turned inward to its original green peace and ordained a cultural hero to vanquish the corrupting West. Traditional kava is triumphant; the colonials and Presbyterians laid low.

Trappist monk, scholar, and poet Thomas Merton heroized cargo cults, including John Frum, along these lines in his poetic cycle *The Geography of Lograire*. His poems "John the Volcano" and others render John Frum into blank verse:

> I John Frum—Volcano ancestor—Karaperamun
> "My Brother here is Joe
> Everything is near to me
> See us two Joe-Captain: Cockle Shell" . . . (Merton 1968, 105)

> I Neloiag
> Am John Frum King
> I level the mountain
> Where my planes will come
> I am King of American Flyers
> I can arrest the British
> With my telegraph
> Though they declare me insane . . . (106)

> Baimbai money belong me he come
> Face belong you fella King
> Take 'em, he go back! . . . (108)

> "Jake Navy he is player and smoker
> Good fella seen in vision

By the faithful
Lives in a beard and a battleship lifebelt
He will send his delegate
(Noah's avatar)
To take the place
Of Agent Nicol"
Is everybody happy? . . . (116)

Merton's tone of poetic dignity surfaces elsewhere in popular John Frum literature (see eg, Rice 1974 who also liked to versify John Frum stories). The ironic stance, though, is the more common manner of popular writing. Many John Frum texts, however, manage to combine Brother Merton's romantic heroism with Englishman Marsh's parody to strike mixed chords of what might be called ironic heroism. John Frum, here, mutates from Che Guevara into Batman or Captain America. Comic irony is doubled in that the Tannese themselves have invented a gang of superhero sidekicks to assist John Frum's good works, including Merton's figure Jake (or Tom) Navy and Captain World. It is no literary accident that the droll off-tones of popular cargoism have much in common with the style of comic books. The question, *pace* Brother Merton, is not "Is everybody happy?" It is "Is everybody amused?"

John Frum for Adventurers

The various styles of popular John Frum writing tend to bleed together. I distinguish three loose subgenres—the adventurer, the journalistic, and the touristic—based on a text's likely readership and whether or not it presents itself as news or entertainment (often a spurious distinction to be sure as the "infotainment" industry understands). Whatever the porosity of subgenre boundaries in this area, popular John Frum stories in general reach far larger audiences than the anthropology texts from which they borrow, if not always much content, at least some ethnographic authority. Foremost among such borrowings is the term cargo cult itself, along with various, more specific John Frum cargoist themes.

The true heyday of John Frum adventure writing only arrived in the 1970s, although the first example of the subgenre dates back to 1960. This, actually, was a textual by-product of David Attenborough's pioneer ethnographic film work for the BBC. Attenborough went to Tanna with movie camera to hunt the cargo cult. "It was the chance of witnessing if not the birth, then the very early stages in the development of a new religion, that drew us to Tanna. I hoped that, when we got there, we might be able to meet the leaders of the movement and discover from them how John Frum's orders and prophecies originated, and perhaps to persuade them to describe in detail the actions and appearance of their mysterious leader" (1960, 49).

Here, Attenborough staked out two of the main motifs of adventurist cargoism: discovery and mystery. Adventurers, like administrators and missionaries, prefer to entertain cultic mystery. Like anthropologists, they make a point to experience personally their literary object. Such personal experience is the basis of adventurist authority, as it is ethnographic authority. Adventurers deal in discovery. They go on quests. They probe the mysterious. Attenborough climbed Iasur, the active, cinder cone volcano behind Sulphur Bay: "On the highest point of the crater's lip, we found the cross" (1960, 62). Climactic acts of finding and discovery recur often in this sort of cargoism.

Adventurers, however, typically are in rather more of a hurry than are anthropologists, and if they want quick cultural and historic detail, they need to draw upon the stories of other John Frum subgenres as well as interviews with available local experts. Attenborough, for example, clearly read his way through some of the extant John Frum archive, as his text repeats several anthropological stories. He also, however, interviewed Australian trader and planter Bob Paul who first settled on Tanna in the mid 1950s and stayed for the next twenty-five years. Affable and commanding, Paul quickly emerged as the John Frum story agent, a go-between mediating rambling adventurers and journalists and John Frum disciples and lieutenants. Attenborough was only the first of many popular cargoists to buy into and circulate Bob Paul's stories. "A tall thin man, with sandy hair, a small mustache, and a deceptively mild manner, he owned more land on the island than any other European and was the only one to run a large plantation. For anybody who wished to talk to the Tannese about John Frum, he was the ideal host" (1960, 51). In addition to John Frum tales, Bob Paul also sold his adventurers their tinned provisions, and rented them his humble tourist bungalows. Returning his favors, the adventurers crowned Paul the "King of Tanna" (eg, Woodcock 1976, 226; Bitter 1976, 61; Dyson 1982, 40).

There is today a powerful lineage of Bob Paul John Frum stories, a narrative genealogy that rivals Guiart's anthropological versions, and one that dominates popular John Frum writing. More conscientious adventurers, like Attenborough, read some way into the thickening John Frum archive. They combine in their texts both the Guiart/anthropological and the Paul/administrative story lineages. Lazy ones just chatted with Bob Paul.

Through trader Paul, certain colonial administrative cargo motifs have crept into popular John Frum literature. While anthropologists brooked neither mystery nor madness, these were stock motifs of administrative cargoism, and Paul traded them readily with eager adventurers. The colonial motif of native ignorance is also prominent in adventurist cargoism's borrowed John Frum tales. Attenborough, for example, repeated Paul's stories of the Tanna Army, concluding: "It might have been that the dummy guns and sham uniforms were just being used for practice in preparation for the day when John Frum would send the real things. It was also at least as probable that these actions were yet another example of the uncomprehending imitation of the white man's activities carried out in the vague muddled belief that it was some form of magic" (1960, 54).

Adventure cargoists likewise follow administrative narratives in blaming the Presbyterians for John Frum madness (eg, Guillebaud 1980, 146). The voice of Bob Paul, perhaps, comes through here as well; his early relations with the mission on Tanna were by no means always cordial (Guiart 1956*b*, 201). Attenborough, however, was also happy to join with mission cargoists and impugn the march of civilization rather than the missionaries per se: "It seems that it is too much to expect a people to make within the space of two or three generations, the transition from a Stone Age culture to the most advanced material civilization that the world has ever known without running the risk of their complete moral disorientation and mental dislocation" (1960, 67). He also echoed the colonial motif of the rascal cult leader. Attenborough encountered John Frum prophet Tommy Nampas and found him foxy (1960, 65); his eyes blazed wildly (1960, 66; see also Gourguechon 1977, 318; Guillebaud 1980, 137): "Did Nambas believe what he was saying? Was he a mystic who had vision? Or was he a charlatan who was claiming special powers so that he could influence his people and make them do what he wished? I could not tell. If he were mad, then he had infected the whole island with his madness" (1960, 67).

It is difficult to have serious adventures with the ordinary. Adventurist cargoism must accentuate, therefore, the grotesque, the eerie, and the mysterious. John Frum is "bizarre" (41). The Friday night dances of the John Frum sabbath are strange, eerie, "the people dancing with a drugging insistent rhythm" (68).

An adventure writer also profits if he finds himself in danger. More than just plain weird, John Frum is sinister. The Tannese stare at Attenborough suspiciously and unsmilingly. "Several times we stopped and asked one of them about the meaning of a nearby cross or gate. Always the answer was, 'Me no savvy' " (1960, 55). There is "an ominous, brooding air" to Tannese kava-drinking grounds (56). Kava itself makes drinkers "moody and irritable" (57). The volcano is "menacing" (61) and "terrifying" (62). Carved figures at a John Frum shrine "were pathetically childish, yet they seemed deeply sinister" (63). The intrepid adventurer braves perilous native and treacherous volcano in his quest "to discover the truth about" John Frum (56).

Adventurist cargoism differs from the anthropological in one of the stylistic markers which it employs to signal its authority. Anthropologists such as Guiart and Bonnemaison call attention to the longer periods of time they spent on Tanna by salting their texts with words taken from Tannese vernaculars. Faster moving adventurers, however, rely on expressions in Bislama, Vanuatu's Pidgin English. Attenborough inaugurated this symbolic usage, reproducing a lot of tortured misrepresentations of Bislama (see also Rice 1974). His Nampas says: "Because *man* stop inside volcano. Many man belong John Frum. Red man, brown man, white man; man belong Tanna, man belong South America, all stop 'long volcano. When time come, man come from volcano and bring cargo" (1960, 66). The resourceful Attenborough, too, can speak Pidgin of this sort: " 'Me walk 'long volcano', I said. 'Me lookim but me no see man'. 'You no see 'im', retorted Nambas scornfully. 'Your eye dark' " (67; Gourguechon 1977, 319 and Theroux 1992, 202 also relied on this device).

The adventuring eye may not be wholly dark, although it is true that adventurers, like administrators but unlike anthropologists, are amenable to discover nothing but even deeper mystery at the end of their quest. John the obscure and his enigmatic followers are, in the end, found to be altogether *too* mysterious to understand (see eg, Rice 1974, 239–243). The adventurer's goal, after all, is to experience rather than to explain. In fact, his experiences and dangers are magnified further if he is lucky enough to encounter the inexplicable. He has braved the mysterious native but survived. The interests of administrators and adventurers run in tandem here. Both desire mysterious natives—the one to justify his administrative powers, the other his adventures. The slippery native evades the adventurer's questions: "Me no savvy" (Attenborough 1960, 58). Attenborough, at last, arrived at the dark heart of the movement to interview the cryptic prophet Nampas. But did Nampas believe what he was saying? In the end, Attenborough "could not tell" (67). Enduring John Frum mystery deflects the sensuous gaze of the adventurer.

Subsequent adventurist John Frum stories of the 1970s took up Attenborough's themes of quest and discovery, eerie novelty, sinister danger, and unfathomable mystery. One of the earliest, and still the most ambitious, of these texts is Rice's book *John Frum He Come* (1974). Notably, Rice along with most of his fellow adventurers continued to call upon Bob Paul to feast on his stories (Rice 1974, 151–163; see also Villaret 1975, 237; Woodcock 1976, 225, 235; Gourguechon 1977, 320; Trumbull 1977, 81; Simpson 1979, 95–99; Shears 1980, 86; Frater 1980, 59; Dyson 1982, 48).

The Tannese are an adventure. They are extraordinarily primitive: "Stone Age ways ruled on Tanna when Capt. James Cook discovered the island in 1774" (Muller 1974, 706). Furthermore, by reviving traditional costume and ritual, Islanders today have headed "back to the Stone Age" (711). For Villaret, also, Tanna

> had practically not changed since 1774, the year of its discovery. The descriptions of Captain Cook . . . could nearly be superimposed with what we saw. The island's welcome is suitably hellish. These are the black Hebrides, with their evil enchantments and their diseases hostile to the white man. . . . There we lived for unforgettable hours in a past that one would have thought finished. We said a final goodbye to the people of John Frum who live, in the middle of the 20th century, confined in a closed universe fascinated with a myth outside time and space. (1975, 233, 237–238, my translation)

Woodcock, observing horses running across the grassy plains of northeastern Tanna, lost his grip on the present: "As I watched them, I seemed to be looking over an unbelievable chasm of time, for it was of the palaeolithic horses of Lascaux that I was irresistibly reminded" (1976, 229). Dripping nudity, rather than wild horses, convinced Theroux that "in the persistent drizzle it was a gloomy little glimpse of the Neolithic Age, complete with muddy buttocks" (1992, 193)—although he at least promotes the Tannese up one age to the Neolithic.

"Back to the Stone Age" is a common adventurer motif—one that structures the manner in which they fathom and write about the people they encounter along their travels away from home. The Stone Age is a popularized adventurer version of the colonial native reaction motif. John Frum, for the adventurer, is the reactive consequence of Stone Age and Space Age encounters (see Simpson 1979, 96; Skole 1986, T20). Furthermore, the Stone Age Tannese exhume and bring into view the prehistoric bones of civilized Europe: "at the end of five minutes, I imagined that I had penetrated, here in this mythic land, those myths which yet stir in the depths of ourselves" (Guillebaud 1980, 139, my translation). John Frum is nothing less than our own dark past: "In the mythopoeic imagination which has vanished from our rational age, John is the embodiment of our primitive shadow" (Rice 1974, 241).

The Tannese are mysterious. John Frum is "bizarre" (Woodcock

1976, 224; Guillebaud 1980, 139); he is "cryptic" (Muller 1974, 704). John Frum is a mystery, and as such we must approach him. We cannot take him at one gulp. So John is revealed layer by layer (Rice 1974, xxii–xxiii). No one knows the origins of his name (Woodcock 1976, 230–231; Gourguechon 1977, 320). Tanna is the island of the "mad" (Guillebaud 1980, 137). The land is full of shadows: "an island without *colons* and without plantations, where reigns a sacred volcano—Yasur—and the impenetrable shadow of a Melanesian prophet" (Guillebaud 1980, 139, my translation). Villaret even sees an ephemeral Tanna melting away: "On a promontory of gleaming rocks furtively appeared, from time to time, the silhouette of Man-Tanna. Then the entire island, with its layers of greenery deluged by rain, seemed again to liquify itself before us" (1975, 233, my translation).

Adventurers, without the conscientious burden of native understanding that anthropologists must labor under, happily confess that they find cultists "elusive": "In the very elusiveness of the followers of Jon Frum we had seen the recessiveness of a cult combining a reverence for the lost past of paganism with a millenarianism of the most eccentric kind, based on the presumably endless resources of American capitalism" (Woodcock 1976, 264). Dyson, too, encountered the opaque native:

In the shade of a bush on the edge of the ash plain where we picnicked there was a strange little stockade in which the Frumites had erected a cross. It was surrounded by crude wooden models of landing lights, a control tower, and aircraft lined up on a tarmac, all painted a red that had faced to pinkish silver. This was one of many shrines of the cargo cult, built with the aim of luring out of the sky John Frum and his great silver birds stuffed with goodies. But it was clear we would get no nearer to the cargo cult than glimpses over the stockades of their shrines. To win the trust of such fanatics might be possible over the course of years but to be privy to all their secrets would probably be impossible for any white man. (1982, 50; see also Bitter 1976, 61)

Opacity and elusive fanaticism in natives raises their narrative value for adventurers, but decreases their utility for anthropologists.

The Tannese are dangerous. Louis Nedjar's John Frum is a "curious movement" (1974, 97), yet one suffused with ominous danger. Nedjar, describing John Frum marchers celebrating the 15th of February, slipped into gentle irony: "They approach, martially, flanked by a sergeant who shouts 'one, two, one, two' in English and, oh surprise! they have on chest and back the letters U.S.A. painted in blood red. Impeccable halt, a change of shoulder for the rifles, half turn, the army displays its knowledge to the huge amazement of the few Europeans who find themselves there" (1974, 106, my translation). Adventurer irony, however, must be confined to the text. It is not safe to be personally ironic while experiencing adventure itself: "The seriousness of the men is sufficiently impressive to dissipate the grotesqueness that such a scene could suggest. Anyway, no one is advised to show his astonishment because the John Frum chiefs don't play around and any manifestation could be wrongly interpreted" (1974, 106, my translation).

Gourguechon, who also wrote with a sort of just-so irony, likewise smelled danger:

> Arriving on Tanna, we were immediately aware that it was an island unlike the others. Everywhere else in the New Hebrides, the people welcomed us with smiles. Here, the smiles were reserved for our little plane, perhaps the same one which will bring John Frum one of these days. The Tannese, who do not work for the airline, emerged with rags in hand and respectfully polished the airplane, an object of veneration. . . . On the surface the atmosphere is fairly gay, because of the island music and the vividly colored costumes. But underneath there is a current of tension, even hostility, which didn't escape us. (1977, 316)

A contrast between dark Tanna and the rest of the archipelago similarly structures Shadbolt and Ruhen's writing: "Tanna disturbs the mind by the rumblings of its volcano and the rebellions of its men, but most New Hebrideans inhabit happy islands" (1968, 170; see Theroux 1992, 201–202).

Along with ironic danger, adventurist cargoism frequently sinks into nostalgic lament. Adventurers travel with white handkerchiefs in their pockets to mourn the imminent demise of their literary objects. They, sad to say, are the last who will be able to sample the adventurous mysteries of Tanna. Lucky for us readers, though, they have suffered to experience John Frum in his twilight hours, and have preserved that personal experience in print for our vicarious pleasure and edification. Such discursive nostalgia, of course, relates to the adventurist motif of the "Stone Age." The Stone Age on Tanna (and it is about time, too) is at last succumbing to the assaults of modernity. Vanuatu's independence and video cassette players are about to kill off John Frum. Nostalgia, we might remark, also adds to the literary capital of the venturesome object; John Frum's death conveniently preserves his mystery.

Adventurer writers, thus, share with missionary cargoism and comparative anthropology the motif of cultic decline, although each prefers to kill off John Frum for its own reasons. Muller, in 1974, wondered "will Tanna's generation of tomorrow continue to ride on today's beliefs?" (1974, 714). Villaret, in 1975, mourned "alas, has John Frum religion already given way to a triumphant tourism? I prefer not to go there to find out" (1975, 237). Woodcock, in 1976, was "told that their cult was disintegrating" (1976, 224) and that "the militant phase is over" (235). Simpson, in 1979, found that "the cult is slowly losing influence" (1979, 96). Dyson, in 1982, informed us that "today the cult is slowly losing impetus" (1982, 48). Happily for adventurism's own future in the cargo cult business, though, John Frum yet defies all reports of his demise. He might, in fact, manage to outlast adventurism itself.

John Frum for Journalists

Journalists, whose first John Frum stories apart from *Pacific Islands Monthly* reportage date to the 1970s, overtook adventurers in the production of John Frum writing in the 1980s. Journalists compose two sorts of cargo texts: human interest stories, and newsworthy reportage. Free-lance writers tend to produce the first type; corresponding staff reporters the second. Human interest cargoism is a sort of distilled mini-adventurism. Journalists, who keep an eye on the numbers of their words, must boil down the main adventurist themes into crowded sentences. The second sort, newsworthy cargoism, is rarer. This gets produced only when John Frum people manage to attract the attention of the international press. They did so, quite successfully, around the time of Vanuatu's independence in 1980 by attempting to detach their island from the new state.

Human interest cargoism goes, as it were, for the reader's jugular —or rather for his funny bone, numbskull prejudice, and occasional libidinous interest. It accentuates outré cultism to seduce reader attention. Tanna is the "home of the weird Jon Frum cargo cult" (Keith-Reid 1984, 13). Despite occasional marvels and gems of incredibility, however, journalist writing is repetitious, stereotypic, and stale. It rehearses again and again a limited thematic repertoire. The titles, often the most interesting part of the text, say it all: "On a Pacific Island, They Wait for the G.I. Who Became a God" (NYT 1970, 7); "The Cargo-cult Chief and the Letters from a God" (Hamilton 1983, 1); "Tanna Islanders Still Waiting for John Frum" (Ashbrook 1986, 2); "Space Age Succeeds Stone Age on Pacific Isle" (Kristof 1987, 1); "Legend of Hat and Rice Brings Hopes for More" (HS-B 1989, A9); and "Waiting for the Skies to Open" (McKee 1989, 26).

Human interest cargoism deals in monsters and superlatives. It promotes itself by boosting the fabulous cargo cult. And, of these, John Frum is the last of the best.

I had come here because I had been told that this was one of the last active centres for the cargo cult in the world. (Hamilton 1983, 1)

The 60,000 islanders of Vanuatu watched in awe as half a million American soldiers—white and black, friendly and, by island standards, fabulously rich—passed through the sleepy colonial backwater on their way to war. And one of the South Pacific's most enduring cults was born. Academics from around the world still travel to study the John Frum movement. The cult, they say, is related to a long line of "cargo cults" that primitive Pacific islanders have founded over the centuries to try to explain and share in the unfathomable material wealth of the Westerners who have come to their shores. (Ashbrook 1986, 2)

The John Frum Custom Movement is believed the world's longest-lasting cargo cult, nearly a half century in existence. (Lansner 1987, 80)

Journalists, who tend to be in an even greater hurry than adventurers, brush by the John Frum archive and pick out a few stories that they twist and squeeze to fit the lines of their newspapers. The persistent appearance of the same motifs and themes might suggest that, if they read or talk with anyone at all, it is only with each other. We should rather assume that they all, thanks to anthropology's worthy efforts, have learned to repeat the same narrative lineaments of the standardized cargo cult. Moreover, they all write to meet the interests and expectations they presume of their audience.

American journalists, for example, understandably play with a twist the American card: Black and white American military servicemen, who were both powerful and generous, during World War II awakened desires within the oppressed native for economic and political progress. Such journalist texts shamelessly flatter the American reader. They function, in a small and occasional way, to uphold an American self-image—The G.I. Who Became a God:

> The west Pacific is dotted with crude wooden crosses painted red in honor of the G.I. who became god in the influential "cargo cult" known as the John Frum Movement. Who John Frum really was, if he ever existed at all, is not known. But one branch of the widespread cult reveres, as a sacred relic of the mysterious white messiah, an old United States Army field jacket with sergeants stripes and the red cross of the Medical Corps on the sleeves. (*NYT* 1970, 7; see also McKee 1989)

Or, journalists hymn the sacred American dream: "the American dream has transcended geopolitics and passed into the realm of bizarre cult religion" (Ashbrook 1986, 2).

> Chief Isaac Won sits in the dirt at the foot of a smoking volcano and dreams of the good old days, when the men of his island could paint "USA" on their bare chests and backs and march, with bamboo poles for rifles, until they could almost see John Frum. Those were great times, he says. The men would drink the intoxicating juice of the kava root and raise the American flag in the field between the village huts and sing out strong for paradise. . . ."The promised land is still coming," says Chief Won. "America will bring it. John

Frum said so." . . ."When the Americans come again to this place, John Frum will come too," says the chief. "John said our brothers are in America. They will come and help us. They are our friends." (Ashbrook 1986, 2)

And beneath the seething red lava of Yasur's crater, Chief Tom Meles says, lives John Frum. From there, leading his legions "of millions and millions," and with American assistance, John Frum will one day march to bring "freedom and all things they have ever wanted" to the people of Tanna and neighboring islands. . . ."I am getting to be an old man," he shakes his wizened gray head, "please tell the Americans they must come soon." (Lansner 1987, 80)

The US has a special place in the hearts of the cultists who believe in John Frum, the king of America, whose return will not only bring a time of unprecedented wealth, but will also rid the islanders of the demanding ways of foreigners, especially Europeans. (Glines 1991, 86)

This final example, which contrasts freedom-loving Americans with oppressive Europeans, appeared in the American *Air Force Magazine*. Here, again, in the 1990s is a strange cargo-cult conjunction of anthropological and military texts. A vestigial military cargoism, in fact, lives on in some of the publications of World War II veterans associations. Aging veterans maintain a lively curiosity about various aspects of the Pacific today, including John Frum for whom they rightly take some credit (see eg, Discombe 1991, 32).

Occasionally, journalists, with an eye for novelty, create rather than merely rephrase. Or they rephrase so far as to generate something altogether new and so contribute fresh stories to the John Frum archive. However, because journalistic authority is weaker than ethnographic or adventurist, their narratives often have an odd smell to them. Many stray too far beyond the bounds of the John Frum canon.

The John Frum party . . . is based on the surrealistic Cargo Cult, a messianic movement which believes in the arrival of a Big Man who will banish illness, confer immortality, and distribute money, cars, boats and consumer durables of every kind. He is also said to enable his followers to acquire, effortlessly, the total sum of the world's knowledge in 14 days—a claim which emptied Tanna's schools overnight. . . . He has been variously identified with President Lyndon Johnson and senior members of the French Communist Party. (Frater 1980, 38,46)

They will explain . . . that the Japanese are now forced to labor making radios and watches for Americans because they lost the war. (Ashbrook 1986, 2)

John Frum, who appears in dreams or visions to comment periodically on contentious issues, is now cited as authority against a thatched grass disco erected in a clearing in the jungle. (Kristof 1987, 6)

After Cyclone Uma ravaged Tanna's east coast in February, emergency relief from overseas quickly arrived. Tents emblazoned with an image of a strong black hand firmly shaking a strong white hand and the words "Gift from the People of the United States of America" are among aid to reach Sulphur Bay. The clasped hands, John Frum followers say, are of two men the same age, being those of Chief Tom Meles and Ronald Reagan. (Lansner 1987, 80)

A hat and a bag of rice presented by the Australian minister [Gareth Evans] to a village chief in Vanuatu has led to a cargo cult on the South Pacific island group. . . . Since then, the chief's "Jon Frum Movement" has claimed the hat and rice symbolize Australian's recognition of its beliefs and that Canberra will send food and other cargo. (HS-B 1989, A9)

Journalists deal in current events as well as human interest, and the candle of Vanuatu's troubled independence in 1980 attracted a rare swarm. The task was to report upon secessionist attempts on Tanna that many John Frum people supported.

The bow-and-arrow rebellion in the New Hebrides spread last week to the island of Tanna, where some of the South Pacific's most primitive people were armed to the teeth with unprimitive weapons.

About 300 separatists lobbed explosives onto the island's grass-covered airstrip. Then, led by an opposition politician named Alexis Ioulou, they attacked the nearby government compound with rifles, shotguns and more explosives. British police fought back with tear gas, but they couldn't stop the rampaging crowd from breaking into the prison and freeing 29 allies. Ioulou himself died in the attack, killed by a shotgun blast at point-blank range. . . . The island is known as the home of the "John Frum" cargo cult, which cropped up after the Allies used the New Hebrides as a base during World War II. Its followers believe that John Frum (as in "John From America") will someday ascend from a volcano, ushering in a work-free paradise in which all material needed will drop by parachute from the sky. (Brecher and Robinson 1980, 42)

A principal motif in this coverage is that John Frum people are dupes. Why else would millennialists involve themselves in bloody politics? The gullible "Frumites" are "easy prey to any kind of manipulation from outside" (Dyson 1982, 49). This is a journalistic version of the old administrative cargo motif of criminal foolery, only the trickster here is not the native prophet but rather the devious French, who scheme to retain their control of the archipelago (Frater 1980, 38; Trompf 1984, 43; Lansner 1987, 80), or dubious American real estate investors.

In 1942 a quarter of a million American GIs arrived in the New Hebrides to pursue the war against the Japanese. With them came such extravagant supplies of food and clothing and new wondrous things from the great country across the water that the islanders acquired a distorted view of a civilisation which had never touched them before. In common with other Pacific islands visited by the American forces, a "Cargo cult"—a belief that the white man will satisfy all needs—evolved and is enshrined in the name "Johnny Frum", pidgin English for "Johnny from America." . . . It has made Tanna vulnerable to the blandishments of American businessmen, who for some years now have been savouring the prospect of developing the New Hebrides. (Dobson 1980, 68)

Or, perhaps it is not the French or shady developers after all, but rather the British and independent Vanuatu's own leaders who are beguiling John Frum: "the British decided to encourage [people of Iounhanan village] in their worship of the Duke of Edinburgh. . . . . The British and [prime minister] Father Walter Lini did not want the islanders losing faith in cargo and turning their devotion to political activities. . . . The problem of former cargo cultists taking political action had appeared on Tanna, and the only peaceful policy was to keep the belief in cargo alive" (Shears 1980, 106–107). The Tannese—the Dupes of Edinburgh—automaniacally follow their strange gods. The French trick them to plunge into serious politics at the very moment when the British are hoaxing them to retire from the scene. Journalism resuscitates the old cargo motifs of criminal foolery and ignorance, but in so doing washes its customary ironic stance with bathos. At least administrative cargoism allowed the clever tricksters to be Tannese! Some anthropologists, too, reverse the dupe motif to argue that the Tannese actually were manipulating the French (see Guiart 1975, 110; Richardson 1987, 8). Still, at least journalistic cargoism approaches John Frum as a problem to be explained. The Tannese, although duped, can still make trouble. One final subgenre of cargoism instead petrifies John Frum into a natural wonder.

John Frum for Tourists

Touristic cargoism, like journalistic, prefers to deal in cozy stereotypes. These most simple forms of popular cargo stories distill the cargo cult down to its essentials. All but the most basic cargoist motifs boil away: "The cargo cult has come to Tanna. Cargo cults happen like spontaneous wildfires among peoples whose knowledge of the outside world is limited mainly to the opaque pages of the Bible" (Fields and Fields 1972, 25).

Touristic writing, which undertakes to attract wealthy visitors to a place and to direct their gaze after they arrive, is delighted with John Frum. Tanna, for prospective tourists, is "The Island of John Frum Myth" (Bitter 1976, 60). Here is a spectacle. Something for visitors to look upon. Tanna is doubly blessed, in fact, since Sulphur Bay village (John Frum "headquarters") is conveniently located at

TANNA ISLAND
REPUBLIC OF VANUATU

*Tanna Island is renowned
for its active volcano,
custom villages,
potent kava,
cargo cultists,
strong traditions,
exciting festivals,
gigantic banyan trees,
magnificent wild horses,
long black and white beaches,
velvet nights, and much more...*

Cargo cultists as tourist attraction. (Courtesy of Tanna Beach Resort)

the foot of Iasur (or Yasur) volcano. Touristic writing uses the volcano to frame John Frum, and John Frum to frame the volcano. Each magnifies the spectacle of the other. Iasur is thrilling because it is the home of the mysterious John Frum; and cargo-cult eeriness is heightened by eruptions of black volcano plumes in the near distance (see Stanley 1989, 630; Harcombe 1991, 129). Iasur is the "world's most accessible volcano," and John Frum the world's most accessible cargo cult. Happily, tourists can take in volcano, cargo cult, and a catered picnic lunch all in one go during a day trip down from the hotels in the capital.

Tanna is one of the most remarkable islands in the Pacific, a broad statement but easy to substantiate. Here one can climb an active volcano, visit villages whose adherence to non-Christian ways is devotedly maintained, observe the behavior and paraphernalia of one of the longest lived "cargo cults", see herds of wild horses, ride beyond the reef in a huge outrigger canoe, visit one of Cook's landing places, and do many of these things in a single day. (Douglas 1986, 85–86)

Tanna "boasts an active volcano, a centuries-old lifestyle, mysterious cargo cult and fields of beautiful wild horses" (*PIM* 1991, 40; see also Hermann and Bonnemaison 1975, 87; Stanley 1989, 627).

Touristic cargoism focuses on what is most easily seen—on "sights." John Frum's mysterious red crosses, not surprisingly, are a particularly popular item:

Red-painted wooden crosses, fences, and crude models of aircraft— symbols of the movement—stood eerily in the volcanic haze. (Shadbolt and Ruhen 1968, 170)

The red cross, which could be photographed but not touched, is the emblem of this religion whose origin is unknown. . . . It is up to you to confirm or invalidate. (Coral Tours Melanesie 1971[?], 79)

At the edge of the crater pit, through the stinking sulphur smoke roiling up from the thundering hellfire below, I saw a huge, faded scarlet cross erected to honor Jon Frum. (Fields and Fields 1972, 25)

The red cross is a tribute to the volcano by the followers of John Frum, the quaint and primitive religion of Tanna. . . . The crude symbols of the John Frum cult such as gates, birds, crosses, all of which are usually painted red, may be photographed, but please do not touch them. When visiting Tannese villages never enter a native hut or man's house unless asked. Your guide may arrange it for you. (Quoted in Rice 1974, 132–133)

Other cargo-cult sights include John Frum headquarters at Sulphur Bay, scattered John Frum "churches," and the annual John Frum 15 February celebrations.

The ceremony of 15th February is looked forward to in an atmosphere of great excitement, amidst lavish preparations. Hundreds of "pilgrims" come with their families from all over the island. . . . They gather round the red cross (symbol of their faith) which stands in a sacred enclosure in the centre of the village. . . . [T]he pilgrims will make their way home in little groups, expecting to meet their messiah at each bend in the road. (Vanuatu Institute of Technology 1981, 180)

Just north of Yasur is Sulphur Bay village, stronghold of the Jon Frum cargo cult. The chief is a funny old guy who speaks not a word of English and thinks all tourists are mad! On one side of the village common is a simple guest house where visitors may sleep free on the dirt floor. Opposite is the John Frum Church with red cross and other iconography. The grave of Nampus, an important chief and Jon Frum leader, is well tended by the villagers. . . . At Yaneumakel, just above Sulphur Bay, is a Jon Frum Church with a picture of Christ about the red cross and a magazine color photo of U.S. space exploration personalities on the moon. . . . Purchase grass skirts made out of *brau* fiber from the Sulphur Bay villagers for v.300, a beautiful and genuine buy. (Stanley 1989, 630)

Touristic cargoism petrifies John Frum into a beautiful and genuine sight—an object and experience of gaze. Cargo-cult observers watch in safety from mobile tourist minivans. Touristic cargoism perpetuates and condenses the popular cargoist themes of John Frum mystery and adventurous primitiveness. Sensibly enough,

A red cross, Sulphur Bay. (Lindstrom)

however, the related motif of cultic danger fades from touristic
texts. It is unwise to alarm one's clients. While adventurers may
profit from frissons of danger, most tourists seek out more relaxing
spectacles. John Frum may be primitive, eerie, and mysterious, but
he is in the end safely "quaint." John Frum freezes into an object of
touristic gaze. His people stand still and smile back into the camera.

   Or do they? A remnant of the cultic danger motif survives in
some tourist writing. John Frum sometimes scowls, not smiles, and
so jeopardizes the touristic experience itself. This inverts the dupe

motif of journalistic cargoism: here, John Frum dupes the tourists. A *PIM* travel piece on Tanna describes circumcision feasts, noting merrily that "visitors are warmly welcomed to these events—to the extent of participation being encouraged!" (*PIM* 1991, 40). Rather ominously, however, the article's title touts the island as a "Minefield of Adventure" (1991, 40). Is the innocent tourist in danger of tromping on buried cultic explosive? One tourist guide offers such a word to the wise:

> An ancient Tannese myth describes a great white ship that will someday anchor offshore and the wealth of the world will be transferred to the beach for them to enjoy without working. Now this vision seems to have arrived, as affluent white visitors line up and pay good money to look at anything and everything of interest on the island. Adventurers, trying to get away from the fun-fair, zoo-like environment of the world's tinsel strips, must contend with operators who consider tourists a resource to be exploited, and locals who are used to being paid fat bucks to smile for the camera. . . . Villagers around Yasur Volcano argue over who is to get the tourists' money, and tour buses are often turned back by rival groups and prevented from seeing the volcano. Tour Vanuatu guides hassle visitors who decline to join their tours or stay in the tourist bungalows. . . . Beware of crooked taxi drivers. And be very careful answering questions about politics and taxes as the most innocent things can be twisted by some. Tanna is well worth visiting, but be forewarned. (Stanley 1989, 627–628)

Here, at last, we reach the ultima Thule of the John Frum archive: the climactic narrative motif of tourists as cargo. Various cargoists, including anthropologists, have occasionally bantered that Islanders have mistaken *them* to be the source of cargo. Self-deification of this sort in a cargoist text, no doubt, is an agreeably ironic diversion. Anthropologist Peter Lawrence, for example, apotheosized himself into one of cargo's strange gods:

> It was believed also that a good European was one who, remembering his brotherhood with the natives through Noah, would fulfil the obligations of the relationship by giving liberally of his own

store of cargo, and ultimately by revealing the secret of its origin. My own case bears this out. I had shown myself liberal and friendly: I therefore remembered my brotherhood with the people. I was a European: I therefore had the [road to] God. It was believed, by some Garia at least, that eventually I would pray to God to send the spirits of my own and the Garia ancestors with cargo to Sydney. From there my living relatives would ship it to Madang, and from Madang it could be flown inland by aircraft. I was approached by several natives and asked to build an aerodrome for this purpose. (1954, 14)

It is one thing to be taken for a prophet or cargo deity such as John Frum. It is quite another to be taken for John Frum's cargo itself. European cargoists on tour are much more comfortable in the role of alien gods than they are as packaged merchandise for avaricious Islanders.

This touristic self-perception of themselves as the cargo testifies to the widespread and powerful functions of cargoism as a dominant Western discourse about the truth of the native. Europeans of all sorts in Melanesia today have cargo in mind. Cargoism is a discursive field from which tourists and others harvest overgrown understandings to frame and interpret their passing relations with Islanders. If Tannese taxi drivers try to stiff the tourists, this must be because Islanders perceive tourists as cargo (see Cockrem n.d., 19). If the people smile at airplanes but scowl at the tourists inside, this must be because they yearn only for John's return. After all, Tanna is known to be the "Island of John Frum Myth," and the "home of the cargo cult."

John Frum for the Tannese

But how do the Tannese know their island? The John Frum archive is predominantly a Western achievement. Few Tannese voices are recorded directly therein. Islanders' own John Frum themes and motifs circulate orally within local conversation, and are stored only in local memory. Some Melanesian movements, such as the Paliau movement on Manus, Papua New Guinea (Otto 1991, 269), have produced their own sacred texts. John Frum, however, still awaits his Saint Paul.

The various subgenres of cargoism, of course, have captured Tannese voices here and there. Guiart (1956*b*, 145, 409) and Rice (1974, 175,201, 207–210, 223–227) transcribed spoken John Frum statements; and Guiart (1956*b*, 409–410) and Lindstrom (1990, 118) reproduced cultic letters written by Islanders. These minor local texts, however, are thoroughly encapsulated within external, literary cargoism. John Frum himself may belong to the Tannese, but John Frum writing is the property of the textualizing West. The John Frum archive, like cargoism in general, does not exist on Tanna. The written cargo cult erupts only in the West.

Cargo Cult for John Frum

Whatever John Frum may be for the Tannese, for us readers who live beyond the reach of volcanic shadows on that marvelous island he is a cargo cult. The discourse of cargoism gives us John Frum. Were it not for cargoism, we would know nothing of Nampas, Nakomaha, red crosses, 15 February, and fifty years of events and excitements on a minor, isolated, South Pacific island. Cargoism packages John Frum stories. It offers a variety of cultic motifs and themes that reflect diverse Western interests to administer, proselytize, understand, adventure, report, and tour.

Thanks to the discourse of cargoism, we know John Frum as blameworthy foolery, madness, ignorance, or sin, either perfectly mysterious or perfectly understandable, reactive nationalism or indigenous millenarianism, universal stage or culturally particularized event, precious irony or romantic heroism, external Japanese and communist subversion or internal cultural creativity, declining or persistent, duped or duping, a Stone Age reaction, and finally a touristic spectacle. All these themes now structure Western experience and stories of the Melanesian other. John Frum, as it were, has been framed. He is now well known as a cargo cult.

John Frum, in some quarters, is even *the* cargo cult. In the early 1970s, free-lance photographer Kal Muller working on an article for *National Geographic* took photographs at Sulphur Bay of the 15 February John Frum holy day. Muller has been peddling these pictures successfully ever since to American textbook publishers. Thanks to Muller/Woodfin Camp and Associates, John Frum stories and photographs now illustrate the generic cargo cult in many introductory anthropology college texts (eg, Aceves and King 1978, 344; Hoebel and Weaver 1979, 327; Ember and Ember 1985, 426; Howard 1986, 377; Haviland 1989, 530, 1990, 377; Harris 1991, 310). Bohannan (1992, 290), instead, reproduced an old black-and-white Attenborough photo of a "Christian cross [sic] and the airplane" to illustrate the cargo cult. But like most of these texts, he did not bother to further identify the cultic objects or the people portrayed as either John Frum supporters or Tannese. Rather, they are merely "cargo cultists." John Frum red crosses and John Frum marching guards now serve to illustrate and represent the prototypic cargo cult everywhere.

Anthropology's cargo cult, furthermore, is unchanging and ahistoric. Since it is always the same, its story never needs updating. The first edition of *Culture, Man, and Nature,* Marvin Harris' introduction to general anthropology, which was published in 1971, notes of cargo cult: "On the island of Tana in the New Hebrides, the John Frumm cult cherishes an old G.I. jacket as the relic of one John Frumm, whose identity is not otherwise known. Like many recent cargo movements, the prophets of John Frumm have directed the construction of landing strips, bamboo control towers, and grass-thatched cargo sheds" (1971, 566). Twenty years later, Harris' third edition of *Cultural Anthropology,* his other introductory text, repeats exactly the same story in the same words. "On the island of Tana in the New Hebrides . . ." (1991, 310). This neglects a generation of events on Tanna, not to mention that the New Hebrides disappeared in 1980 with the independence of Vanuatu. Ember and Ember (1985, 426) and Bates and Plog (1990, 418) also misplaced John Frum in the New Hebrides.

Also disturbingly, one text (Kottak 1978, 377) reproduces yet another Muller photograph of "land divers" on Pentecost Island of northern Vanuatu. This is labeled "Cargo cult in the New Hebrides. . . . Here they look to the sky for airplanes bearing desired possessions." The crowd, actually, is looking up to a man

John Frum worship before the red cross. (Lindstrom)

about to jump from a tall tower with elastic lianas tied about his ankles. Once a firstfruits celebration, the land dive more recently is connected with contemporary tourism as a mecca of the forerunner of bungee jumping. No one, save possibly the introductory anthropology student, is searching the sky for airplanes. Such pictorial confusion in a prominent anthropology text is a modest, if obvious, example of the powers of a static and rigidly thematic cargoist discourse to frame our vision of Melanesians.

Anthropology, following through its program of total understanding of Melanesian culture, comes at last to denounce cargo cult, as we have seen in the development of the anthropological subgenre of cargoism. Latter-day anthropology protests that John Frum is *not* a cargo cult. In effect, however, anthropology protests against its own success. Anthropology was largely responsible for the definition and standardization of cargo cult, a standardization that prepared the way for cargo cult's slippage into more popular discourses. Cargoist storytellers of all subgenres have taken from anthropology both the label cargo cult itself, and also more recent notions of Melanesian "cargo mentality" (see eg, missionary Calvert 1978, 220). Despite anthropology's second thoughts, John Frum is trapped within a web of its own cargoism.

The only noticeable effect of anthropology's recent objections to cargo cult is a writer's occasional qualification of the term. Coates, for example, notes that Tanna's "secret world produced the Jonfrum, or John Frum, movement, which is sometimes described as a cargo cult, though it is not exactly so" (1970, 275; see also Douglas 1986, 88; Ryman 1987/88, 93). Despite such passing qualification, these authors invariably cannot resist repeating stock cargo themes. These they borrow from anthropology and also one from another. In so doing, they contribute to the further standardization of the John Frum story. Two minor cargoist motifs, for example, bounce from subgenre to subgenre within the John Frum archive. Unlike some more generically restricted themes, all subgenres of cargoism repeat these narrative figures. They are obligatory parts of the John Frum story. The first of these motifs consists of catalogs of desired cargo. Strangely enough, these cargoist shopping lists of coveted goods typically fixate upon refrigerators. It is clear, however, that this narrative reiteration of refrigerators reflects the history and dictates of the John Frum story itself rather than any real desire in the hearts of the Tannese:

. . . are based on a fundamental envy of European goods—those highly exciting things like calico and electric torches and refrigerators. (Priday 1950, 67)

. . . the white form spoke, saying: "Basis, I am about to make delivery to you of a big ice box, an outboard motor, a pair of pointed shoes, and a coil of barbed wire." (Marsh 1968, 83)

Irving Johnson . . . explained to the leaders of the cult that jeeps and refrigerators and canned food are not produced by magic. (Coates 1970, 278)

Meanwhile, news of the impending arrival of fabulous shiploads of refrigerators, jeeps, bulldozers, bottles of coca-cola and all manner of hitherto unheard of riches, reached all the natives. (Hermann and Bonnemaison 1975, 92)

Over the years, the objects they had become more and more surprising—up to radios and refrigerators. . . . How do you shape or weave or build an enameled refrigerator? (Gourguechon 1977, 312)

I will send him cargo, refrigerators and pocket knives, sewing machines and mosquito nets and everything he desires. (Steinbauer 1979, 87)

. . . the extraordinary John Frumm cult, a pagan group that awaits the return of the white man bringing material goods such as refrigerators and jeeps. (Shears 1980, 85)

The [Tannese] are cargo cultists: they believe that one day they will receive material goods such as refrigerators, television sets and washing machines. (Shears 1980, 105)

Primitive villagers like those on the island of Tanna were stunned by the sudden appearance of things like canned food, axes, cameras and refrigerators. (Hamilton 1983, 1)

. . . American troops arrived, and the people saw all the equipment being brought ashore, such as trucks, jeeps, refrigerators, provisions for the whiteman so the Tanna people thought, well, why can't we have the same. (Discombe 1991, 32)

Adherents of the sect drilled with wooden rifles, awaiting the . . . liberating cargo of trucks, jeeps, houses, fridges, tables, chairs and cigars. (Evans 1992, 130)

A messiah by the name of John Frum would come with ships and even airplanes . . . bringing the Tannese the same goods that they had seen unloaded from [Pacific War] Liberty ships, radio sets, refrigerators, cartons of cigarettes, etc. (Pouillet 1992, 38; my translation)

This strange appearance of refrigerators again and again in four decades of cargo shopping lists is at once peculiar and suspicious. Such lists clearly answer to the internal demands of cargoism as a discourse. They are not accurate, in the ethnographic sense. It is obvious that the desires which cargo catalogs reflect and enumerate are European fancies rather than Tannese. It is true that people on Tanna, like all Melanesians, remark the existence of important social relationships with an exchange of food. But this food is in no manner refrigerated, nor do people desire it to be so. The Tannese are farmers. They appreciate the agricultural origins of food. We are the ones who seek food and comfort behind the white enameled door, not the Tannese, who go off instead to their gardens. Refrigerators, on Tanna, have yet to come to symbolize human relations. The lists of desired objects I occasionally receive in letters from Tanna, rather, include wristwatches, video cassette tapes, English dictionaries, cigarettes, clothing, guitars, sewing supplies, asthma medicine, and the like. No one asks for refrigerators.

The more recent cargo shopping lists show some movement in the sorts of goods they enumerate. Televisions and cameras first make an appearance in the 1980s. On the whole, however, cargo stories recycle along with refrigerators the same limited set of goods. If such cargo lists aim for ethnographic accuracy, they would today have to include video cassette players and electric generators—recent prestige goods highly desired on Tanna. It is apparent, though, that cargo lists and the stock sorts of goods they record are a necessary narrative fixture of cargoism as a discourse, and are far removed from whatever John Frum desires might actually be. One may instead suppose that refrigerators once symbolized certain immediate postwar European desires and fears. For us, not the Tannese, solid white refrigerators concatenate a variety of images: the wonders of mass production; modernity and progress; the cleanliness of white enamel; the psychological security of tomorrow's dinner; the mechanized focus of familial commensalism. This frigid symbol, reflected upon the Tannese by early cargo writing of the 1940s, has today become fossilized within the John Frum archive. It continues to be reiterated as a part of the standard John Frum story.

Like fossil symbolic refrigerators, a second popular narrative figure within the John Frum archive also betrays underlying European interests. This is the motif of endless waiting. John Frum people may be tragic, but they are also hopeful and familiar because, like us, they must wait for the millennium. Attenborough set this motif in play, in his inimitable Pidgin English: " 'But, Sam, it is nineteen years since John say that the cargo will come. He promise and he promise, but still the cargo does not come. Isn't nineteen years a long time to wait?' Sam lifted his eyes from the ground and looked at me. 'If you can wait two thousand years for Jesus Christ to came an' 'e no come, then I can wait more than nineteen years for John' " (1960, 58; also repeated by Lansner 1987, 80).

This narrative figure clearly resonates with the Western cargoist sensibilities that infuse cargoism because it continues to recur often throughout the John Frum archive.

> A white journalist pointed out to me that I had now waited 20 years for my cargo of dental supplies to arrive and they were still not in sight. I asked him how long he had waited for Jesus Christ to arrive, and he replied that it must be nearly two thousand years; so I informed him that I was prepared to wait a further 20 years for John but was he prepared to wait another two thousand years for Jesus? He said that he would not be alive then—so I have far more chance of seeing my god than he has. (Marsh 1968, 87)

> "People have waited nearly 2,000 years for Christ to return, so we can wait awhile longer for John," a mission-educated village chief told [a] visitor here. (NYT 1970, 7)

> [Nampas'] dark eyes looked beyond me, at a vision I could not see. Was it that glorious future that enabled him and his people to endure the impoverished present? He spoke again, "You Christians —how long . . . you wait . . . for your Jesus?" (Fields and Fields 1972, 24)

As the Tannese remark to whites who needle them about John's failure to return, "You have waited two thousand years for Christ, so we can wait for John." (Rice 1974, 231)

A John Frum village chieftain interviewed in 1970 noted that "people have waited nearly 2,000 years for Christ to return, so we can wait a while longer for John Frum." (Harris 1974, 136)

When several officials attempted to explain that John Frumm would most likely never return, the cult believers had a ready reply in that although he seemed to be taking a long time, the Christians had been waiting a good deal longer for the return of Jesus Christ! (Hermann and Bonnemaison 1975, 93)

I asked Sam if he really believed, after so many years, that John Frum would return to Tanna. Sam smiled gently and answered in a soft voice, "People have waited two thousand years for Christ—we can wait a few more years for John." (Trumbull 1977, 81)

If you suggest that Jonfrum is a long time coming, they are quick to point out that Christians have been waiting nearly two thousand years for the return of Christ. (Simpson 1979, 96)

Officials who have tried to gently dissuade the cultists by saying that John would probably never come have been given a brilliant reply. Although he seemed to be taking a long time, the Christians have been waiting much longer for the second coming of Jesus Christ. (Shears 1980, 107)

"One day John will come back," cult leader Isac Wan told me. . . . After more than 40 years, the Tannese are still awaiting their Messiah—but then the Christians have now been awaiting *their* saviour's return for almost two thousand years. (Ryman 1987/88, 93)

John Frum did not return to his followers at Sulphur Bay this year . . . but as one villager explained, "the people had been waiting a long time for Jesus, too." (McKee 1989, 30)

When will he come? His followers have waited since the early 1940s and nothing has happened yet. "How long have Christians waited?" they ask. "Nearly 2000 years, yet we've waited only 50!" (Harcombe 1991, 132)

The waiting motif, which repeats across the pages of three decades of John Frum writing, is situated in the mouths of a variety of Islanders: Attenborough's Sam, the prophet Nampas, cult leader Isac Wan, and anonymous native villagers. The actual identity of the person making this comment, or whether any Tannese ever uttered the statement at all, is clearly unimportant. The figure functions rather as a stylistic marker of cargoism as a genre. This is one of the fundamental leitmotifs of cargoism: a sort of forlorn, unfulfilled waiting for a cargo that will never arrive.

The subtext of this motif, of course, is that *we* are cargo cultists too. The Tannese wait for John, but we wait too. This subtext only reveals the obvious. The story of the cargo cult recounts European desire, not Melanesian. Who else but we await the white-gleaming, ever-filled, always giving, softly humming refrigerator that never will arrive? Cargo stories describe ourselves more accurately and sometimes in better detail than they do the Tannese. John Frum is ours. We have spirited away this island spirit. Although a few literate Tannese may also dip into the John Frum archive from time to time to deploy his texts for local purposes, John's texts speak mainly to us.

The unavoidable effect of this cultural appropriation, our narrative kidnapping of John, is that we cannot help reading Tanna except in terms of John Frum, and John Frum in terms of cargo cult. Our subtexted cargoist desires demand that we locate people somewhere in Melanesia whom we can call the *real* cargo cultists. They must exist as cultists insofar as they tell us who we are, and also who we are not. They must want refrigerators to show us why we want refrigerators. They must wait patiently so we can better know why we wait patiently.

Latter-day anthropologists may protest that John Frum is not a cargo cult, but this protest is enfeebled by the remnant legitimacy of the term within anthropology itself and by its growing presence within popular narratives. Discursively, John Frum *is* a cargo cult, and John Frum writing is composed according to the dictates, motifs, and standard figures of cargoism. But cargoism as a discourse frames more than Tanna's singular John Frum. The next chapters explore the recent return of cargo cult throughout Melanesia today, and the hidden treasure of those lost John Frum files: their subtexted secret that we are the true cultists, still forlornly but faithfully waiting for our cargo.

5 THE RETURN OF CARGO CULT

Now in its fifth decade, the term *cargo cult* continues to prosper as an artifice for representing Melanesians. The stamina of the term is especially remarkable in the face of increasing resistance to its usage in certain quarters. Anthropologists, for one, have attacked from two directions. Theoretically, cargo cult should soon disappear. Peter Worsley predicted that "more advanced, secular political movements" will inevitably replace millenarian cults that are destined to dwindle away into quiescent sects among "backward elements" (1957, 255). If we but wait, cargo cult will decay into quaint historic memory. Concurrently, anthropology's etiquette of labeling now counsels that the term really ought to be retired.

> "Cargo cult" has become a term of disparagement and one which affronts Melanesians. . . . Government officials, expatriate settlers and missionaries all used it to damn any Melanesian activity which departed from the ideal of the docile, acquiescent "bus Kanaka" [hillbilly] and which thereby threatened their hegemony. . . ."Cargo cult" is therefore an inadequate expression to describe the complex of ideas, actions and aspirations intrinsic to the millenarian movements of Melanesia. (Hempenstall and Rutherford 1984, 120)

But despite ninja anthropologists' darkened attempts to assassinate the term through erasure, cargo cult has returned to the islands. Neither the happy march of political evolution in Melanesia, nor better anthropological manners, has yet had much of an effect. Cargo cult still glitters; and Melanesia is still "the world's centre of cargo cultism" (Loeliger and Trompf 1985, xi).

This chapter reads through three sorts of texts that bring back cargo cult to make sense of Melanesian culture, desire, and mentality. Journalists, notably, continue to evoke the cargo cult to frame their stories of contemporary political unrest in the postcolonial Pacific. The cargo cult is also a fecund literary resource for novelists, playwrights, songwriters, and film makers. It makes for dramatic island stories.

We start, though, with another return of cargo cult: the term's use today by Melanesians themselves. Islanders have learned from anthropologists that they are cargo cultists. A self-application of the term requires adroit negotiations of identity. What does it mean to be a cargo cultist? The expression delineates obvious boundaries between Melanesians and outsiders, and also within island communities themselves. In these acts of negotiation and self-understanding, a cargo-cult identity can be both revered tradition and punishing abuse.

Cargo Cult at Home

Anthropology's cargo narratives have come home to Melanesia. The prodigal cargo cult, though, bears strange gifts. The term's tricky evaluative charge and its narrative halo of ambiguous motifs provide both opportunities and dangers for island discourses about local identity. When the task is to define oneself against non-Melanesians, Islanders may embrace cargo cult as their mother culture. When the task is to accentuate political, religious, regional, or other difference among themselves, however, Islanders can revile and denounce one another for being cargo cultists. Both these projects of self-identification and self-differentiation are served by the capacious cargo archive to which island writers turn for noble as well as ignoble cargo stories (Hermann 1992).

One local strategy is to deny the reality of cargo cult and its applicability in Melanesia—to cast this mote back into the eyes of anthropologists. The term is culturally libelous; Melanesians are in no way cargo cultists. It is very difficult, however, to write against the ethnographic authority of anthropology and the mass of the overgrown cargo archive. Most island writers accept the term's validity for *some* Melanesians, if not always for themselves (see

Waiko 1973, 420; Kaima 1989, 41; Gesch 1990, 219). Even anthropology's nativized reading of cults as *pre-European* appears in Melanesian writings: "cults in many parts of Melanesia before 1942 should not be seen solely as direct results of contact with the white man. They should be seen as an instance of traditional responses, be it in the form of beliefs or ritualistic practices, associated with facing a challenge or an enemy" (Waiko 1973, 420; see also Waiko n.d.; Opeba 1987, 61). Some Islanders have bought into the most mature version of cargoism. They recognize themselves as cultists not merely in response to European oppression, but cultists by hallowed tradition.

The term's conspicuous presence in commonplace representations of Melanesia demands of island writers that they either exercise or exorcise their cargo-cult culture. Knowing themselves, now, to have such a culture, many island writers have pressed to revalue cargoism. The independence of Papua New Guinea (1975), the

"Car-go-kult" returns to Papua New Guinea's House of Parliament, Port Moresby. (Lindstrom)

Solomon Islands (1978), and Vanuatu (1980) saw a general revaluation of tradition *(kastom, kastam, kastomu)* throughout the region. New political elites evoked shared culture and tradition to foster sentiments of national unity and national distinctiveness vis-à-vis Europeans and other outsiders. Perforce, cargo cult was pulled along in this sort of charged nationalist discourse: If we Islanders are cargo cultists, then cargo cults must be good.

Anthropology and the other subgenres of cargoism furnished several useful motifs for the ideological construction of nationality. Missionary and anthropologist claims that cargo cultism is really a sort of protonationalism already had helped rehabilitate the term. Melanesian cargoists, in this thematic, are akin to freedom fighters. Cults are honorable ways to resist domination. The Melanesian

> believed that an enemy must be fought and defeated or his life would never be safe. The necessity never to give up in the face of an enemy is a deeply ingrained characteristic of the Northern District [Papua New Guinea] people. He considered that one day he would conquer, and take his revenge on the white man. The frequent recurrence of cults supports this argument and the constant attempts to repress the cults helped maintain the response. . . . In other words, the response was a mechanism for some Melanesian societies to adapt to and cope with change. The response not only helped the people to cope with the situation, but also it helped them adapt to the permanent changes that were brought about by the situation. The response led to social changes that were adaptive. Thus, one of the frequent features of the cults is that they united previously separate social groups. This, in fact, if allowed to develop, was exactly the social change needed to combat the whites. (Waiko 1973, 419; see also Hannet 1970, 25; Kerpi 1975)

An honorable cargo-cult culture is useful *after* independence, too. Ferea suggested that "cargo cults can and have contributed to development in a broader sense. Development in a broader sense encompasses economic, social, spiritual, cultural and intellectual development" (1984, 1). The cargo cult "introduces disciplines based on consensus. It creates in its followers a purpose and raises consciousness of their own resources. It puts them on an equal footing with other people in the achievement of the higher goals. It instills confidence, pride, and initiative which had been taken away by the white man" (Pokawin 1984, 79).

The Melanesian nationalist's "Cargo Cult Is Beautiful" motif also resonates in the writings of island Christians. The church's ancient hostility to cargo evaporates away. Instead, Islanders must embrace their cargoist identity as a proof of their authentic Melanesian Christianity. This sort of writing borrows from latter-day mission cargoism that also portrays cults as both reflecting and encouraging the human search for salvation. Melanesian tradition and the Bible alike thus foretell the good life: "Not only did the Bible uphold and prophesy a good and attractive way of life, but there were also points of continuity in Melanesian tradition and in the biblical message. . . . Given this continuity, Melanesian thinkers supposed that fundamental principles governed both Melanesian and biblical traditions" (Opeba 1987, 64). Since Melanesians are naturally religious, perhaps even proto-Christian in all but name, cargo cults "reveal the essentially religious nature of Melanesian societies, societies that are clearly not pagan, evil-dominated, or lacking in morality, even if made to look that way by the early missions and the government" (1987, 66).

Not surprisingly, island cargoism has scorned the common motifs of sinfulness, madness, and criminal foolery. To the contrary, "there is nothing sinful, heretical, or mad about [cargoism]; it was quite normal and acceptable" (1987, 62). Local cargoism, here, borrows the pronounced romantic and heroic thematics of the cargo archive's tragic as opposed to its comic face. Cults are a form of noble resistance to the world system. Cargo prophets are national heroes: "The prophets or cultic leaders who have sought to protect pre-Christian religious forms, moreover, far from being mentally sick, are worthy of praise as true prophets for refusing to accept their people's loss of their own destiny in the face of Western civilization" (1987, 66).

Cult prophets are not crazy, nor are cult followers deluded or ignorant. Melanesian cargo mentality is not at all a kind of chronic racial madness, but is a dignified, genuine "philosophy" (Narokobi 1974, 96). It is a "natural, useful, constructive and creative process in the development of ideas in the mind" (94). As such, cargo cult is protoscience just as it is protonationalism: "Cargo believers could transform themselves into native geniuses of the Melanesian philosophy of life. Genuine science and technology have developed from apparently crazy beliefs. Genuine Melanesian scientists can come from the cargo believers" (101). This nationalist paean to cargoism evokes cultural authenticity, genuineness, resistance, and adaptation as well as personal initiative and self-confidence. Cargo culture is honorable and authentic; cargo sentiments are adaptive and resistant; and cargo mentality is nothing but natural philosophy. Melanesians, who are now citizens of the new nation, should both take pride in and profit from their genuine cargo-cult culture.

Alongside its rejection of the common cargo motifs of sin, madness, ignorance, and so forth, nationalist cargoism is understandably much more judicious in its use of irony and ridicule than are the other cargoist subgenres. Even journalists, for whom irony is a favored voice, tread warily here. It is instructive to consider the Papua New Guinea *Post-Courier*'s coverage of events that took place during August 1983 on the island of New Hanover. Lyndon Johnson never arrived, but Islanders were waiting still (see also Billings 1969).

HANOVER AWAITS CHRIST

Hundreds of people are pouring onto the island of New Hanover off New Ireland for "the return of Jesus Christ" on Friday.

Supporters of the Tutukuval Isukal Association are expecting to receive K200 million on that day, according to people in Kavieng, the main town of New Ireland.

The people of New Hanover are best remembered for their support of the bizarre activities of the Johnson cult in the 1960s.

Thousands of people on the island dropped all normal activities to await the arrival on a mountain top of the then US President, Lyndon Johnson.

They expected President Johnson to rule over them and bestow all of the wealth of the United States on their island.

Later investigations found the mass indoctrination of villages stemmed from distortions of conversations with US Army surveyors who spent a short time on the mountain top preparing for the establishment of communications equipment.

In later years, activities of the cult followers were steered into business ventures within the operations of the TIA [Tutukuval Isukal Association].

Their leader Mr. Walla Gukguk served a term in Parliament as the Member for Kavieng.

Mr. Gukguk was removed from his seat late last year for failure to attend meetings of Parliament.

The MV Danlo has been sailing between Kavieng and Taskul since Monday taking people for Friday's "celebrations."

The boat has been travelling fully loaded, and many disappointed followers have been left at Kavieng.

Details of the proposed celebrations could not be confirmed yesterday, but officials in Kavieng expect Taskul to host the occasion.

The cult's quasi-religious aspects have often been linked to the strong influence on the island of the Catholic Church, but members of the church maintain that any involvement by priests has only been to assist the TIA member[s] to start their business ventures. (PC 1983c, 3)

"AUSSIES GO HOME"

The Tutukuval Isukal Association of New Hanover, New Ireland, is pressing for the removal of all Australians from PNG for having "ignored requests for presidential government for New Hanover people."

Hundreds of association members have been gathering at Kuligei village to celebrate their "hamamas day" [happy day] and to await the arrival of former American President Lyndon Johnson.

They expect the late Mr. Johnson or a US representative to arrive in a helicopter on Mount Pativung on Friday to declare for New Hanover people a "matanitu" or government base[d] on the US presidential system.

In a special meeting this week, leaders of the association unanimously agreed to press Mr. Johnson for the removal of all Australians, because the Australian government had ignored their request for a separate Presidential government.

The demand is one of a number of issues contained in a circular being distributed widely in New Ireland in the past week.

The New Ireland Provincial Government is playing a "low key" with the celebration at Kuligei village.

"We do not want to interfere with their program, although we fear there would be some trouble if Mr. Johnson or whoever the Americans decide to send do not arrive to meet the people," [a] provincial government spokesman said. (PC 1983a, 3)

EDITORIAL: HAPPY EVENT ON HANOVER

What can one say about the multitude assembled atop a mountain on New Hanover Island except that it seems highly unlikely that either Lyndon Baines Johnson or Jesus Christ will arrive there today by helicopter.

To many people no doubt the vision of the Tutukuval cultists awaiting the event—and it seems K200 million—will be weird. But the cargo cult has its place in contemporary Papua New Guinea mythology. It is not an embarrassment.

The difficulty with cargo cults is that many of them mask political objectives which, in our overburdened democracy, ought logically to find a place in some official forum. Some of the expectations expressed by cultists are not too far removed from ideas raised in supposedly sober debate in many assemblies.

But whether political or not in their basis, essentially harmless ideas such as those expressed on New Hanover this week do very little damage to the national psyche—and might even boost our tourist image.

Let's hope the weather stays fine for the celebrations at Kuligei village today. Apinun! (PC 1983b, 4)

MISSION FAILED: CULTISTS LEFT

Devoted cult followers deserted New Hanover Island by the hundreds during the weekend after being "stood up" by Christ.

But the followers have been urged to retain their faith and continue worshipping because Christ had merely postponed his visit until September 1985.

The followers left New Hanover as early as Thursday after the leader of the Tutukuval Isukal Association, Mr. Walla Gukguk, announced that Christ would not arrive to meet them on Mount Pativung as planned.

A provincial government spokesman in Kavieng said food short-
ages and accommodation problems forced many to leave the island
early.

"The only real ceremony which took place on Mount Pativung
was the unsuccessful transfiguration of Mr. Gukguk, who could not
disappear into the clouds as expected by his followers.

"Mr. Gukguk was to have been picked up by some UFO or a
cloud to go to heaven but this did not eventuate.

"His promise to heal the sick and give sight to the blind also did
not eventuate," the spokesman said. (*PC* 1983*d*, 3)

In this reportage, *Post-Courier* journalists worked hard to cultivate a marked neutrality of style. The prophet, a former member of
Parliament, is introduced politely as Mr Walla Gukguk. The writers, although they recalled the label "Johnson cult" and *cargo cult*
itself, were careful also to use the group's own name: the Tutukuval Isukal Association. The articles also report that the Catholic
Church and the New Ireland Provincial Government have likewise
taken a neutral stance vis-à-vis the cultic "celebrations."

Post-Courier editors, however, abandoned journalistic neutrality in
an editorial which, applauding these mountain top celebrations,
salutes the cargo cult. The editors wished the faithful gathered atop
Mount Pativung happy, rainless days. They editorialized: cargo
cults, perhaps, to the uninstructed may appear bizarre, even weird.
But they are nothing more than honest, collective political action in
other form. Cults are not an embarrassment. They consist of
"essentially harmless ideas." Echoing cargoism elsewhere, the *Post-
Courier* concluded cheerfully that the cargo cult "might even boost
our tourist image." The nation might profit from such renown:
Papua New Guinea—the Land of the Cargo Cult.

We might compare the *Post Courier*'s neutral style and its cargo-
cult boosterism with another report on the Johnson cult that
appeared five years later in the American tabloid *Weekly World
News*. This piece, which removes the cultists to the New Guinea
mainland, is advertised on the tabloid's cover as "Headhunter tribe
thinks that former prez LBJ is a big-eared god!" Inside, the article
itself is titled "Wacky tribe thinks ex-prez LBJ is a god!: Savages
worship Johnson and his flop-eared mutts":

Tabloid cargo. (Courtesy of *Weekly World News*)

A Stone Age tribe of cave dwellers in the rugged and remote Bismarck Mountains of central Papua New Guinea worships a former U.S. president as a god-king, reports the stunned leader of a recent anthropological expedition to the area. A fading and wrinkled color photograph of Lyndon B. Johnson hangs garlanded with flowers in the mammoth, cathedral-like cave of the primitive tribe's high priest, said Dr. Ulrich Ritterfeldt of the University of Utrecht in Holland. "It's absolutely mind-boggling," he told newsmen in the coastal city of Madang. . . ."Through a combination of sign language and pidgin English, the high priest, Ken Ma, told us the tribe has been venerating LBJ as its 'holy, wise and generous' deity for about 20 years," Ritterfeldt said. . . . The high priest told the anthropologists that an ancient tribal legend predicted that a pale-faced god with large, protruding ears and his long-eared hounds would descend from heaven—from nearby Mt. Wilhelm, which towers above the clouds at 14,793 feet—to shower blessings on the simple savages and help them form a great society. (O'Neill 1988, 29)

Comic-book irony here is heavy indeed: Stone Age headhunters, savages, primitives, wacky tribe, and the big-eared god-king LBJ and his floppy beagle dogs. The *Weekly World News*'s version of the Johnson cult rehashes journalism's self-indulgent motif of America as cargo god: President LBJ brings the goods. We should not overlook, also, the implicated equation of Johnson's Great Society with cargo cult, the ironic subtext that blurs the identity of the real cargo cultists.

The *Post-Courier*'s cheerful hopes to boost tourism on the back of Papua New Guinea cargoism are, no doubt, furthered by these popular tabloid images of Johnson cultists. International stories of wacky primitives, however, violate local cargoism's themes of the honest, unembarrassing cult that is nothing more than ordinary politics. Local cargoism's neutrality and celebrations founder against international cargoism's sharper, ironic burlesques.

Cargo cultism at home, however, can also tell contentious stories. Ferea's nationalist cargoism, for example, calls for a new approach that would "help us to see how cargo cults can and have contributed to development in a broader sense" but, more problematically, at the same time would "help to erase cargo beliefs from peoples minds" (Ferea 1984, 1). Island cargoism has borrowed as well from the darker, comic side of the cargo archive.

Nationalistic cargoism, emphasizing the bounds of new Melanesian states and the unity of their citizenry, celebrates freedom-fighting cargo cultists and the economic, philosophic, and scientific benefits of a cargoist culture. Where the contested social boundaries are internal, however, cargo cult can serve to label and denigrate behaviors or communities within the new nation that challenge the young powers that be. This other strand of local cargoism adopts a number of darker motifs from the cargo archive: notably, the themes of blame, spies, and cargo dupes. These cargo stories are not at all celebratory or neutral in tone. Instead, surpassing the *Weekly World News'* comedy, their accent is one of condemnatory ridicule.

Cargo cultists, rugged and independent protonationalists as they are, have a bad habit of maintaining their opposition to centralized political authority even after national independence has been secured. In such cases, home cargoism performs a discursive about-face. Freedom-fighting cult nationalists rapidly mutate into obnoxious cabals bent on subverting the new state. Cargo cult returns home as Melanesians slander one another for being cargo cultists. The term cargo cult, which bleeds perpetually from various semantic stigmata, is an extremely useful term of abuse: One's cultic political opponents are not serious. They are not even an opposition. They are merely deluded, mad cargoists.

At the time of Vanuatu's independence, for example, John Frum people on Tanna were opposed to a Vanuaaku Pati national administration. Party leaders turned to a discourse of cargoism to account for such unseemly local resistance: "The membership of the Jon Frum and Kapiel movements are concentrated mainly on the island of Tanna. Their membership is mainly Melanesian and many of their characteristics are the same as cargo-cult movements of the Solomon Islands and Papua Niu Guini" (Weightman and Lini 1980, 183–185).

This strategic, political cargoism borrows the motifs of blame and duping from the cargo archive. Someone must be behind this untoward political resistance. The good people of Tanna plainly have been duped into not supporting their new political elites. In Vanuatu, the French, luckily, were at hand to blame.

The Vanuaaku Party has warned people to be careful of outside influences who use Melanesian people in order to promote their own interests and achieve their own aims. . . . [T]he so-called moderates and independence opposition are not really moderates. They are terrorists and leaders who are hungry for power and will not tolerate any democratic system. (Lini 1980, 52)

The leadership of both movements [Tanna's John Frum and Espiritu Santo's Nagriamel] has also been manipulated and used by the French administrations to oppose the Vanuaaku Pati. (Weightman and Lini 1980, 185)

The Bislama version of this last statement puts the dupe motif even more starkly: "Franis Kafman ikivim help long tufala, mo i mekem olgeta i akensem Vanuaaku Pati. Hemia i mekem tingting blong olgeta i mix ap tumas we bambai oli save stretem nomo afta long Independs [sic] [The French government provided aid to the two groups and it caused them to oppose the Vanuaaku Party. This made their thinking so mixed up that it can only be straightened out after independence]" (Weightman and Lini 1980, 180–182).

In Papua New Guinea, politicians at the national and provincial levels have also decried their rivals as merely cargoist:

A firm stand will be taken against organisations in the North Solomons which "smack of cargo cults." The warning came yesterday from the North Solomons Premier, Dr. Alexis Sarei. . . . He said cargo cults would not be tolerated in North Solomons and the provincial government was moving now to stamp them out. . . . Dr. Sarei said such organisations did not fit into the North Solomons society and were a danger to social and economic development. He said some of the cult followers were known to come from outside villages in the province and moves would be made to have them repatriated. (PC 1976a, 3; see also Laboi 1972)

Similarly, in Papua New Guinea's East New Britain Province, members of the Provincial Government

spoke strongly yesterday against cargo cultism, the digging-up of bodies, and illegal organisations. . . . A legal officer advised that it was a criminal offence to recover a body from a grave and the same applied to unauthorised courts, unauthorised magistrates and unauthorised taxes. . . ."These people are creating and practising illegal governments, illegal courts and fines, and illegal taxes. Have we got power to stop the cargo cults?" (*PC* 1976*c*, 7; see also 1977*a*, 11)

National politicians, not surprisingly, are disturbed by village attempts to circumvent provincial powers to legislate and adjudicate, not to mention to fine and tax. Such local resistance "smacks of cargo cultism" that must be stamped out. This politics of labeling is spiced with cargoist tales of digging up the buried dead and sundry strange rituals.

Accusatory cargo cultism has also served Melanesian religious as well as political leaders. Incoming missions can threaten the positions of the more established churches. Embattled pastors and priests, whose congregations are melting away, sometimes fight back with stories of cargoism:

> Religious cargo cults in Papua New Guinea could lead to mass killing to pardon sins, the Member for Milne Bay, Sir John Guise, has warned. Sir John said the Government must crack down on "bible-bashing Christian churches" entering the country "through the back door." . . .Sir John said he had deep respect for freedom of religion as enshrined in the Papua New Guinea constitution. However, if this freedom allowed the entry of increasing foreign Christian sects hostile to the established churches, it could be bad for the nation. . . . That sort of religious teaching and behavior was nothing more than a cargo cult movement at its worst, he said. "It uses Jesus Christ as a scapegoat, assisted by the ever-present collection box." He said it was a pity any outbreak of cargo cult received bad publicity in the Western Press and portrayed a bad image of the country. "On the other hand, Christian sects which practise these sorts of religious cargo cults under European leadership in the nation, do not get any publicity at all . . . only expatriate church workers who belong to nationally-established churches [should be] allowed entry permits. (*PC* 1978, 1,4; see also Mosoro 1975)

Cargoism's primal blame motif continues to have rewarding political uses for Melanesian leaders. In the North Solomons (Bougainville), Dr Sarei's blame falls partly on "outsiders" who support subversive and dangerous cargo cults. Or, one can blame disloyal, local opponents for fomenting cargoism: "Deputy Speaker, Mr. Joe Eko, said he had witnessed the effect on the local economy at Pomio with coconuts and cocoa trees reverting to bush as the people waited for the 'cargo' to come by ship, allegedly to be piloted by a well-known local representative" (PC 1976c, 7). And, "The Provincial Commissioner, Mr. Joseph Nombri, said [cargo cult] was the fault of the leaders of the community who collect money from the people and who never co-operate with the council carrying out projects in the area" (PC 1976b, 8). National elites have seized upon blameworthy cargoism as a useful narrative motif to discount local political resistance and to rebuke their opponents, despite the unavoidable thematic associations of Melanesian foolishness and ignorance that such strategic usage evokes. Cargo cult, here, returns home with some vengeance.

Local stories of cargoism also serve political elites by excusing their failures with national economic development, as Buck (1989, 168) has observed. Theoretically, economic development will finish off the cargo cult. In practice, though, cargo cult kills development despite the honest efforts of national leaders.

> New Ireland politician Mr. Noel Levi has urged the Lihir Island people to abandon any "cargo cult-type" beliefs. He warned them against thinking that development would come easily to them because their Members of Parliament were the Prime Minister, Sir Julius Chan, and himself, the Minister for Foreign Affairs and Trade. "No, that is cargo cult-type thinking and I can tell you that achievement comes only from hard work and co-operation between yourselves," Mr. Levi told the people at Londolovit, Lihir, during a recent flying visit. . . . "In many parts of Papua New Guinea people sit on their backsides and just cry for help," Mr. Levi said. "But if we in Government heed all such appeals, we will waste all the funds and have nothing achieved. . . . You can't expect the New Ireland Provincial Government or the national Government to seemingly wave a hand and create anything you want." (PC 1980, 13; see also Hannet n.d.)

Cargo cults are "a danger to social and economic development" (*PC* 1976*a*, 3). Where cults hold sway, coconut and cacao plantations revert to bush (1976*c*, 7). Pernicious cargo thinking frustrates the best efforts of national leaders to develop the country. Cargoism torments national elites otherwise as well. It can oblige them against their will to travel in VIP automobiles in order to be worthy of popular cargoist expectation.

"If people see us travelling in taxis or PMVs [Public Motor Vehicles, ie, buses]," [Member of Parliament] Mr. Torato told parliament, "they are going to wonder what has gone wrong with the system. 'He is supposed to be travelling in a VIP car because he is a bigman'. I am ashamed because of this. When the people elect me to parliament," he went on, "they think I own the Bank of PNG. People demand you buy them motor vehicles or give them money because they have been your campaign managers or cast their votes in your favour. They demand you produce K10,000 and buy them a car. . . . People have this kind of mentality that when we become MPs, we inherit wealth. I call this cargo cult." (Dorney 1990, 54–55)

Cargoism coerces harassed national elites both to motor about in their own luxury vehicles and to purchase more cars for their supporters—onerous and costly duties to reconcile. And they call this cargo cult.

Kaima, along these lines, suggested that "political campaign tactics and platforms in themselves promote a cargo cultic mentality among the people" (1989, 4). Politicians appear as cult prophets (28); party platforms as cult doctrine (59); campaign ritual as cultic ceremony; and political parties themselves "are considered more powerful versions of cargo cults" (55). In this oddly reflective politics of identity and labeling, national elites excuse their failures and chastise their enemies in terms of cargoism only to turn around and find that the voters recognize and elect them as conspicuously powerful cargo-cult leaders!

Islanders have applied the cargo cult label to a variety of threatening political and other sorts of irregularity. Kaplan noted: "I even heard an official of the Fijian administration call some Fijian villages 'cults' because they did not fit the patterns recorded by the Lands Commission" (1990, 16). In Papua New Guinea, a craze for card playing threatens "development and the country's Eight Point Plan" (Lamang 1976, 2). Such unruly card playing is actually nothing but cargo cult in different guise: "Cards are a nuisance and a hinderance [sic] to progress. Card gambling is only another type of a nation-wide cargo cult practice" (1976, 2). Or perhaps highway robbery is really cargo cult?

> The coastals have their magic spells to reach the whiteman's riches: cargo cult. The Highlands have the same idealistic dreams for the same purpose. Robberies which (like cargo cult) stem from the same source: Frustration and incomprehension of the outside world. . . . The lasting help will have to come from education, particularly moral education. Once our youngsters learn how to get rich in a proud and honest way (and Papua New Guinea has a tremendous asset of rich reserves outside highway trucks!) this Highland version of cargo cult will disappear. (PC 1977a, 19)

Here, again, are the familiar cargoist motifs of native ignorance, need for moral education, and eventual cultic decline.

But home cargoism, as a naturalized discourse at least, today serves too many valuable local functions within the new Melanesian states to decline very soon. Cargo cult has come home. There now is a Melanesian subgenre of cargoism. Islanders today know and label themselves as cargo cultists. Cargoism serves, positively, as a metonym of Melanesian culture. Cargo stories record a proud history of resistance to colonial domination. As a philosophy and protoscience, the cargo cult distinguishes Melanesians as Melanesian.

More ominously, however, cargoism serves negatively within island political debate to label and denigrate anything that may threaten established orders. Cargo cult is an extremely flexible term of abuse. A wide range of oppositional or subversive behavior and opinion can be explained away and contained as mere cargo cult. Island cargoism, here, eschews tones of easy comic irony, typical elsewhere, for cruel ridicule. Ridiculous cargo cultism, discursively at least, is made no longer threatening.

Jimmy Stevens, for example, the jailed leader of Vanuatu's Nagriamel movement—himself commonly labeled a cult prophet (see eg, Hours 1974)—once abused John Frum followers for being cargo cultists: "He spoke with contempt of Jon Frum—with whom it was quite evident he did not intend to associate—and of cargo cultists in general. 'I no waiting for steamer. I rather have black steamer than white steamer. Land my steamer' " (Woodcock 1976, 242–243). Here is a fine state of affairs! One cargo cultist mocks other cargo cultists for being cargo cultists.

These abusive, ridiculing uses of cargo cult might be called Birdism. This is the return of Mr Bird: the legacy of cargo cult as a term of political abuse. Cargo cult returns home to Melanesia as Islanders develop their own cargoist stories. It also returns home to its original political functions of scaremongering and low argument. Mr Bird's advocacy of a particular political program, and his move to belittle and frighten his enemies and political opponents with the specter of cargo cult, continues as a familiar strategy today.

Melanesians, even those who use the term positively for purposes of national identity construction, unavoidably inherit all the darker as well as the lighter motifs of the genre: blameworthiness, madness, native ignorance, primitivism, touristic spectacle, criminal foolery, need for moral education, it goes on. These home narratives of cargoism invite not only the return of cargo cult, but also the revenge of cargo cult.

"Cargo Cult Won't Die Quietly"

Melanesians nowadays may call one another cargo cultists, but the main engines of cargoist discourse clatter along outside the region. Western accounts of Melanesia return again and again to the cargo cult to make sense of remarkable events and occurrences in these islands.

The *Pacific Islands Monthly*'s 1958 plaint that "cargo cult won't die quietly in the Pacific" was duplicitous. A generation later, it turns out that *PIM* itself, along with its journalistic and anthropological compeers, keep cargo cult alive by exercising it regularly to describe their Pacific subjects. Journalism's popular archive of cargo-cult stories converges with anthropology's postwar construction of a systematic Melanesian cargo-cult culture to ensure frequent cargo-cult sequels, remakes, and further installments. A quiet death for the term is increasingly unlikely.

Cargo cult returns particularly alongside movements of political protest in the contemporary Pacific. Earnest anthropologists and others once tried to provide the unseemly cargo cult a little social respectability by claiming that it is actually an honorable form of millenarian political protest. Hempenstall and Rutherford, to give a typical example, declared:

> Such movements, in the form of cults, sects and churches, continue to flourish throughout Melanesia. They flourish in spite of repeated failure to deliver cargo in its narrowest sense. But that is, perhaps, not important. In the widest, all embracing sense of cargo they can point to successes. . . . The construction of these alternatives has been an example of successful protest employing religious symbols and in the process people have developed new corporate solidarity and emotional satisfaction. (1984, 149; see also Keesing 1978; May 1982, 439)

But this worthy argument to politically ennoble the cargo cult reverses too easily. Cargo cult returns to cast its shadow on contemporary Melanesian politics. If cargo cults are actually movements of political protest, then perhaps today's protest movements are really only cargo cults.

People on Tanna, objecting to their island's incorporation into the new state of Vanuatu in 1980, marched to the government offices at Isangel to free imprisoned friends and relatives. A fire fight broke out when protestors confronted national police and an irregular posse of government supporters sheltering within the district agency. Under cover, some of these partisans shot and killed protest leader and Member of Parliament Alexis Ioulou. The British resident commissioner, in an initial press statement, was careful to claim (inaccurately) that "the dead man was one of the leaders in the John Frumm cult" (cited in Shears 1980, 92). Cargo cult, inserted into official texts such as this, functions as an excuse for both unfortunate protest and botched government response. An equation of cargo cult with protest movement may raise the social value of the former, but it also serves to lessen the political consequence of the latter. Cargo cult similarly haunts journalistic and anthropological accounts of one of the most consequential Pacific movements of political protest of the late 1980s and early 1990s. This is the attempt by people on Bougainville Island to secede from the state of Papua New Guinea. In late 1988, a Bougainville Republican (or sometimes Revolutionary) Army, the BRA, led by Francis Ona and Sam Kauona, called for either the closure of Panguna copper mine, one of the world's largest open pits, or massive reparation payments of ten billion kina. The following year, BRA military action shut down the mine. Subsequently, the Papua New Guinea government sent in, and then withdrew, its army several times and has engaged in intermittent and protracted negotiations about the future status of the island.

Cargoism has distinctly stained reportage of Bougainville's secessionist movement. The *Far Eastern Economic Review* reported that

> more worrying still, said some observers, was information suggesting the movement had been joined—and possibly is dominated by—a charismatic "cargo cult" leader, Damien Damen, who has lived in isolation with several hundred followers ever since PNG became independent in 1975. . . . The bodies of some recent victims of rebel attacks are reliably reported to have carried axe cuts on arms and legs which are believed to be a sign the cultists were responsible. If the cultists are fighting alongside or in parallel with the landowners, they now have a common aim—secession from PNG and an end to mining operations, which they believe have not benefited them. (Malik 1989, 21)

A *Los Angeles Times* article, in similar cargoist vein, took note of "ritual killings" on the part of BRA militants: "They've chopped ears and fingers off, shot at ambulances, threatened hospital workers" (Drogin 1989, A14).

Anthropologists as well as journalists have been unable to forget their past investments in a language of cargo when writing about the BRA. Ogan, for example, in an opinion piece published in the *Canberra Times* told us that some of the BRA's violent protest "draws its energies from 'cargo cult' attitudes developing out of earlier dissatisfaction" (1989, 14; see also Hyndman 1987). Ogan doubted that the BRA could be a real revolutionary force. Rather, it was probably just prosaic, familiar cargo cult that was disguised behind a sophisticated rebel mask.

> There is no evidence that the violence constitutes an organised effort with any common objective, leadership or administration. One should not be misled by the pronouncements of any individual. For decades, there has been widespread Nasioi [a Bougainville community] dissatisfaction with their lot. Frequently, this dissatisfaction has led Nasioi to seek supernatural solutions to their problems. Manifestations have varied over time, but "cargo cult" is a catch-all term, useful in this case. A problem here is that some cult leaders have adopted terminology suggestive of political sophistication but have either not understood the accepted Western meaning of these terms or else consciously used them simply to manipulate followers. Thus "business," "secession," "referendum" and the like take on for cultists connotations quite different from Western legal usage. In the Nasioi case, "cargo" sentiment does seem to motivate some of those carrying out violence against the mine. However, this is by no means the same as an organised effort to overthrow the existing government. . . . Cultists are most unlikely to fit the definition of an organised force out to supplant an established authority. (Ogan 1990, 38)

Connell, likewise, discounted BRA militants as including "landowners, cultists, and some 'rascals' (small-scale criminals)" (1990, 31).

Academic commentators have put into play the language of cargoism also to explain the BRA's seemingly exorbitant monetary demands, along with axe chops, attacks on government institutions, and disorganized leadership. Standish, writing in *Pacific Research,* suggested that the BRA's ten billion kina compensation claim, "more than the mine has earned in over half its project life . . . was ignored as unrealistic. . . . Some see Ona, a former BCL

[Bougainville Copper Limited] surveyor, as messianic; he has teamed up with a local cargo cultist" (1989, 5). May, similarly, argued:

> there seems little doubt that the "irrationality" of the military land-owners' demands . . . goes a long way towards explaining the alliance, from early 1989, between the militant landowners—the core of the Bougainville Revolutionary Army (BRA)—and the followers of Damien Damen's "Fifty Toea" [cents] cult movement and, apparently, various local *raskol* [criminal] groups outside the mine area. The continuing association of these elements, especially the millenarian elements of Damen's followers, will make a negotiated settlement difficult. (1990, 56)

The BRA cannot *really* mean ten billion kina. This must be only the fevered influence of irrational cargo cult. A language of cargoism functions to shrink not only the BRA's monetary demands, but the political consequence of the rebellion as a whole.

Cargoist discourse has returned to color descriptions of other protest movements in the Pacific besides Bougainville's war of secession (see eg, Trompf 1981). Tucker analyzed various operations of the Free Papua movement of Indonesian Irian Jaya as actually just a series of cargo cults: "the rebel movement in Irian Jaya is energised by cargoistic/millenarian ideology, and is therefore primarily a millenarian movement manifesting itself as a political liberation movement" (1988, 177). Cargoist discourse, occasionally, can even taint accounts of governments in power as well as reckless island secessionists. The *Voice of Vanuatu,* for example, once headlined one of its articles (in a bit of poetic justice for John Frum), "V[anua'aku] P[ati] Platform—A New Cargo Cult? 'Custom' is the name of the ship which will bring the cargo. [Prime Minister] 'Lini' is the name of her captain" (1981, 4).

Cargo cult, in fact, sneaks back to inform our understanding of a spectrum of Islander plans, programs, demands, interests, protests —almost any sort of active Melanesian desire (see Hermann 1992, 68). Such island longing and planning need not always be tragic or futile, either. The cargo storyline can account for political party platforms infused with Weberian bureaucratic rationality equally as well as it can unreasonable secessionist monetary demands. Melanesian cargo-cult culture, as an explanatory device, thus functions to illuminate a wide variety of contemporary island interests and practices. Cargo cult, to give just a few examples from many, has returned to Melanesia in recent analyses of Christian revivalism (eg, Flannery 1983, 176; Schwarz 1984, 259–260; Weymouth 1984, 204; Jebens 1990). Personal epiphanies of the Holy Spirit are cargo cult. Participation in business and economic development schemes is likewise cargo cult (eg, Walter 1983; Clark 1988). Going to school is cargo cult (Swatridge 1985, 148; Smyth 1975, 45–46). Filling in forms and writing letters are cargo cult (Kulick and Stroud 1990, 294). Popular stories of cargo-cult, and anthropology's more elaborated notions of cargo-cult culture, work to apprehend, delimit, and in part explain away all sorts of conspicuous Melanesian desire that comes to outside attention.

Cargo cult as an explanatory device is strangely commodious. It is roomy enough to harbor complex and bloody ethnonationalist protest movements like the Bougainville Republican Army. Yet, it is also cozy enough to digest small urges such as filling out mail-order catalog forms. Given this remarkable explanatory utility, it is no surprise that cargo cult returns, and returns again, in popular as well as anthropological stories of Melanesian social organization (cult) and aspiration (cargo).

Cargo Cult Goes to Hollywood

Anthropologists, journalists, and Islanders themselves share the cargo-cult archive with more popular, and often more literate, observers of the Melanesian scene. The entertainment industry very quickly seized upon cargo cult as a winning story line. Not two years after cargo cult made its debut in *Pacific Islands Monthly*, the magazine in 1947 published "Cargo," a short story by Lorna Crouch.

Cargo cult, after all, was born in popular colonial discourse, and only adopted subsequently by anthropology as a proper social scientific label. It is not surprising that the term maintained some currency back in its native, nonacademic community. Both academic and popular discourses have endowed cargo cult's semantic portmanteau. These discourses, moreover, have informed one another. There has been, to use a recent term, considerable intertextuality between cargoist fictions of the popular novel, and anthropology's artful cargo monographs. Some of the same cargo themes and motifs structure both idle romance and solemn ethnography. Both tell stories of cargo-cultic Melanesia.

Australian novelist Olaf Ruhen, for example, employed the standard cargoist motifs of waiting, trickery, and madness in his short story "The Village of Phantom Ships" (1957). Young Kudgil, returned from a year's plantation labor, is waiting. He desires to marry the pert and wealthy Talua but cannot afford her shell-money brideprice. Luckily, Kudgil dreams up a cargo message. This, and latent cargo mentality, ignites madness among his village neighbors: "Tombarap came forward, dancing to his chant, self-hypnotized in fury, and shaking his spear. There was a chanting behind him too, now, that grew faster and faster. Tombarap became an automaton, moved by the chant" (Ruhen 1957, 156). Ruhen's debt to the anthropological literature is obvious. He has fictionalized Francis Williams's disingenuous Vailala Madness prophets and his automaniacs (ie, "automatons").

An Australian district officer paddles up river, shoots down the cargo maddened village chief, and promotes Kudgil, the cult prophet, to be headman—a fictional reflection of Australian colonial policy to co-opt cargo leaders such as Yali of Madang, and Paliau of Manus: "[The district officer] explained to Robins afterward: 'Apparently this was the Joe who started all the trouble. He's found out how to use people now—not many natives do. So we might as well use him' " (1957, 158).

Enjoying his new status, Kudgil's neighbors, still cargoist in their mentality, bring him pearl shell just in case cargo, after all, arrives to fill the village's newly built storehouse. Kudgil cuts a deal with Talua's father, and the story ends with the line: "He found Talua waiting at the rim of the bush; and all his dreams came true" (1957, 160). Kudgil's prolonged waiting climaxes, successfully, when he at last makes love to Talua in the bush. This literary metamorphosis of cargo dreams into love and copulation, as we shall see, reflects a peculiar European rather than Melanesian desire (chapter 6).

A pair of playwrights have also explored the cargo cult. Both these writers borrowed themes of nationalism and resistance from the cargo archive. Papua New Guinea author Arthur Jawodimbari's 1971 play, *Cargo,* tells of the "Pure tribe" that tragically misunderstands a missionary's teachings and the source of his cargo. The missionary calls in colonial police who rout the uprising cultists. After the police retire, however, one unsubdued warrior stands up for stubborn cargoism. He speaks the play's last lines that evoke a continuing protonationalist struggle and also a stubborn cargoism: "Hear, O my people, the white Father is gone and his magic sticks too. Arise, take up your spears and shields and be men again. Remember, only this village is defeated, but the whole tribe of Pure is large and spreads over all this land. Tomorrow we will carry out the job of making canoes. Until then go back to your village, and let it be known throughout the Pure people when the work will begin. We will get our cargo" (Jawodimbari 1971, 19).

British playwright David Lan also exercised the nationalist motif, although he enfeebled this with the theme of tragic waiting, in his 1979 play *Sergeant Ola* (reprinted 1990). Lan drew upon Peter Lawrence's descriptions of the Yali movement in *Road Belong Cargo.* The play, in fact, echoes dramatically Lawrence's utilitarian disapproval of cargo cults. In an introduction, Lan stated that his play is about religion as "an unlimited and perpetually fruitful resource. In times of material and spiritual hardship people can draw on it to fuel resistance. Some kinds of religion will be more effective than others. 'Cargo' leads into a brick wall" (1990, xii).

Actually, Lan's cargo leads to tourism. He borrowed as his moral and his denouement the ironic motif of tourists as cargo. At the play's climax, Joana, a polygamous wife who has killed herself to ensure the arrival of cargo, makes a darkened and ghostly appearance to Ola, the cult prophet, and some of his followers in order to show them "what will come." (Lan's Papua New Guineans speak a sort of simple English decorated with occasional Pidgin words.)

The stage lights come up suddenly and "we see a view of the sea from an island in the Pacific. Palm trees, atolls, turquoise sea—just as on the postcards and in the movies" (Lan 1990, 120). The future's cargo turns out to be a deculturated, commodified society replete with Western tourists, sunglasses, cameras, ice cream, and radios blaring loud music (reggae, presumably).

> JOANA: You got cargo. Did it bring you happiness?
> YIM: You bet your life! I got ten black boys working for me now . . .
> PIOBA: . . . Look at me now. I got a uniform. I got some words here on my sign. When did I ever get such good, good pay? . . .
> JOANA: Do you love cargo?
> SWANSI: Sure. We love cargo.
> MAMBA: His Uncle's got a night spot on the beach. Those tourist chicks!
> SWANSI: They sure mean business. (1990, 120)

Besides enterprising tourist chicks, Lan's cargo, like Jawodimbari's, also leads to political co-option. The Australian district officer offers to free the prophet Sergeant Ola from prison if he joins a newly established local council. Ola agrees, but only because he continues to think with a cargo mentality. He believes the new council house to be a secret cargo house. The play ends, again like Jawodimbari's, with stubborn cargoism. Sergeant Ola once more searches the horizon for cargo's arrival. He still yearns forlornly: "OLA: So now we got a local government council. We got a small, small government just for us. We tell the Australian government. The Australian government tells the Queen. A woman will do anything we tell her. So now we got a council. We got democracy. These beautiful new wetmen's [whiteman's] things will bring us what we need. *(He walks down to the shore and looks out. To himself)* Cargo. Cargo" (Lan 1990).

Ola's final cargo chant is a refrain of many others in the play (eg, 1990, 66). Two of Lan's characters, who stand for modern capitalism and socialism, are as cargoist as the mad prophet Ola. Joana, in fact, is the only character who manages to escape pervasive Melanesian cargo thinking. But she only does so by killing herself. By dying and becoming a real ancestor, she sees the future. She knows that the ancestors will never bring anything like cargo, and that cargo thinking terminates in a corrupt society modeled upon a poor man's desires and Western materialism. Joana the ghost warns Ola: "You got to wake the people, Ola. It's dawn! The sea is white! Ola, you *got* to wake them. I got to go back to my mud. Don't lose your life in waiting, Ola" (1990, 121).

Joana sees the truth because the dead are awake and the living asleep: The white sea carries not cargo but corrupt European materialism to island shores. Joana pleads with Ola to stop waiting. But Ola refuses. He waits because he knows his ancestors will bring cargo. This persistent, futile waiting furnishes the play's tragic drama. Cargo desire leads headlong into the brick wall of deculturation, cultural inauthenticity, materialism, and touristic incursion. Melanesians are poignant, but stubborn and instinctive cargo cultists. They refuse to awake to the dawn. They do not care if the sea is white. Even a crash course in moral education won't help. Death can be their only escape from the drama of coming misery. Cargo is the Melanesian's tragic flaw.

Fictional cargoism shares with other cargoist subgenres this recurring theme of Melanesians as normal, stubborn cargo cultists. From the beginning, however, popular cargoism also has told stories of cargo-cultic Europeans. In blurring the identity of the real cargo cultists, it introduces a motif that anthropology has only belatedly arrived at forty years later.

Lorna Crouch, for example, began her 1947 story of cargo with images of Melanesian dirt and infirmity: "He was an old man and he sat alone on the veranda of his house. The dirty village stretched before him, to the right and to the left of him. A dozen filthy dogs lay easily in the sun below him, too weak to move much, half-starved, and sick with running sores" (Crouch 1947, 48). The old man is musing, exercising his cargoist mentality: "He frowned. He remembered the fable that the white man's cargo rightly belonged to the native man, and that his ancestors put it on the ships. It was the white man who always went on board first and changed the names on the cargo from theirs to those of the well-known stores. . . . One day it would not be necessary to work. Thousands were waiting for the day when the native would find himself master of the magic that produced ships from the far horizons filled with this good cargo for Papua" (1947, 48).

Into this waiting scene speeds Jim on the motorboat he has just sold to the old man's sons for £200. Suddenly, Jim (rather carelessly) crashes into two native sailing canoes, sinks the motorboat, but manages to swim ashore and meet his wife Cecile who is screaming on the beach. She exclaims: " 'But this is awful!' He only laughed. 'I sold it this morning to some native chaps who live in this village. They paid the money to me in cash. It's their funeral —not mine!' " Jim plans to keep the money and use it to go South, home to Australia with Cecile.

Understandably, the villagers are quite peeved and they begin to remonstrate and shout. Perhaps it *is* Jim's funeral after all: " 'Better get out of here, Cecile'. . . The girl was trembling. . . . Suddenly a jeep appeared, 'Thank Heaven!' Jim said as he assisted Cecile on board. 'You're here just in time,' he said to the white man. 'Thought I was about to be hung, drawn and quartered!' " (Crouch 1947, 48). The natives remain dangerous. They gather around the old man that night, stimulated and maddened by chewing betel nut. The old man reveals his cargo dream: "So much tinned food. So many clothes. Cars. Trucks. Blankets."

Only one young man protests—a morally educated one of course: "They talk like that in the far villages, but it is not true. I know. I have been to school." He, or perhaps one of his brothers, instead takes direct action. He slips away and steals back the £200 from sleeping Jim. Next morning, disheartened and poor again, Jim and Cecile forego their trip "South" and return in disgust to their plantation.

Crouch, however, next made a significant move. She concluded her romance by twisting the identity of the cargo cultists. Is the old man the true cargoist? Or are Jim and Cecile? Sometime later, a policeman appears on the couple's plantation veranda. He reveals that the police have caught the thief and secured the money—only this proves to have been counterfeit. The money is revealed, in the end, to be false cargo. Crouch applied the theme of hopeful, stubborn but ultimately tragic waiting to *both* Melanesian Islanders and

Australian planters. When the policeman appears on the veranda, "a faint wave of hope swept Jim and then, as quickly, faded away." Jim and Cecile wait in vain to go south; the natives wait for cargo ships full of trucks and blankets. Unrequited desire fixates upon illusory, inachievable objects.

The story concludes: "The old man sat in his chair and watched the children and the dogs play beside the straggling village path. He was ashamed. The police had put his son in gaol. What did the white man want with money? It was bad anyway" (1947, 48). A bad desire for natives and, implicitly, bad for whites as well. The blurred identity of colonials and natives within this cargo story, however, is incomplete. Real differences remain. Jim at least gets back his boat. The natives end up in jail without their £200.

The secret that Europeans—or humans in general—are the true cargo cultists gets revealed in an assortment of subsequent novels. Australian author Randolph Stow, for example, set his story *Visitants* (1979) in Papua New Guinea. Colonial officer Alistair Cawdor has become involved in a cargo cult. Dalwood, his assistant, chances on a hidden cargo shrine decorated with airplanes:

> The house was a church, it had a cross at the peak of the gable. . . . I walked nearer, and looked up the cross. It wasn't a cross at all. It was a plane, a nasty-looking sharklike plane, carved in ebony. Inside, from all the rafters, planes hung from cords and revolved in the faint breeze . . . at the end where an altar might have been in the God-times, a huge black plane, another ebony one, hung upright from a rope. As I came near a puff of wind hit the wings and twisted it round, and I was looking into eyes. . . . It was a pilot, there could be no doubt about his being a pilot: he was wearing all his gear, I made out the straps of his parachute and the goggles, pushed up on his helmet. He hung there by the neck, with his arms stretched out, crucified on his plane. (Stow 1979, 93)

This symbolic forerunner of a bad, cargoist ending climaxes in Cawdor's gory suicide. Cawdor, like the natives, is obsessed with alien "visitants" who arrive in a different sort of aircraft. He is certain, and exhilarated, that extraterrestrials have been watching him from hovering flying saucers. The natives fixate on Western planes and cargo; but Westerners are likewise preoccupied with space aliens and the hopes they provide. But these obsessions lead to madness and death. Cawdor commits gruesome suicide to join the stellar visitants: "Down the tunnel. My body. Atoms. Stars" (1979, 185; see Tiffin 1981; Wright 1986). Europeans, too, search the skies for signs that portend an end to desire.

Poet John Thorpe also employed the aerial cargo motif, one that evokes an ultimate tragedy of desire, with a beached, abandoned airplane crashed on the cover of his book of poems, *The Cargo Cult* (1972). Planes also figure in Ayi Armah's novel *Fragments* (1970), although here the desiring cargo cultists have been located in Africa: "We saw the line of people, many many white people but also others who were black, go like gentle ghosts into the airplane" (1970, 16; see Wright 1985). Baako, the tragic hero, takes the plane to America for an education. When he returns home to Ghana, he realizes that he is surrounded by people fervidly expecting that he has brought home cargo. The story ends typically: Baako goes mad, asking "So how close are we to the Melanesian islands? How close is everybody?" (1970, 229).

A story of popular cargoism turns up once more in an adventure tale by Australian historian and writer Peter Corris, first created as a television script for the Australian Broadcasting Corporation's TV drama *Pokerface*. With a playful twist of the term, Corris entitled his book *The Cargo Club*. The cargoists, here, turn out to be a gang of European businessmen and investors living in a fictionalized Pacific country called Vitatavu, one that shares certain features with Vanuatu. One of these characters explains the name: " 'Informal group,' Wilson said. 'We've been called the Cargo Club. Silly name, but it's stuck. We're progressive, go-ahead. This place has potential, but it's being held back' " (Corris 1990, 38). Like Melanesian cargo cultists, these melancholy European cargo clubbers wait and scheme futilely to profit from tourism and land developments that never arrive.

And universalized cargo cult appears once more in the science fiction *cum* murder mystery *Dream Park*, by Larry Niven and Steven Barnes (1981). The cargo plane, here, turns out to be Howard

Hughes' Spruce Goose. The dream park is a Disneyesque fantasy land where the jaded yuppies of the future act out their fantasies within a computerized playhouse that simulates virtual reality. A group of game players sets out upon a fantasy quest among Papua New Guinea cargo cultists (Niven and Barnes have read closely their Peter Lawrence). They seek a lost cargo plane with a secret World War II weapon on board.

The book, however, hints that the *real* quest is to locate an alternative reality that can satisfy and thereby end our desires. The players, who appear to be only fantasy cargo cultists are, in fact, the real thing: "He hugged her with one arm as they moved down the trail, the shrubbery closing behind them like a healing wound. 'I'm a city boy, Cas. What am I supposed to want? Six days from now I'm back at work copying blueprints eight hours a day. Hell, I . . . guess my expectations are a little unreasonable. I can't really expect an amusement park to undo in a week the damage a dull job does in fifty, but I do' " (Niven and Barnes 1981, 73). The fantasy cargo quest ends in a lot of death all around. The real cargo quest also fails, ultimately, to satisfy human desire: "Illusions . . . all there was in this world were lies and dreams, and that was just the way it was" (1981, 94). Dream Park computers blur the lines between reality and fantasy, but cannot in the end quiet the endless yearnings of players whose desires return anew when the game ends.

The theme of Melanesians as cargo cultists, and the accompanying, shadowing theme that we Europeans are natives too, twist through Gualtiero Jacopetti's 1961 film *Mondo Cane*. (An English version was released in 1963.) This film, whose introductory statement purports an objective interest in the human species, juxtaposes images of curious natives with shots of equally bizarre Westerners. The narrative pose is an anthropological one that suggests that humanity is one.

Jacopetti ended his film with cargo cult. The final image is of cargo cultic Melanesia. He filmed Papua New Guineans in paint and feathers staring through the fence at airplanes taking off from Jackson Field in Port Moresby. Jacopetti's intrusive cameras next shift to "Roso (?) and Mekeo" people who wait, searching the skies, around a dummy airplane and control tower at a makeshift airfield

Mondo Cane, a dog's world. (Courtesy of Vidcrest)

9000 feet up in the mountains above Port Moresby. The film's pontifical narrator orates a Hollywood version of cargo cult:

> As [the native] gets closer to the coast, he jumps hundreds of centuries in only a few days. . . . . Here in Port Moresby airport where his trip through time ends, and where he cannot find a reason for all that he has been taught and seen so hurriedly, the seeds of the cargo cult, the cult of the cargo plane, is born in him. . . . They believe that planes come from paradise. Their ancestors sent them. But the white man, a crafty pirate, manages to get his hands on them by attracting them into the big trap of Port Moresby. . . . You build your plane too, and wait with faith. Sooner of later, your ancestors will discover the white man's trap and will guide the planes on your landing strip. Then you will be rich and happy. (Jacopetti 1963)

Some contemporary reviewers of the film swallowed Jacopetti's narrative social evolutionism and read cargo cult to be the primitive beginnings of all the other sorts of more civilized, human excesses portrayed in the film. For example, a review in the *New York Times* queried: "The final sequence, showing cliff dwellers in the dark New Guinea wilds and the practice of the 'cargo cult', or worship of the airplane by naked natives in this deep, benighted land, bring the film to a brilliant conclusion on a strong anthropological note. So this is the way it all started! Will society return itself to this state?" (Crowther 1963, 58) Cargo cult, here, stands as a savage past that warns of a dread future. This interpretation reflects Jacopetti's jabs at modernity. His miscellany of degraded images and savage/civilized juxtapositions indict comfortable notions of social progress. Similar attacks on modernity and on the ideology of progress, of course, were to become increasingly common throughout the 1960s. The *New York Times,* however, continued to read cargo cult in evolutionary terms, only suggesting that we all could someday regress back to a benighted and dark cargo worship on some lonely, homemade airstrip.

Other reviewers of the film, however, highlighted Jacopetti's civilized-is-savage but savage-is-civilized juxtapositions without his evolutionary overlay. Parallels between the final cargo-cult sequence

Cargo planes and tragic love: Islanders wait forlornly. (Courtesy of Vidcrest)

and an introductory scene of young Italians from Rudolf Valentino's hometown who wait to be discovered by Hollywood help cue this reading: "as the camera moves through the [Italian] crowd it picks up, one after another, loutish young faces. . . . Their future lies in lounging about in ignorant squalor, waiting to be discovered by a Hollywood which itself has long been dead" (Hatch 1963, 334). Jacopetti's Italian louts and Papua New Guinea cargo cultists alike are both tragic waiters, full of unrequited desire. The film ends with a surge of celestial music and the lines: "They wait motionless. Searching the sky. . . . And here they are, waiting faithfully, at the doorway to the sky." Hatch, reviewing for the *Nation*, picked up this universalized motif—of waiting natives and waiting Europeans—but faulted Jacopetti for not developing it as he might have: "The pain and ugliness that result from an apparently universal human search for a short-cut to bliss could have made a subject" (Hatch 1963, 335).

Although the film's equation is one between New Guinea cargo cultists and young Italian "louts" (and is thus still at one remove from readers of the urbane *Nation*), the "apparently universal human search for a short-cut to bliss" must imply that we, too, can be cargo cultists. And not in the *New York Times*' devolved future either, but today. Whitemen, as playwright Lan's Pidgin English instructs, are *wetmen* "waitmen" too.

It is perhaps no accident that echoes of cargoism also haunt *Mondo Cane*'s popular theme song, "More," that weaves together the film's collage of scattered images. The song's themes of hyperdesire and prolonged, melancholy waiting flash us back to Jacopetti's New Guinea mountaintop airstrip where yearning, stubborn natives anticipate the opening of their "doorway to the sky":

> . . . More than the simple words I try to say
> I only live to love you more each day
> More than you'll ever know
> my arms long to hold you so
> . . . Longer than always is a long long time
> But far beyond forever you'll be mine . . .

Mondo Cane's juxtapositions climax with an equation of cargo and love. The maddened Melanesian cargo cult is nothing but a shadow of inflamed, crazy, unrequited love. The following chapter looks at how our incessant, seductive, and powerful ways of talking about and experiencing love have bled into stories of the cargo cult.

This blurring of cargoist identity and cargo/love already reaches deep into popular culture. An American rock band calling itself Cargo Cult issued an album in 1986 entitled *Strange Men Bearing Gifts* (see also Cora and Moss 1983). An eponymous song surveys the cargo archive to find in there the American Dream:

> I kneel on the ground
> I pray to the sky
> The Lords have frowned
> I don't know why

Strange Men Bearing Gifts. (Courtesy of Cargo Cult and Touch and Go Records)

Yankee go home
Yankee come back
Yankee go home
Yankee come back
Come back

They gave us guns
And bibles too
But now they're gone
What do we do? . . .

I love you America
My beautiful America
You came to me from a big silver bird in the sky
And I?
A lonely native here in the jungle
Who had never had the miracle
of Tictacs, linoleum, cottage cheese
Oh America
I love you
I love you
I love you

The equation of the desirous self with cargoist native, drawn
with right-handed ridicule or left-handed irony, is increasingly common in Western popular discourse. It is critically important to
understand how cargo cult continues to inflect our vision of
Melanesians and of Melanesian aspiration and organized protest,
such as the Bougainville Republican Army. But, equally important,
we must acknowledge how cargo cult also has come to inflect our
understanding of ourselves. This is the real homecoming of cargo
cult: the term's return not to Melanesia, but to ourselves, its crea-
tors. Western colonialists and anthropologists invented cargo cult
in 1945 to describe the Melanesian other. The term now has
boomeranged back into the hand that once pitched it. We are the
cargo cultists. And we? We are the lonely natives here in the jungle
who have never had the miracle.

6 CARGO CULTS EVERYWHERE

Outbreaks of the cargo cult continue, although strangely not so much anymore in Melanesia. Cargoism has percolated out of these islands into the wider world. Nowadays, almost anyone anywhere might be a cargo cultist. This is not much of a puzzle, of course. Cargo cult, as a term, has proved both useful and provocative. Anthropologists along with other observers of human hope and folly find a language of cargo cult productive. They extend the term to describe cultlike ritual and cargolike belief worldwide. In these descriptive extensions, Melanesia unwittingly donates its cargo cult to us all.

In this final chapter, I read through uses of the term to describe events outside the region, seeking the logic of such extension. What is it about certain events, and what is it about cargo cult, that permit such extension? The hodgepodge of cargo extensions here and there around the world strip down the term to its core essence. An eruption of distant cargo cults in Kansas, Moscow, Australia, and Japan must accent the term's lowest common denominators that each so-described cult possesses.

Beyond the basic meanings of cargo cult that permit its employment outside Melanesia, certain interests must motivate that usage. I return, here, to the question of cargo cult's allure. Why is cargo cult so captivating? Why are we seduced to use the term beyond Melanesia? We do not have to brand, for example, wayward small town Arizonans as "cargo cultists." We could instead pull a hundred other descriptive labels from the stock of existing social science jargon, or we could invent new terminology.

There is something about cargo cult, though. It evokes an emotional frisson, a faint thrill, an uneasy glee. Cargo cult keeps returning. I conclude by suggesting that we are motivated to use the term, and use it widely, because it palpates and animates our own diffuse but powerful discourses of desire and of love, particularly the melancholy of unrequited love. The cargo cult is an allegory of desire. And desire itself, as an emotion, an interest, a future, another self, an unending problem, is desirable. Stories of desire have emotional and intellectual currency, and cargo cult pays with interest.

This is, of course, not an uncommon charge in recent, postmodern deconstructions of anthropological theory and language. We think we are staring deep into the dark eyes of the native but, in fact, we see reflected in those eyes mostly an image of our cargo-cultic self.

Creeping Cargoism

Cargo cult popped up outside Melanesia even before Worsley, Burridge, and Lawrence popularized the term within anthropological circles of the late 1950s and early 1960s. In 1953, just eight years after Mr Bird's felicitous commentary in *Pacific Islands Monthly,* Annette Rosenstiel had already located cargo cult in Kenya. Rosenstiel first discovered cargo cult when writing her Columbia University PhD dissertation, "The Motu of Papua-New Guinea: A Study of Successful Acculturation." (The acculturated success of the Motu, a periurban community of fishermen and traders living near Port Moresby, was certified by their lack of interest in cargo cult.)

Her horizons broadening, Rosenstiel carried the term with her to Africa. She discovered there too cargoist affinities in Kenya's postwar Mau Mau "problem," including "native dissatisfaction with things as they are, a feeling of inferiority, of having had withheld from them the things which they believe are rightly theirs" (1953, 427). Rosenstiel recommended to harassed Kenyan colonials New Guinean administrative policy and experience in combating cults. Citing F. E. Williams and the foiled Vailala Madness in particular, she suggested that incipient signs of Mau Mau would have been better handled by a colonial government that "from the outset operated under a long-range, scientific policy, and has based its actions and regulations on the reports and suggestions of trained anthropologists in its employ" (1953, 429). One certainly might be suspicious, here, of anthropological opportunism. The more cargo cults located, the more needful an employment of anthropologists to combat such cults. Happy the anthropologist were he or she in the medical doctor's position of both diagnosing and curing disease!

Worthier motivations, though, both of theory and of fashion prompted anthropology's discovery of cargoism worldwide. For one, cargo cult, a catchier term, sometimes substituted generically for the "nativistic," "millenarian," or "revitalization" movement —particularly when people were beseeching ancestral or otherwise supernatural redress of economic deprivation. Lowell Holmes, for example, proclaimed that the Siovili movement of 1830s Samoa was "Oceania's first true cargo cult" (1980, 478) although Jehovah, not Samoan ancestors, was to ship the goods. This historical relocation of cargo cult is hyperbolic, as we have noted, given that cargo cult did not exist until 1945. Others have found cargo cults among peoples as diverse as twentieth century Australian Aborigines (Glowczewski 1983) and seventh century Japanese (Ellwood 1984).

The extension of the term outside Melanesia demands its simplification. A small set of distinctive core features remains to define cargo cult. An anthropological discovery of some or all of these features can key the exercise of the term to describe cultic events in various societies worldwide.

Cargo cults, first, comprise the desire for wealth of some sort. The Mau Mau sense "withheld from them the things which they believe are rightly theirs" (Rosenstiel 1953, 427). The Samoans experience a "great desire to acquire the material wealth apparently associated with the god Jehovah" (Holmes 1980, 478). Ancient Japanese shout "The new riches are coming!" (Ellwood 1984, 222).

Second, cargo cults entail some sort of collective behavior. Cultists need not be formally organized into an obvious group, but application of the term at least implies widespread, public involvement in irregular ritual and belief. There must be some notable, popular manifestation for an observer to deploy the label "cult."

Third, cultic behavior and belief invoke supernatural means to achieve collective ends. This is the foremost defining feature of cargo cult, underwriting its extension beyond Melanesia and its infiltration into the West. Cargoist discourse very easily paraphrases "supernatural" as irrational at the same time as it reads desire for increased wealth, moral betterment, or political sovereignty as "rational." The distilled essence of cargo cult, in this most simplified delineation of the term, is a tragic relationship between rational ends and irrational means—between genuine desire and ineffective practice.

The Mau Mau, for example, seeking to dislodge the British from Kenya, relied on traditional oath-taking to ensure the loyalty of movement supporters. The oath, Rosenstiel stated, "became a tool of black magic [ie, irrational] instead of an aid to the administration of justice [ie, rational], as it had been in traditional times" (1953, 428). The Samoan Siovili movement "stressed spirit possession, adventism and a return to customs which newly arrived London missionary teachers had outlawed" (Holmes 1980, 479). The Ancient Japanese, experiencing "a mood of rising expectation combined with hopelessness" supposed that "the right sort of magic could as suddenly and unexpectedly bring the new riches in their own direction" (Ellwood 1984, 436).

This clash between rational goals and irrational means enacts a tragedy of unfulfilled desire. The object of cultic desire, whether this is money, industrially manufactured goods, or freedom from oppression, demands less explanation, for Westerners, than does the irrational, magical practice of its fulfillment: cargo, in the West, has long made better sense than cult. We can understand the desire, but we read the means as magical, mystical, and ultimately ineffectual in serving that desire. We look at cargo cult and we forecast a bad end. Cults must end in tragedy. The cargo never comes. The future is melancholy. There is a familiar, underlying language, here—a language of an inflamed love that must remain unrequited.

An actual location of working cargo cults outside Melanesia is less common than the metaphoric usage of the term. Cargo cult is extended to label a variety of public desires and schemes for material betterment insofar as these plans are impotent and irrational. One very common extension of the term targets misguided and abortive attempts to develop Third World economies. Postwar faith in modernization and international development has failed, and what once looked like clever global economic strategy now stinks of cargo cult. Dreams of Third World economic development are as substantial as the arrival of ghostly white cargo ships.

In Africa, in Cameroon, for example, an international development expert worries "without going so far as to consider development as a cargo cult could it be that the underlying mechanisms of the latter are also to be found in development processes?" (Langley 1986, 31). Langley, *pace* himself, did go so far: "The picture which emerges from the discourse of [Cameroon] institutional representatives in this study is closely akin to the prayers made in the cargo-cult, going so far in one case to inform European donors of their 'prayful interest for greater things to come' " (1986, 30). Langley also evoked cargo cult, and *Mondo Cane,* with the cover photograph on his ENDA Third World Report: "scale model of a Concorde airplane made by children out of wire" (1986, 2). The cargoist conjunction of motifs of airplane and of simple wire and children is conspicuous.

Similarly, a lead piece in *Anthropology Today* laments that "many development projects have lapsed into cargo cults" (Thornton 1991, 2). Micronesia is a case in point. American attempts to develop these islands economically have climaxed in a cargoist tragedy: "They came for good, all right, and in their desire to make things better . . . they turned 'a fish-and-taro subsistence economy into a Spam-and-cheese cargo cult' " (Kluge 1991, dust jacket).

The *Economist,* honoring cargo-cult "pioneers," even brings back our friend John Frum to satirize international disaster and development aid efforts.

Anyone reluctant to open his purse endures guilt feelings promoted by the ever-expanding industry of cargo-cultism, with its easy access to newspapers and television. . . . The islanders of Tana deserve some practical advice. Their basic thinking is correct. If handouts have arrived out of the blue in the past, it is reasonable to expect that they will arrive again. But dancing under a tropical moon, however charming, is not going to deliver the goods. The gods the islanders seek to please want reports, statistics and programmes of action—preferably sent by fax. For a start, the islanders should con-

Saki, cargo pioneer, waits by the sea at Sulphur Bay. (Lindstrom)

sider employing a public-relations expert. It would be a shame if, like so many pioneers of a new trend, the people of Tana were deprived of its benefits. (1991, 20)

Such metaphoric extension of cargo cult to international development schemes rhetorically mourns the tragedy of their failures, but can also ridicule the comedy of their ineptitude.

Nativizing Ourselves

It is one thing to discover actual or metaphoric cargo cults among sundry Third Worlders here and there beyond Melanesia. It is something else to discover cargoism here at home. When the term pivots about and attaches to oneself, to Western practices and beliefs, its edge and political consequence sharpen.

A variety of desires for collective benefit coupled with apparently irrational strategies to attain those desires have attracted the label cargo cult. Such labeling occasionally evokes tragedy, playing upon the melancholy future of unfulfilled desire. But most often, cargo-cult labeling highlights an irrationality of practice rather than sorry futures. The cargoistic Tannese, advises the *Economist,* should "first master the fax" (1991, 20). Tragedy, here, transforms into comedy, sometimes even mean irony. The closer cargo cult comes to the self, the more the tone of such extended usage slides from melancholy to mockery. Comic book cargoism returns. A cargo-cult label is frequently a grenade thrown to protect the dominant, the normal, and the genteel.

Employments of cargo cult to label one's own poor can still suggest tragedy. This is the local version of Third World development schemes as cargo cult. The poor, as internal natives, are yet distant enough that the combination of noble economic goals with unwise and ineffective means can evoke a discursive melancholy rather than derision. Newspaper columnist William Raspberry, for example, criticized American social welfare policy that teaches the poor, "like New Guinea's 'cargo cultists', to become mere clients" (1986, A9). Raspberry cited John McKnight, a Northwestern University professor who had located cargo cults erupting in the neighborhoods of Chicago.

> There are many people in Chicago today who are *waiting* for a Saturn [automobile] plant to drop down. They are waiting for a parachute load of transistors to come and save us. It's a *tragic* mistake. We need a harsh, clear look at who we are, what we have, and what we can make that we and others need, a kind of understanding about a renaissance in our own productivity that will depend very little upon help from the Federal Government and the major corporations. I don't think they are going to drop plants down from the sky. (Quoted in Chandler 1985, 203, my emphasis)

Cargo cult is tragic because it is a falsely expective, facile, confused understanding of self and of economic reality. Ultimately, it leads to a bad end.

Whereas McKnight's Chicago cargo cultists merely wait tragically, searching the economic skies, Douglas Dean (1970) located a more dangerous mob in Kansas City. Here, he suggested, "a large 'cargo cult' exists within the minority black culture" (1970, 156). This Kansas City extension harks back to Mr Bird, drawing trickily upon the more sinister, jungle drum themes of cargoist stories. Dean fretted that "if the system becomes more rigid as a response to industrialization and 'Cargo Cult' energy, the reaction and therefore new stimulus of the next evolving stage may be a cry for revolution" (1970, 165).

This is cargo-cult tragedy with an apocalyptic edge to it. African Americans are cargo cultists insofar as they demand "their share of the technological innovations flaunted before their eyes of [*sic*] a WASP-dominated mass communications system" (1970, 157). A variety of strategies taken by the black community to achieve economic parity are all cultic: " 'Cargo Cultism' is currently taking other forms," including economic boycotts, bank loans to black entrepreneurs, and even shoplifting. Finding other channels closed, many blacks condone stealing: "This may be interpreted as the 'Court of Last Resort' for blacks instilled with 'Cargo Cult' energy that must be released" (159). Blacks who reject dominant

WASP culture, "preferring not to assimilate and consequently lose identity are forming a 'Cargo Cult' of their own, demanding economic equality and cultural separatism" (163). The 1960s Black Power cry itself is a "unifying manifestation of 'Cargo Cultism' " (159; see also Merton 1979, 88–89).

A cargoist prognosis of systemic collapse is a different sort of tragedy than the melancholy of unfulfilled, honest desire. Clearly, although Dean no doubt intended his use of cargo cult to be read as the neutral language of social scientific analysis, his extension of the term to label economic boycotts, black capitalism, shoplifting, and the Black Power movement at large not only highlights the comic irrationality of such strategies but deprecates them as well. If irrational means evoke the workings of cargo cult, a cargo-cult labeling in turn can impugn madness.

Cargo cults continue to erupt in more places than just Chicago and Kansas City. The collapse of communist governments in the former Soviet Union and Eastern Europe, and associated attempts to cultivate a capitalist economy, have precipitated cargo cults all over Europe. Actually, European cargo mentality begins with the devastations of World War II: "Americans were looked at as if they were men from Mars, and their belongings were treated with a reverence reminiscent of the cargo cults of Polynesia [sic]. Europeans displayed attitudes like those found in the Third World" (Enzensberger 1990, 119). Now it is happening all over again. The East fervidly waits, in ultimate tragedy of course, upon the cargo of the West. The *Manchester Guardian Weekly* reported that

> the new Soviet religion is the cargo cult. . . . On the ground floor of the Hotel Pekin there is a credit-card-only Spar supermarket with all its prices in Deutschmarks, a cargo cult temple on Mayakovsky Square. . . . I felt affronted by these places, and it is easy to see them provoking riots one day soon by frustrated and hungry people. That is one of the popular scenarios for the coming crisis, when the troops disobey their orders, the Politburo flees the Kremlin, and the mob storms the Oktyabraskaya Hotel to seize the free toothpaste. (Walker 1989, 21)

The *Spectator* headlined Poland's "Cargo Cult Candidate," Stanislaw Tyminski, who promised "wealth, high salaries, and instant happiness. The audience cheers" (Applebaum 1990, 12). Like Pacific Island natives who ritually worship "whatever flotsam and jetsam that the modern world may happen to cast upon their shores" (including, Applebaum notes, old refrigerators), today's Poles are maddened by desire for cargo (1990, 12).

The Western Europeans, too, are going cargoistic as fast as their Eastern cousins. A gross cargo shrine has newly risen from the plains of central France: "Euro Disney is a multi-layered, £2.2 billion cargo cult where nostalgia for the cinematic America that never was joins hands with consumer fanaticism. Disney priests know every prayer in this fascinating religion, where dad could end up with a cowboy hat worth £100 while disputing juvenile extravagances like a pair of cardboard Mickey Mouse ears" (Webster 1992, 7). In the city of Nîmes, mad and silly cargo-cultist city fathers are "pushing a seemingly rational idea to the point of utter irrationality" (Buchanan 1992, 4), having lost their grip on sensible city planning.

And the Japanese likewise, canny in business though they are, "have developed a cargo-cult mentality about Western pop culture" (McDonell 1991, 41). Sony and Matsushita corporations spent fanatically to acquire Hollywood movie studios that will never repay their investment. Modern Japanese pop culture cargoists are emulating their ancient, seventh century forefathers.

Like contentious Melanesian politicians, many Westerners have found *cargo cult* a useful term of abuse for excoriating rivals. This sort of political cargo story is deployed against claims that menace social order. The certain tragic future of desiring but misguided cultists is backgrounded. Rather, it is the future of existing systems, order, and ruling norms that worries those who discover cargo cults erupting all around them. As cargo cults close in upon us, they appear less and less tragic, and more and more crazy. Polish candidate Tyminski is a "genuine religious maniac" (Applebaum 1990, 12). Cargo cultists are foolish, irrational, and often mad.

Former Australian Prime Minister Bob Hawke, for example, introduced his plans for Australian higher education as "building a clever country." This was a most inauspicious alliteration in that it opened the door, eurhythmically, for charges of irrationality. His opponents hit back with "The Clever Country as a Cargo Cult": "[the plan's] arguments do not go beyond the first stage of simplistic assertion. There is no economics in it at all, despite its reliance upon economic language. Instead there is a crude cargo cult: train the population in technology and the pot of gold will follow. . . . It is a cargo cult because of the missing steps" (Quirk, Duncan, and De Lautour 1990, 49). Cargo subverts clever. Australian higher education is perverted with cargo thinking: Bob Hawke desires gold but his means are simplistic, crude, and missing steps. Australia—that outpost of the West which most closely neighbors Melanesia—has slipped away into cargo madness: "Our so-called 'revolution of rising expectations' was cargo cult writ larger and on a more gigantic scale of irrationality. . . . [W]ho ever paused to ask whether all this was either rational or affordable? Our national symbol of cargo cult is Canberra's repulsive and extravagant Parliament House. I saw its prototype in 1943, in an outbreak of cargo cult on the Rai Coast, not far from Madang" (Ryan 1992, 2). And the "cargo cult mentality which dominates Australian government and business thinking about the future" (Harwood 1991, 214) surfaces again in schemes to tap into Japanese capital and technology and build a "multifunctionpolis" in South Australia. Although billed as a "science city," this is really only a cargo bad dream—an "irrational megaproject," "high-tech fantasy," a "flight from reality" (Harwood 1991; see also Trompf 1990, 61–63).

Prime Minister Hawke's cargo mentality, sad to note, is all too common today—and not just among Australians either. Literature critics suffer from it. Critic Derek Wright, for example, blasted his fellow specialists who misread Ayi Armah's novel *Fragments:* "In their confusion of the material and the mythological, these critical misreadings . . . fall into the trap of the very cargoist thinking which is the novel's target" (1985, 57).

Demographers, too, are infected, although "the pursuit of demographic goals by 'cargo cult' methods in anthropology was short-lived" (Howell 1986, 224). Cargo cult bubbles over in Boston offices when white-collar workers encounter the magical computer:

"Boston Cargo Cult handles the contradiction of an office with precomputer human skills that has added computers" (Ballester 1982, 258). The president of California Institute of Technology takes pains to alert his school's graduates to the dangers of "cargo cult science" (Feynman 1974, 10). Such crazed science comprises "educational and psychological studies [that] . . . follow all the apparent precepts and forms of scientific investigation, but they're missing something essential, because the planes don't land" (1974, 11). American belief in the powers of subliminal persuasion, for example, is proof that our science has already decayed into cargo cult (Pratkanis 1992).

This abusive employment of cargo cult to denounce and disparage fools, and anyone else who misses something essential, already might be just whistling in the dark. Perhaps it is too late. Cargo cult, nowadays, is everywhere. In an address, again presented at the California Institute of Technology (it is agreeable to note that Caltech is so attentive to creeping cargoism), Ruben F. Mettler, a onetime chairman and chief executive officer of TRW Inc, decried "the cargo cult mentality in America": "Like South Pacific Islanders who thought that talking into little boxes made the planes come, the U.S. is responding to its problems with magic rituals instead of rational planning and hard work" (1980, 22). American cargo mentality consists of "a failure to perceive reality or an unwillingness to act upon it" (1980, 22). Chairman Mettler and other American businessmen are alarmed: "the problems that confront our country today are survival problems that will not yield to a cargo cult mentality. We urgently need to recognize and remove the unexamined assumptions and myths underlying so much of our contemporary thinking" (1980, 22). Cargo-cult mentality is unexamined political assumption and irrational economic myth that threaten our future. The planes don't land. But will the mere sting of cargo-cult labeling cure the raging national madness?

Cargo cults flare around the country. The Mormons, an American religious denomination, are essential cargo cultists (Bracht 1990). The Brotherhood of the Sun, a Californian sect, is likewise cargoist (Trompf 1990, 38). The entire state of New Mexico itself is a cargo cult, possessing "a version of 'Cargo Cult' dependency common to parts of the Third World, where the good things of life are expected to drop from the sky, as part of foreign aid, or in New Mexico's case large-scale federal defense projects" (Lupsha 1988, 82).

The citizens and boosters of the small town of Willcox, Arizona, too, are cargo cultists. Their feverish attempts to develop their community have brought about "Rex Allen Days"—a local festival celebrating a now deceased homeboy who made good as country-western singer and television spokesman for Purina Dog Chow: "The Rex Allen Days ceremony was based on the belief that Willcox could be socially and economically transformed if people acted like cowboys and cowgirls. The eventual emergence of this nativistic cargo cult closely followed the stage development of New Guinea cults" (Burns 1978, 172–173). Instead of ritual cargo runways, the citizens of Willcox built tourist rest stops along a nearby interstate highway. Instead of ancestral bones, cult sacra included Rex Allen's boots, shirt, saddle, and his trousers (1978, 173). Instead of a cargo of refrigerators, Willcox sought outside capital. But it is not just demented Willcox, AZ. "In what has allegedly become the most highly advanced society in the world technologically the coming of the Cargo has become a natural expectation" (Trompf 1990, 60). We Americans *all* are covert cargo cultists: "In the United States, an ethic of a 'better tomorrow' and a world view that emphasized the richness and never-ending supply of resources were fertile grounds for the growth of rural cargo cults" (Burns 1978, 177).

America, the land of the cargo cult, here usurps the claims of Tanna and Papua New Guinea. Melanesia's cargo-cult culture moves halfway around the globe to transform into America's cargo-cult culture—or was it the other way around? Conforti (1989) discovered, in American schools, that our native cargo-cult ideology has now beaten down an enfeebled Protestant ethic. We really believe, nowadays, that fortune depends on episodic luck, animated by ritualistic strategy, rather than in the old truths of steady, progressive effort and hard work.

We nurture both our cargo desires and our faith in magical practice, kneeling daily at the altar of television (see Merton 1979, 92). Children's cartoons and adventure series "continually reinforce the idea that things come into existence fully formed; there is little or no process depicted, no growth, no development, no accumulation; there is also neither ambivalence nor compromise, something either is or it is not, one does something or one does not" (Conforti 1989, 6). Advertisements, similarly, "most clearly reflect a cargo cult orientation, in that the advertised product is presented as representing the simple catalyst that would bring about the desired state of affairs. At some point the lines between traditional reality and fantasy seem to fade into an emergent amalgam, a new reality. If this new reality is not yet a fully formed cargo cult, it may at least be understood as constituting a cargo cult orientation" (1989, 5).

Thomas Merton, too, had earlier already sniffed out our essential cargo-cult mentality: "Man wants to go through the Cargo Cult experience and does so repeatedly. Not only the natives of New Guinea, the Solomon Islands, the New Hebrides, and South Africa, but the blacks, the young Chinese, the white Westerners—everyone—all of us find the Cargo experience, in whatever form, vitally important" (1979, 86). We all are engulfed in a "tidal wave of Cargo mentality, whether primitive or highly sophisticated, that is sweeping the world in all directions" (1979, 86). The stigmata of our cargo cult mentality include fabulous consumer advertising, ritualistic buying and consuming, the adoration of the new, and repudiation of the old (83–84).

We have become, in fact, the natives: "a true understanding of the Cargo mentality can tell us much about ourselves" (Merton 1979, 83). We are, at last, ourselves nativized by the erosive forces of modernity: "We may in fact be experiencing the impact of the accretions of the West upon the West, the impact of America on Americans, and this experience defines a situation of alienation! It is an alienation of Westerners from the West and of Americans from America . . . we are experiencing the descent of America into the reality of the myth" (Long 1974, 413). In fact, readers may be encouraged to know, "there are similarities between the behaviors of the natives of the island societies and the professors of universities. . . . Professors are painfully unaware of the means through which their universities obtain their operating budgets. . . . They seem to prefer a belief in the 'goods' somehow obtained magically" (Ramsey and Lutz 1975, 30–31). I myself, a professor of a university, must be roused to write this story of the cargo cult because I am a cargo cultist. And we professors are particularly obstinate in our madness: "It is only slightly more likely that this portrait of the cargo culting of professors will divert them from the predicted fate of all Cargo Cults. They will continue to believe, however" (1975, 33). Charles Long, along these lines, advised his fellow religious experts that their academic association, the American Academy of Religion, itself is per se perhaps not a cargo cult, "but there is in fact something to be learned about ourselves from this kind of religious experience and expression" (Long 1974, 413).

As native, if naive, cargo cultists, it profits us to contemplate the experiences of those of the chosen, like Tanna's John Frum "pioneers," who have gone before: "The cargo cultist in his strange and bizarre behaviour, his Vailala madness, in his myth-dream had probably outlined a modality of modernity, a modern world where the fragility of a new human dimension was making its first gentle gesture" (Long 1974, 414). Vailala Madness is our postmodern future. Shopping malls, television, Hollywood, and Walt Disney have made natives, and cargo cultists, of us all. The Tannese are indeed religious pioneers. But, nowadays, *both* Melanesia and America are the lands of the cargo cult. In Westernizing the native we have nativized ourselves.

But enough is enough. Let's face it. It is almost as silly to find cargo cults in America, Japan, Australia, and Europe as it is in present-day Melanesia. Why, though, is cargo cult so appealing that we are anxious to employ the term lavishly not only upon Pacific Islanders, but upon ourselves as well? Why can't we help ourselves? Why is cargo cult so intellectually and emotionally seductive? Why is it everywhere?

Crazy Love

> Men and women today can look to nothing but the everlasting return of an ardour constantly being thwarted.
>
> (de Rougemont 1956, 285)

Western discourses of love are also stories of aching melancholy. Here we have a much more familiar language of tragic waiting:

Sweethearts anticipate forlornly the arrival or the return of love. They, in popular romantic verse, wait so patiently for the postman to look and see if there is—at last—a letter in his bag. Perhaps cargo cultists are just unrequited lovers, and the cargo story is an allegory of love gone wrong. As a native cargo cultist myself, I believe I now can permit myself to reveal cargo's true secret. There is a metadiscourse of desire itself within Western culture that powerfully informs how we think and feel about our yearnings. This script, or master trope, structures both love stories and cargo stories so that each may be read in terms of the other. The story of the cargo cult is just another avatar of the prosaic Western romance. Cargo cult is thus an old friend. We already know the tricks and thrills of this genre; we already know the denouement. Isolde was Tristan's cargo (de Rougemont 1956). We know cargo, and are cargo cultists ourselves, just as we know love, and are lovers ourselves.

In this metadiscourse of desire, cargo equates not with ordinary, "real" or "true" love but with desire that is in some fashion untoward, unsuccessful, irrational, or unending. Ordinary, "real" love is boring. We know it never lasts. Instead, the most interesting, most captivating love is a love that is ultimately unrequited or futile. The desire that we desire most never gets fulfilled.

A poem published in the Papua New Guinea literary magazine *Kovave* links the two terms to assert that cargo does not buy real love.

> What is it you want
> my black brother
> property, cargo, a slave
> or the love of a woman? . . .
> Love is free
> freely given and freely received.
> Does freedom frighten you
> my black brother?
> White man's cargo is black man's brideprice
> neither guarantees love. (Power 1972, 8–9)

This is generic cargoism. Although the poem idealizes "true" love freely given, its animating, seductive tension is really about the ultimate failure of cargo/love: "property, cargo, a slave." The rational ends—love, cargo—pose for us no problem. Instead, the irrational means and the ultimate failure of desire are the real story. Cargo, like Melanesian marital brideprice customs, seems as if it promises love, but this is only an illusion. Cargo/love is a tragic or an evil dream. Cargo/love is love gone bad. It is unrequited and leads to bad ends. It causes pain. Desperate cargo/lovers (forlorn boyfriends, girlfriends, the Tannese) lose hold of their traditional identities, and become alien to themselves.

Paul Willis quoted two British teenaged girls on unrequited desire:

> RACHEL: Have you ever really fancied somebody and know that they wouldn't go out with you? . . .
> KATY: It makes you feel ugly, doesn't it? . . .
> RACHEL: It makes you feel bad on the inside.
> KATY: It makes you feel like you're an alien. (1990, 117)

This is an obsessive, misplaced love that brings tragedy, alienation, and madness. Cargo cultists, like women who love too much, are in trouble. Testimonies of cargo/love proliferate in popular magazines: "I wanted David so badly, I thought I was going to lose my mind." Alison is fascinated by David: "In fact, she thought about him so much that she became obsessed. All of us have shared, to some degree, Alison's experience. You meet a man and . . . if he doesn't reciprocate your yearning, you'll go mad" (Levine 1989, 68–69).

This cargo/love is familiar; it is an old story. "All of us have shared" the experience. But *Cosmopolitan* warns, "Such an all consuming amour can be *destructive*, so go get unfixated—now!" "Your love is becoming obsessive. You feel an odd pressing sensation in your chest, followed by an intense longing that convincingly imitates suffocation. You will die" (Meade 1988, 171). Or rather, you will go mad: " 'It isn't your heart that breaks,' Carla says now. 'It's your mind. I think I was crazy for six months after we broke up. I slept in his pajamas. I made love to his photograph. I called his answering machine to hear his voice and recorded it on my tape recorder. I would play it over and over' " (1988, 172).

We are not surprised that Carla, just as if she were from Tanna, turns to irrational, repetitious, ritual practices to regain lost love. The Tannese clear airfields more than once for the return of American wartime cargo; Carla makes love to photographs. But such mimicry and ritual facsimile are a form of madness—"pathomimetic behavior," as Schwartz (1976) called this among Melanesians. "When the desire to love and the need to be loved coexist with the terror of abandonment, you are in one of the dangerous, dark places of life . . . there is no happy ending. What you are experiencing as passion may look to your friends very much like lunacy" (Meade 1988, 172).

Psychologists also tell the cargo/love story—a story with no happy endings. Jessica Benjamin, for example, to explain women's complicity within "bonds of love"—within relations of sexual domination—suggests that women, tragically, are drawn into such relations as substitutes for an ideal love they never experienced with the father: "a father-daughter identification in which their own desire and subjectivity can finally be recognized and realized" (1988, 116). A woman, thus, "loses herself in the identification with the powerful other who embodies the missing desire and agency" (116).

Here, again, the love-gone-bad script comes back around to cargo cult. Compare a typical anthropological accounting of similar tragic identification and self-alienation in Melanesia.

> Though often ordered in indigenous patterns, the ritual practice of cargo cults was in many cases no less than a massive effort to mime those European social forms that seemed most conducive to the production of European goods. In a kind of reverse fetishism, what was replicated was what was seen as the most potent of European social and linguistic forms in an effort to increase the likelihood of the arrival of European commodities. (Appadurai 1986, 52)

A weak self/female/native seeking desire/agency/cargo identifies (through sex or mimicry) with a powerful other/male/European and comes to a bad end, dominated by that other within a wretched, fetishistic relationship. Benjamin's bonds of love are Appadurai's bonds of the world capitalist system.

Let's go back to Tanna for two final John Frum texts of cargo/ love. The first is Maurice Guy's novel, *Le Souffle de l'Alizé,* published in English translation in 1959 as *So Wild the Wind.* Robert de Guenchy, the product of his mother's love affair with a Presbyterian missionary, returns to Tanna after her death to inherit her coconut plantation. He returns, too, seeking to revenge himself on his half-brother Henri who, with his father, had made his life miserable for being a love-child. Henri has his own plantation on Tanna, and has married Muriel, the half-brothers' childhood friend.

Guy saw the future, and his book evokes the gloom and unease of the approaching final days of colonialism. He wrote as Algeria and Vietnam were in revolt. The French civilizing mission had petered out. The white man was no longer master of the world, but was now blown about by the wind, *l'alizé:* "a dead leaf in the grip of slow, indomitable currents" (1959, 134). The book climaxes in a fatal hurricane. John Frum and Tanna's mysterious, unknowable natives are part of this deadly, gusty Third World chaos. John Frum is also the savage mirror of Robert's ambitions. Robert's desires both to redeem and to revenge himself with his half-brother and the French *colon* community are ultimately as unsatisfying and illusory as John Frum longings for cargo, refrigerators (1959, 177), and freedom—for the "great white ship" (33). In a preface, Guy described this correspondence of Tannese native and European self: the New Hebrides, "a lost archipelago in the Antipodes. Lost, one says. . . . Yet in the long run, even out there, what we of the West find will be ourselves, true enough; but selves still hindered by the shirt of Nessus which we are as far as ever from shaking off" (1959, 8).

Against all local expectation, Robert succeeds in putting his plantation to rights, and he also seduces Muriel. At first, like the Tannese, he is obsessed with desire: "But now all he could think of was her unclad body. And if he was stung by anything, it was simply by the hold it had on him. He would have liked to dispel the image, to ignore it. To dominate that too. Yet it was he who felt dominated. Not by Muriel herself but by this need which she had aroused, by this desire which dried up his throat and impregnated his being" (1959, 271). Muriel at last, a great white ship, does come ashore. The two make love hungrily, and madly, on the beaches of

"Shark's Bay." "What they sought in each other, more than anything else, was the appeasement of that shared hunger which, as it
seemed to them, they would never be able to satisfy. And in their
quest and exertions there was a methodical greed" (1959, 273).

But, in the end, our hunger cannot be satisfied. Cargo, when it
arrives, is never really what one wanted: "But if the end of the
chase brought them anything, then it was a feeling of weariness followed by the disillusioned discovery that, although they had conducted it jointly, their furious searching had not brought them
together in any true sense. The tide which had borne them up was
now receding, leaving them side by side but still alone, on a beach
as deserted as the real one which now stretched before them"
(1959, 279). Muriel and Robert, the French and the natives, the
Tannese and John Frum always remain alien to one another. They
fail continually to consummate and thereby extinguish their desires
for each other. Robert's cargo conquests evaporate: "His success,
his revenge, the taming of the plantation, the possession of Muriel
suddenly lost all point and meaning. These aims after which he had
striven month after month, these aims at long last achieved crum-
bled and fell away, disclosing a vacuum into which, feeling little but
a faint nausea, he was imperceptibly absorbed" (1959, 282–283).

The hurricane strikes. Philip Tenmu, a Tannese onetime Presbyterian teacher and Robert's plantation foreman, has a vision that he
is John Frum, and, in a mad trance, he kills Robert with a slash of
his bush knife. Henri dies, too, in a flooded stream. Madness or
death are the only effective answers for cargo yearning. Desire for
Muriel, for love, for legitimacy torments Robert. Desire for cargo
torments the Tannese. But these desires can never be quenched.
Even when the great white ship appears to arrive, this is only an
illusion because desire for cargo/love cannot end.

A second John Frum text of cargo/love is *La Mort sur un Volcan*
(*Death on a Volcano,* my translation), a *roman spécial-police* that Pierre
Nemours set on Tanna. Nemours' reading of the John Frum story
also illustrates how easily cargo narratives slide into love-gone-bad
stories. Alain Conan, the young hero, has been posted to Tanna to
assume temporarily the position of French *délégué* (district agent).
Like his real adventurer cargoist counterparts, he finds himself

Death and cargo/love on a volcano. (Courtesy of Editions Fleuve Noir)

drawn into the dark mysteries, the strange perfumes, and heady tropical aromas of the island (1974, 85)—and he is drawn into the standard cargo story, as well. (Nemours blurred the fiction/travelogue boundary with footnotes that certify the truth of his story; this also blurred the hero/author boundary.) Spooky John Frum, *des réfrigérateurs* (76), red crosses (84), Negro soldiers (77), nostalgia for America, everything—it is all there.

Conan has initial prickly encounters with the resident British colonial community, and then trouble begins. Rumors sweep the island that John Frum has returned. The dour, inflexible Presbyterian pastor Cooper is discovered dead in his Land Rover—squashed, it seems, by a flying lava bomb from Iasur volcano. But why has John Frum returned? Has he, and his volcano, killed Cooper in retaliation for mission-supported persecution of the cargo faithful (1974, 125)? Does this reflect a "xenophobic current" (78) on the part of the Tannese, bent on insurrection (the protonationalism motif)? If so, why attack the British instead of the French, in that it is the latter who are resisting island independence (104, 138)?

With commendable French logic, Conan solves the mystery. Luckily for the French colonials, it turns out that John Frum is a hoax. Hobson, a former British civil servant has returned secretly to Tanna and tricks the Islanders into believing he is John Frum—it is the dupe motif, not nationalism after all (Nemours 1974, 247). Some years before, Hobson had a love affair with lonesome Cynthia Cooper, the missionary's wife. The British district agent and Pastor Cooper covered up this stain upon British honor by falsely accusing Hobson of embezzlement, deporting and imprisoning him. Cynthia, out of cowardice, was unable to confess to her love and Hobson's honesty, and she remained behind on Tanna in cold comfort with her stern Presbyterian husband.

Now, Hobson has returned seeking revenge. It was he who killed Cooper, not John Frum, although in self-defense. He howls at Conan as the two scuffle atop Iasur volcano: " 'I have returned to revenge myself not only on Cooper, but on the cursed church that he represents, and on the evil administration that he serves, on this whole system that condemned me in the most sly and unjust fashion. When I finish, the natives will chase the last missionary and the last Englishman from Tanna. This is what I am going to do, Froggy, whatever you do, and you can't stop me because I am obliged to kill you' " (1974, 202). This John Frum, who only appears to be the prophet of cargo, is in reality the child of love-gone-bad. What looks like cargo is unrequited love, and this cargo/love, of course, leads to madness. Cynthia, cowering nearby in the volcanic fumes, has gone insane: "a woman with the empty look of madness, an absent smile, cradles in her arms an inanimate man like a small child and sings to him" (1974, 207).

Conan, shot but only wounded by Hobson, chases down the false John Frum in the far north of the island. But there he cuts a deal with Hobson. In return for Conan's help with escaping British justice, Hobson must kill John Frum and the cargo madness for good: "You will say goodbye to your devotees at Ipekel and will explain to them that it is necessary for them to earn the White [cargo] Ship through their work and their progress. The White Ship, in sum, is themselves" (1974, 249). Nemours attempted to resolve both crazy love and crazy cargo at once at the end of the novel. The male takes revenge on the female; John Frum kills John Frum with yet another hoax upon the benighted Tannese; and Westernized hard work and progress quiet mad yearnings for the White Cargo Ship.

Or will they? Nemours' narrative resolution can only be temporary. Is it possible for us to still our mad longings for crazy cargo/love? Hobson departs, but readers can expect for him a bad end beyond the narrative. More than this, though, the next time Nemours writes another *roman spécial-police,* crazy love must come back to carry that story as well. This is the manner we have, and enjoy, for talking about desire. Like John Frum, crazy love always returns.

If cargo cult is a poetics of desire, then I think we understand why cargo seems at once so strange, yet so familiar, so emblematic of the alien native, but also so characteristic of ourselves. Cargo stories are romances. Or rather, both cargo and love stories together are reflexes or versions of a powerful, underlying master discourse about desire. Cargo stories and crazy-love stories seduce and captivate us because they speak to us and remind us about the truth of desire.

But what is that truth? If we listen to cargo/love stories, we may be troubled by what they say. These are stories of unrequited love, of loving too much, of cargo that never arrives, of madness. We seem most attracted to stories of desire that is never fulfilled (Burke 1952, 274–275). The most interesting sort of desire is, in the end, tragic. "Happy love has no history" (de Rougemont 1956, 52). Sam Girgus (1990) quoted W. B. Yeats: "Does the imagination dwell the most upon a woman won or a woman lost?" He might have also quoted Little Richard: "We all long for love that cannot be, including aging rocker Little Richard, who told USA Today that he still pines for his ex. 'Ernestine was the sweetest person I ever met in my life,' he says. 'If I was going to marry again, I would marry Ernestine' " (*Honolulu Sunday Star-Bulletin and Advertiser*, 21 July 1991, A2). American television has figured this out. *TV Guide* asked "what are we to make of this peculiar pattern that love, true love, only exists on television in a state of frustration? . . . [F]rustrated love is dramatic; so is loss of love and falling in love, but the act of loving is not high drama" (Gaylin 1986, 7–8). Thus, "a sexual, romantic tension is created by creating couples who are never allowed to consummate their love. . . . We are now back in the frustrated world of 'no touch' " (1986, 6).

Gaylin suggested that "modern television has rediscovered the Middle Ages" with its contemporary stories of frustrated desire. And, sure enough, frustrated "lovers in the Middle Ages had a tendency to go mad" (Hood 1990, 20). But this discourse of desire always thwarted is modish, not antique. Television teaches us daily that "the search for romance is a never-ending process" (Toner 1988, 13). Contemporary artists say the same:

> The content and narrative of their work address the ideal of desire as a longing for the unattainable and also serve as a critique of the social, cultural, and political structures that stimulate or deny desire. For Phyllis Bramson, the location of desire is the pressure point between the pleasure of fulfillment and non-fulfillment. . . . Vera Klement's paintings speak of the universal desire for the unattainable and a longing for the lost. (Suhre 1990, 23–25)

What is this "pleasure of non-fulfillment?" Why is melancholy so sweet and "sensuous" (Suhre 1990, 24)? Why is the desire that we desire most always frustrated and therefore unending? If we could answer these questions, we would have arrived at last at the deepest secret of cargo—or at least the secret of why cargo-cult stories seduce us so.

Perhaps our psyche is just bent. We could listen to Freud. The processes of individuation demand the real or symbolic death of our parents. We are reflectively nostalgic of childhood, longing for the return of what never can return. With Freud, we could also take a hard look at Western cosmology. The Tannese themselves, as we have seen, in their teasing fashion have made the connection between John Frum and Jesus Christ. They may wait eternally for John Frum, but we wait too—equally forlornly—for the return of our own deities, among whom we should recently number space aliens, saucer pilots, and a miscellany of extraterrestrial Third Kind. There is cargo cult in the New Age (see Trompf 1990, 59). We also engage in hopeful waiting for a visitation that will consummate and quiet desire.

Or perhaps we await the advent of a perfect body with ritualized dieting. But that body never arrives. This form of cargo/love, too, can lead to madness—a frantic fear of ugliness that psychologists nowadays label "body dismorphic disorder."

We may say we seek finitude, real love, and the ultimate end of desire, but we dream and act oppositely. Television shows the desirous viewer that "the search for an all-encompassing love will never end" (Toner 1988, 12). But, as a consequence, "the viewer is forced to withdraw further into his individual (voyeuristic) fantasies to find the satisfaction that is apparently not available in the real world. [Fantasy] lovers are created to be subservient to the individual and provide an unending and unrealistic list of services. . . . As Freud put it, 'the pleasure-principle triumphs over the reality-principle' " (1988, 12). We keep on searching for love because even true love never satisfies desire (de Rougemont 1956).

Perpetually unrequited love, moreover, breeds "erotomaniacs" characterized by "intense yet tumultuous, attachment to their love objects" (Meloy 1989, 482). Western erotomaniacs shadow Melanesian automaniacs. Constant desire itself becomes desirable as a form of delicious punishment: "masochism is inherent in erotomania because of the pleasurable suffering of unrequited love. This pathological infatuation with an unattainable love object would be appropriate unconscious punishment for the hysterical character's devalued oedipal meanings of all sexual interest" (1989, 485). Meloy prescribed neuroleptic medications for symptomatic relief of erotomania (489). But are psychotherapeutics a cure for cargo/love? Can lithium carbonate kill John Frum?

We instead might follow Lacan who suggested that no cure is possible: "In the movement whereby the child in one form or another translates his need he alienates it in the signifier and betrays its primary truth. The real object of lack, of need and of the instinct is lost for ever, cast into the unconscious. . . . This is also the reason for man's radical inability to find anything to satisfy him" (Lemaire 1977, 163). The attempted relief and resulting transfiguration of our primal "lack" in symbolic language ensures that our desire remains always thwarted and unending. It keeps returning. "The conversion of such needs into a symbolic relationship constitutes an alienating process that promises some degree of continual unhappiness, incompletion and dissatisfaction" (Girgus 1990, 5; see Levinas 1979, 34; Žižek 1989, 173–175). It is impossible to remove the lack. We can only conceive and deal with desire symbolically, moving from love object to love object as each fails in turn. We keep trying, love after love, White Ship after White Ship. Cargo/love "is intransitive and eternal and is not concerned with any specific object in a stable manner, no object being capable of replacing the lost object" (Lemaire 1977, 169).

If so, we are cornered. The human condition itself fixates us necessarily upon constantly frustrated desire. If at some point we come to believe that we have at last found "true" love, a return to mother, the end of desire, or the arrival of the White Cargo Ships, we are, in fact, sicker than we think.

Or perhaps it is our economy that is bent. We might blame cargo/love on capitalism's demands for never-satisfied consumers.

Unrequited desire is usefully unending. Here, the metadiscourse of desire serves systemic economic needs rather than reflects internal psychic lacks and gaps. We can never get enough. Desire cannot be sated. Capitalism and commodity packaging make "the anticipation of use value into an aesthetic" (Willis 1991, 6). They make waiting itself enjoyable (see Modleski 1982, 88). Love of commodities must remain unrequited. If we could possess everything we desire, just as if we could find true love, the psychological economy would grind to a halt. No one would go shopping just as, on 11 May 1941, no Tannese went to church. Why go? Desire was soon to end; John Frum and the Americans were on their way.

These economic functions of unrequited love take us back to cargo conspiracy theory: European colonialists cook up the cargo cult to sustain their colonial and postcolonial empires. Mr Bird impugns the New Guinea militia with cargo cult. Only, now, we are the natives. We conjure up stories of cargo/love to sustain our own psychological economy that, if not always comfortable, is at least accustomed. We hoax ourselves. The madness motif—erotomania—and the dupe motif both come home.

These speculations into the origins and functions of unrequited cargo desire are no doubt too simple; or perhaps too complicated. Let me just argue that the ways we have of thinking desire, talking desire, and desiring desire animate both love stories and cargo stories so that each may be read as versions of the other. Yes, cargo cult is an efficacious term to blast our enemies, the foolish, the mad, and the dangerous, or to lament those who are misguided by their aspirations. But this abusive or pitying usage betrays our own melancholy. Melancholiacs and Melanesians: At a general, more diffuse level, we all are cargo cultists in that we wait eternally for an end to black desire that will not end.

The tragic truth of desire is that *none* of our means are rational in that the ultimate object (love, cargo) is impossible to obtain. Madness potentially awaits us all. There is no finitude to desire. We tell the same love story again and again; and we keep on discovering cargo cults. The story is the same. The cultic Tannese wait for John

Frum and the White Ship; the unrequited lover waits for the post-man and the letter. Both may be foolish, or mad, but both nonetheless cannot—and must not—stop waiting.

Our metadiscourse of desire makes cargo cult for us both believable and emotionally compelling. Whatever the ethnographic truths of Melanesian cultic practice may be, we look their way through a screen of cargo/love stories that we ourselves have written. We love to love. We once found the cargo cult only in the Pacific, splitting the discourse geographically: they seek cargo, we seek love. Now that the Pacific has changed politically, and Islanders today at once both reject and embrace the cargo cult, we are moved to extend the term globally. Cargo cult returns home to America—the true land of cargo—to rejoin with love. Cargo cult, like love, is everywhere. The unrequited desire of cargo/love is unending. We cannot divert ourselves from telling this story over and over again. Like crazy love, John Frum will always return. This particular tragedy is our own.

References

Aceves, Joseph B., and H. Gill King
   1978   *Cultural Anthropology.* Morristown, NJ: General Learning Press.

Allen, Bryant C.
   1976   Information Flow and Innovation. PhD dissertation. Dept of Anthropology, Research School of Pacific Studies, Australian National University, Canberra.

Andrew, Brother
   1984   A Psychiatrist Looks at Religious Movements. In *Religious Movements in Melanesia Today (3),* edited by Wendy Flannery, 80–91. Point Series no. 4. Goroka: The Melanesian Institute for Pastoral and Socio-Economic Service.

Appadurai, Arjun
   1986   Introduction: Commodities and the Politics of Value. In *The Social Life of Things: Commodities in Cultural Perspective,* edited by Arjun Appadurai, 3–63. Cambridge: Cambridge University Press.

Applebaum, Anne
   1990   The Cargo Cult Candidate. *The Spectator,* 8 December, 12.

Armah, Ayi Kwei
   1970   *Fragments.* Boston: Houghton Mifflin Company.

Armstrong, William
   1952   News from the Field, Lenakel, Tanna. *Quarterly Jottings from the New Hebrides* 233 (Jan): 8–10.

Ashbrook, Tom
   1986   Tanna Islanders Still Waiting for John Frum. *The Boston Globe,* 23 October, 2.

Attenborough, David
   1960   *People of Paradise.* New York: Harper & Bros.

Australian Presbyterian Board of Missions
   1964   "Jon Frum" Movement. *Encounter* (Mar): 26–27.

Ballester, George
1982   Magic for Think. *Datamation* 28 (3): 254–258.

Barrow, G. L.
1951   The Story of Jonfrum. *Corona* 3 (10): 379–382.

Bastin, Ronald
1980   Cash, Calico, and Christianity: Individual Strategies of Development on Tanna, New Hebrides. PhD dissertation, Department of Anthropology, University of Sussex.

Bates, Daniel G., and Fred Plog
1990   *Cultural Anthropology.* 3d ed. New York: McGraw-Hill.

Beckett, Jeremy
1989   *Conversations with Ian Hogbin.* Oceania Monograph no. 35. Sydney: University of Sydney Press.

Bell, H. M.
1941   From the Rev. H. M. Bell. *Quarterly Jottings from the New Hebrides* 194 (Oct): 8–11.

Belshaw, Cyril
1951a   The Cargo Cult. *South Pacific* 5 (8): 167.
1951b   Recent History of Mekeo Society. *Oceania* 22:1–23.

Benjamin, Jessica
1988   *The Bonds of Love: Psychoanalysis, Feminism, and the Problem of Domination.* New York: Pantheon Books.

Berndt, R. M.
1952/   A Cargo Movement in the East-Central Highlands of New
1953   Guinea. *Oceania* 23:40–65, 137–158, 202–234.
1954   Reaction to Contact in the Eastern Highlands of New Guinea. *Oceania* 24:190–228, 255–274.

Biersack, Aletta
1991   Prisoners of Time: Millenarian Praxis in a Melanesian Valley. In *Clio in Oceania: Toward a Historical Anthropology,* edited by A. Biersack, 231–295. Washington, DC: Smithsonian Institution Press.

Billig, Otto, and B. G. Burton-Bradley
1978   *The Painted Message.* New York: Schenkman.

Billings, Dorothy K.
1969   The Johnson Cult of New Hanover. *Oceania* 40:13–19.

Bird, N. M.
1945 Is There Danger of a Post-War Flare-Up Among New Guinea Natives? *Pacific Islands Monthly* 16(4, Nov): 69–70.
1946 The "Cargo-Cult." *Pacific Islands Monthly* 16(12, July): 45.
1947 How NGVR Hung On Near Muba, in 1942. *Pacific Islands Monthly* 18(1, Aug): 62–66, 71; 18(2, Sept): 38–40, 51–52.

Bitter, Maurice
1976 *Iles Merveilleuses du Pacific.* Aubina, France: Fernand Nathan.

Bohannan, Paul
1992 *We the Alien: An Introduction to Cultural Anthropology.* Prospect Heights, IL: Waveland Press.

Bonnemaison, Joël
1987 *Les Fondements d'une Identité, Territoire, Histoire et Société dans l'Archipel de Vanuatu (Mélanésie): Essai de géographie Culturelle (Livre 2), Tanna: Les Hommes Lieux.* Collection Travaux et Documents no. 201. Paris: Editions de l'ORSTOM.

Bracht, John
1990 The Americanization of Adam. In *Cargo Cults and Millenarian Movements: Transoceanic Comparisons of New Religious Movements,* edited by G. W. Trompf, 97–141. Berlin: Mouton de Gruyter.

Brecher, John, and Carl Robinson
1980 The Revolt of the Cargo Cultists. *Newsweek,* 23 June, 42.

Brunton, Ron
1981 The Origins of the John Frum Movement: A Sociological Explanation. In *Vanuatu: Politics, Economics, and Ritual in Island Melanesia,* edited by M. R. Allen, 357–377. Sydney: Academic Press.
1989 *The Abandoned Narcotic: Kava and Cultural Instability in Melanesia.* Cambridge: Cambridge University Press.

Buchanan, Peter
1992 Cargo-cult City Planning. *Architectural Review* 190 (1139): 4–8.

Buck, Pem Davidson
1989 Cargo-Cult Discourse: Myth and the Rationalization of Labor Relations in Papua New Guinea. *Dialectical Anthropology* 13:157–171.

Burchfield, R. W., ed
1972 *A Supplement to the Oxford English Dictionary.* Oxford: Clarendon.

Burke, Kenneth
1952 *A Rhetoric of Motives.* New York: Prentice-Hall.

Burns, Allan F.
1978 Cargo Cult in a Western Town: A Cultural Approach to Episodic Change. *Rural Sociology* 43:164–177.

Burridge, Kenelm
1960 *Mambu: A Study of Melanesian Cargo Movements and Their Social and Ideological Background.* London: Methuen.
1993 Melanesian Cargo Cults. In *Contemporary Pacific Societies: Studies in Development and Change,* edited by Victoria S. Lockwood, Thomas G. Harding, and Ben J. Wallace, 275–288. Englewood Cliffs, NJ: Prentice-Hall.

Burton-Bradley, B. G.
1970 The New Guinea Prophet: Is the Cultist Always Normal? *The Medical Journal of Australia* 1:124–129.
1972 Human Sacrifice for Cargo. *The Medical Journal of Australia* 2:668–670.
1973 The Psychiatry of Cargo Cult. *The Medical Journal of Australia* 2:388–392.
1974 Social Change and Psychosomatic Response in Papua New Guinea. *Psychotherapy and Psychosomatics* 23:229–238.
1976 Cannibalism for Cargo. *The Journal of Nervous and Mental Disease* 163:428–431.
1978 Kung Fu for Cargo. *The Journal of Nervous and Mental Disease* 166:885–889.
1986 Psychiatry, the Law and Acculturation. *American Journal of Forensic Psychiatry* 7:41–51.

Calvert, Ken
1978 Cargo Cult Mentality and Development in the New Hebrides Today. In *Paradise Postponed: Essays on Research and Development in the South Pacific,* edited by A. Mamak and G. McCall, 209–224. Sydney: Pergamon Press.

Cargo Cult
1986 *Strange Men Bearing Gifts.* Dearborn, MI: Touch and Go Records (audio recording).

Carson, Donald G., and Samuel M. Patten
1943 JonFrum Uprising on Tanna in October 1943. Unpublished report to Army Headquarters, III Island Command, APO 932

(Efate Island). US National Archives, Washington National Records Center, Suitland, MD. File 98-IC3-2.6.

Chandler, Christopher
1985   Chicago Interview: John McKnight. *Chicago* 34 (11): 202–207.

Christiansen, Palle
1969   *The Melanesian Cargo Cult: Millenarianism as a Factor in Cultural Change*. Copenhagen: Akademisk Forlag.

Clark, Jeffrey
1988   *Kaun* and *Kogono:* Cargo Cults and Development in Karavar and Pangia. *Oceania* 59:40–58.

Clifford, James
1983   On Ethnographic Authority. *Representations* 1:118–146.

Clifford, James, and George E. Marcus, eds
1986   *Writing Culture: The Poetics and Politics of Ethnography*. Berkeley: University of California Press.

Coates, Austin
1970   *Western Pacific Islands*. London: Her Majesty's Stationery Office

Cochrane, G.
1970   *Big Men and Cargo Cults*. Oxford: Clarendon Press.

Cockrem, Tom
n.d.   The Magic of Tanna. *Pacific Paradise* (Air Vanuatu), [no volume or issue number]: 17–21.

Conforti, Joseph M.
1989   The Cargo Cult and the Protestant Ethic as Conflicting Ideologies: Implications for Education. *The Urban Review* 21 (1): 1–14.

Connell, John
1990   Perspectives on a Crisis (4). In *Bougainville: Perspectives on a Crisis,* edited by P. Polomka, 28–34. Canberra Papers on Strategy and Defence no. 66. Canberra: Strategic and Defence Studies Centre, Research School of Pacific Studies, Australian National University.

Cooper, S. J.
1958   White Sands Tanna. *Quarterly Jottings from the New Hebrides* 258 (April): 8–9.

Cora, Tom, and David Moss
1983   *Cargo Cult Revival*. New York: Rift (audio recording).

Coral Tours Melanesie
1971?   *New Hebrides: Islands of Ashes and Coral.* Paris: Editions Delroisse.

Corris, Peter
1990   *The Cargo Club.* Ringwood, VIC: Penguin Books Australia.

Counts, David, and Dorothy Counts
1976   Apprehension in the Backwaters. *Oceania* 46:283–305.

Counts, Dorothy E.
1972   The Kaliai and the Story: Development and Frustration in New Britain. *Human Organization* 31:373–383.

Crouch, Lorna
1947   Cargo. *Pacific Islands Monthly* 18 (2, Sept): 48.

Crowther, Bosley
1963   Mondo Cane (film review). *New York Times,* 4 April, 58.

Davies, D.
1972   *A Dictionary of Anthropology.* New York: Crane, Russak.

de Rougemont, Denis
1956   *Love in the Western World,* revised and augmented edition. New York: Pantheon.

Dean, Douglas H.
1970   Economic Sources of Transcultural Conflict in Kansas City, Kansas. *Kansas Journal of Sociology* 6:156–168.

Discombe, Reece
1991   Vanuatu (New Hebrides) Member Tells Us About the "Cargo Cult", U.S.S. Tucker and Pentecost Jumpers. *Guadalcanal Echoes* (July): 32.

Dobson, Christopher
1980   Independence—and Paradise Lost? *Now!* 29 February, 67–69.

Dorney, Sean
1990   *Papua New Guinea: People, Politics, and History.* Sydney: Random House.

Douglas, Norman
1986   *Vanuatu—A Guide.* Sydney: Pacific Publications.

Drogin, Bob
1989   "Mine of Tears" Imperils a Nation. *Los Angeles Times,* 17 December, A12–A14.

Dyson, John
1982   *The South Seas Dream: An Adventure in Paradise.* Boston: Little, Brown.

Economist
1991   The New Cargo Cults: Don't Forget the Pioneers. 4 May, 20.

Eliade, Mircea
1965   *Mephistopheles and the Androgyne.* New York: Sheed & Ward.

Ellwood, Robert S.
1984   A Cargo Cult in Seventh-Century Japan. *History of Religion* 23:222–239.

Ember, Carol R., and Melvin Ember
1985   *Anthropology.* 4th ed. Englewood Cliffs, NJ: Prentice-Hall.

Enzensberger, Hans Magnus
1990   Europe in Ruins. *Granta* 33:113–139.

Errington, Frederick
1974   Indigenous Ideas of Order, Time, and Transition in a New Guinea Cargo Movement. *American Ethnologist* 1:255–267.

Evans, Julian
1992   *Transit of Venus: Travels in the Pacific.* New York: Pantheon Books.

Eveille, Nancy J.
1953   Lenakel. *Quarterly Jottings from the New Hebrides* 257 (Jan): 8–9.

Fabian, Johannes
1983   *Time and the Other: How Anthropology Makes Its Object.* New York: Columbia University Press.

Ferea, William B., ed
1984   Cargo Cults and Development in Melanesia. Unpublished ms, University of Papua New Guinea, Port Moresby.

Feynman, Richard P.
1974   Cargo Cult Science. *Engineering and Science* 37 (7): 10–13.

Fields, Jack, and Dorothy Fields
1972   *South Pacific.* Tokyo: Kodansha International.

Firth, Raymond
1951   *Elements of Social Organization.* London: Watts.
1953   Social Change in the Western Pacific. *Journal of the Royal Society of Arts* 101:804–819.

Flannery, Wendy
  1983　Bilip Grup. In *Religious Movements in Melanesia Today (2)*, edited by W. Flannery, 155–193. Point Series no. 3. Goroka: The Melanesian Institute for Pastoral and Socio-Economic Service.
  1984　Mediation of the Sacred. In *Religious Movements in Melanesia Today (3)*, edited by Wendy Flannery, 117–157. Point Series no. 4. Goroka: The Melanesian Institute for Pastoral and Socio-Economic Service.

Foucault, Michel
  1972　*The Archaeology of Knowledge and the Discourse on Language.* New York: Pantheon Books.
  1979　What Is an Author? In *Textual Strategies: Perspectives in Post-Structuralist Criticism*, edited by Josué V. Harari, 141–160. Ithaca: Cornell University Press.

Frater, Alexander
  1980　Pandemonium Beneath the Palms in the Isles of Bali Ha'i. *London Observer Magazine* (June): 38–59.

Gaylin, Willard
  1986　A Psychiatrist Wonders What's Happening to Romantic Love. *TV Guide*, 4 October, 5–8.

Geertz, Clifford
  1988　*Works and Lives: The Anthropologist as Author.* Stanford: Stanford University Press.

Gesch, Patrick
  1990　The Cultivation of Surprise and Excess: The Encounter of Cultures in the Sepik of Papua New Guinea. In *Cargo Cults and Millenarian Movements: Transoceanic Comparisons of New Religious Movements*, edited by G. W. Trompf, 213–238. Berlin: Mouton de Gruyter.

Gill, S. R. M.
  1946　Effect of War Upon Papuan Natives. *Pacific Islands Monthly* 16 (Jan): 52.

Girgus, Sam B.
  1990　*Desire and the Political Unconscious in American Literature: Eros and Ideology.* New York: St. Martin's Press.

Glines, C. V.
  1991　The Cargo Cults. *Air Force Magazine* 74 (1): 84–87.

Glowczewski, Barbara
1983 Manifestations Symboliques d'une Transition Économique: Le "Juluru", Culte Intertribal du "Cargo" (Australie Occidentale et Centrale). *L'Homme* 23 (2): 7–35.

Gourguechon, Charlene
1977 *Journey to the End of the World: A Three Year Adventure in the New Hebrides.* New York: Charles Scribner's Sons.

Griffin, James, Hank Nelson, and Stewart Firth
1979 *Papua New Guinea: A Political History.* Richmond, Vic: Heinemann Educational Australia.

Guiart, Jean
1951a "Cargo Cults" and Political Evolution in Melanesia. *South Pacific* 5 (7): 128–129.
1951b Forerunners of Melanesian Nationalism. *Oceania* 22:81–90.
1952 John Frum Movement in Tanna. *Oceania* 22 (3): 165–177.
1956a Culture Contact and the "John Frum" Movement on Tanna, New Hebrides. *Southwestern Journal of Anthropology* 12 (1): 105–116.
1956b *Un Siècle et Demi de Contacts Culturels à Tanna, Nouvelles-Hébrides.* Publications de la Société des Océanistes no. 5. Paris: Musée de l'Homme.
1975 Le Mouvement "Four Corner" à Tanna (1974). *Journal de la Société des Océanistes* 46:107–111.

Guidieri, Remo
1988 Two Millenaristic Responses in Oceania. In *Ethnicities and Nations: Processes of Interethnic Relations in Latin America, Southeast Asia and the Pacific,* edited by Remo Guidieri et al, 172–198. Houston: Rothko Chapel Press.

Guillebaud, Jean-Claude
1980 *Un Voyage en Océanie.* Paris: Editions du Seuil.

Guy, Maurice
1959 *So Wild the Wind.* London: Jonathan Cape.

Hamilton, John
1983 The Cargo-cult Chief and the Letters from a God. *Brisbane Courier-Mail,* 1 December, 1–2.

Hanneman, Emil F.
1945 Village Life and Social Change in Madang Society. MA thesis, Department of Anthropology, University of Chicago.

Hannet, Leo
  n.d. Em Rod Bilong Kago. *Kovave* (pilot issue): 47–51.
  1970 Disillusionment with the Priesthood. *Kovave* 2 (1): 22–28.

Haraway, Donna
  1989 *Primate Visions: Gender, Race, and Nature in the World of Modern Science*. New York and London: Routledge.

Harcombe, David
  1991 *Vanuatu: A Travel Survival Kit*. Hawthorn: Lonely Planet.

Harding, Thomas
  1967 A History of Cargoism in Sio, North-East New Guinea. *Oceania* 38:1–23.

Harris, Marvin
  1971 *Culture, Man, and Nature: An Introduction to General Anthropology*. New York: Thomas Y. Crowell.
  1974 *Cows, Pigs, Wars and Witches: The Riddles of Culture*. New York: Random House.
  1991 *Cultural Anthropology*. 3d ed. New York: Harper Collins.

Harwood, John
  1991 Technopolis in Australia: The Rise of a Millennial Cargo Cult. *The Ecologist* 21 (5): 214–219.

Hatch, Robert
  1963 Films (Mondo Cane). *Nation* 196 (16, April 20): 334–335.

Hau'ofa, Epeli
  1975 Anthropology and Pacific Islanders. *Oceania* 45:283–289.

Haviland, William A.
  1989 *Anthropology*. 5th ed. Fort Worth, TX: Holt, Rinehart & Winston.
  1990 *Cultural Anthropology*. 6th ed. Fort Worth, TX: Holt, Rinehart & Winston.

Hempenstall, Peter, and Noel Rutherford
  1984 *Protest and Dissent in the Colonial Pacific*. Suva: University of the South Pacific.

Hermann, Bernard, and Joël Bonnemaison
  1975 *New Hebrides*. Pape'ete: Les Editions du Pacifique.

Hermann, Elfriede
  1992 *The Yali Movement in Retrospect: Rewriting History, Redefining 'Cargo Cult'*. *Oceania* 63: 55–71.

Hoebel, E. Adamson, and Thomas Weaver
1979 *Anthropology and the Human Experience.* 5th ed. New York: McGraw-Hill.

Hogbin, H. Ian
1951 *Transformation Scene.* London: Routledge & Kegan Paul.
1958 *Social Change.* London: Watts.

Holmes, Lowell D.
1980 Cults, Cargo and Christianity: Samoan Responses to Western Religion. *Missiology: An International Review* 8 (4): 471–487.

Höltker, G.
1946 How "Cargo-Cult" Is Born: The Scientific Angle on an Old Subject. *Pacific Islands Monthly* 17 (4, Nov): 16, 70.

HS-B, Honolulu Star-Bulletin
1989 Legend of Hat and Rice Brings Hopes for More. 8 April, A9.
1991 Oh, Lonesome Him. 21 July, A2.

Hood, Gwenyth E.
1990 Medieval Love-Madness and Divine Love. *Mythlore* 61:20–34.

Hours, Bernard
1974 Un mouvement politico-religieux Néo-Hébridais: Le Nagriamel. *Cahiers ORSTOM, Séries Sciences Humaines* 11:227–242.

Howard, Michael C.
1986 *Contemporary Cultural Anthropology.* 2d ed. Boston: Little, Brown.

Howell, Nancy
1986 Demographic Anthropology. *Annual Review of Anthropology* 15:219–246.

Hyndman, David C.
1987 Mining, Modernization, and Movements of Social Protest in Papua New Guinea. *Social Analysis* 21:20–38.

Inselmann, R.
1946 "Cargo Cult" Not Caused by Missions. *Pacific Islands Monthly* 16 (11, June): 44.

Jacopetti, Gualtiero
1963 *Mondo Cane.* New York: Times Film Corporation.

Jarvie, I. C.
1964 *The Revolution in Anthropology.* Chicago: Henry Regnery.

Jawodimbari, Arthur
   1971   Cargo. In *Five New Guinea Plays,* edited by U. Beier, 11–19. Brisbane: Jacaranda Press.

Jebens, Holger
   1990   Cargo-Kulte und Holy Spirit Movements. *Anthropos* 85:403–413.

Kahn, Miriam
   1983   Sunday Christians, Monday Sorcerers: Selective Adaptation to Missionisation in Wamira. *Journal of Pacific History* 18:96–112.

Kaima, Tua Sammyuel
   1989   Attitudes Towards Changing Leadership Patterns in Papua New Guinea. MA thesis, Center for Pacific Islands Studies, University of Hawaii, Honolulu.

Kaplan, Martha
   1990   Meaning, Agency and Colonial History: Navosavakadua and the *Tuka* in Fiji. *American Ethnologist* 17:3–22.

Keesing, Roger
   1978   Politico-Religious Movements and Anti-Colonialism on Malaita: Maasina Rule in Historical Perspective. *Oceania* 48:241–261; 49:46–75.

Keith-Reid, Robert
   1984   Vanuatu: A Nation in Gear. *Islands Business* 10 (8): 12–16.

Kelly, John D., and Martha Kaplan
   1990   History, Structure, and Ritual. *Annual Review of Anthropology* 19:119–150.

Kempf, Wolfgang
   1992   'The Second Coming of the Lord': Early Christianization, Episodic Time, and the Cultural Construction of Continuity in Sibog. *Oceania* 63: 72–86.

Kerpi, Kama
   1975   Cargo. *Kovave* 5 (1): 30–36.

Kilani, Mondher
   1983   *Les Cultes du Cargo Mélanesiens: Mythe et Rationalité en Anthropologie.* Lausanne: Le Forum Anthropologique/Editions d'en Bas.

Kluge, P. F.
   1991   *The Edge of Paradise: America in Micronesia.* New York: Random House.

Kohn, Tamara
1988   A Text in Its Context: F. E. Williams and the Vailala Madness. *Journal of the Anthropological Society of Oxford* 19:25–42.

Kottak, Conrad Phillip
1978   *Anthropology: The Exploration of Human Diversity.* 2d ed. New York: Random House.

Kowalak, Wladyslaw
1982   *Kulty cargo na Nowej Gwinei.* Warsaw: Akademia Teologii Katolickiej.

Kristof, Nicholas D.
1987   Space Age Succeeds Stone Age on Pacific Isle. *New York Times,* 19 July, 1, 6.

Kulick, Don, and Christopher Stroud
1990   Christianity, Cargo and Ideas of Self: Patterns of Literacy in a Papua New Guinean Village. *Man* 25:286–304.

Kuper, Adam
1988   *The Invention of Primitive Society: Transformations of an Illusion.* London and New York: Routledge.

Laboi, Anton
1972   Cargo King. *Papua New Guinea Writing* 6:3–5.

Lamang, Keith Bawon
1976   Gambling with Cards Is a Cargo Cult. *Post-Courier,* 25 March, 2.

Lan, David
1990   Sergeant Ola. In *Desire and Other Plays,* 59–129. London: Faber and Faber.

Langley, Philip
1986   *Popular Participation as a Cargo Cult?* African Environment. Third World Occasional Paper 96. Dakar: ENDA.

Lansner, Tom
1987   Letter from Tanna. *Far Eastern Economic Review,* 20 August, 80.

Lattas, Andrew
1992   Introduction. Hysteria, Anthropological Discourse and the Concept of the Unconscious: Cargo Cults and the Scientisation of Race and Colonial Power. *Oceania* 63: 1–14.

Lawrence, Peter
1954   Cargo Cult and Religious Beliefs among the Garia. *International Archives of Ethnography* 47:1–20.

1964   *Road Belong Cargo: A Study of the Cargo Movement in the Southern Madang District, New Guinea.* Manchester: Manchester University Press.

1987   Cargo Cults. In *The Encyclopedia of Religion,* vol 3, edited by Mircea Eliade, 74–81. New York: Macmillan.

Leavitt, Stephen C.

1989   Cargo, Christ, and Nostalgia for the Dead: Themes of Intimacy and Abandonment in Bumbita Arapesh Social Experience. PhD dissertation, University of California at San Diego.

Leeson, Ida

1952   *Bibliography of Cargo Cults and Other Nativistic Movements in the South Pacific.* South Pacific Commission Technical Paper no. 30. Sydney: South Pacific Commission.

Lemaire, Anika

1977   *Jacques Lacan.* London: Routledge & Kegan Paul.

Levinas, Emmanuel

1979   *Totality and Infinity: An Essay on Exteriority.* The Hague: Martinus Nijhoff.

Levine, Beth

1989   Obsessed by Love. *YM* 37 (8): 68–70.

Lidz, Ruth W., Theodore Lidz, and Burton G. Burton-Bradley

1973   Cargo Cultism: A Psychosocial Study of Melanesian Millenarianism. *The Journal of Nervous and Mental Disease* 157:370–388.

Lindstrom, Lamont

1989   Working Encounters: Oral Histories of World War II Labor Corps from Tanna, Vanuatu. In *The Pacific Theater: Island Representations of World War II,* edited by G. White and L. Lindstrom, 395–417. Pacific Islands Monograph Series no. 8. Honolulu: University of Hawaii Press.

1990   *Knowledge and Power in a South Pacific Society.* Washington, DC: Smithsonian Institution Press.

Lini, Walter

1980   *Beyond Pandemonium: From the New Hebrides to Vanuatu.* Suva: Institute of Pacific Studies, University of the South Pacific.

Loeliger, Carl, and Garry Trompf, eds

1985   *New Religious Movements in Melanesia.* Suva: University of the South Pacific; Port Moresby: University of Papua New Guinea.

Long, Charles H.
1974   Cargo Cults as Cultural Historical Phenomena. *Journal of the American Academy of Religion* 47:403–414.

Luke, Harry
1945   *From a South Seas Diary, 1938–1942.* London: Nicholson & Watson.

Lupsha, Peter A.
1988   The Role of Politics and Political Culture in New Mexico's Economic Development. In *An Economic Development Strategy for New Mexico,* edited by Hank C. Jenkins-Smith and Gilbert K. St. Clair, 78–85. Albuquerque: University of New Mexico Institute for Public Policy.

Maahs, A.
1956   A Sociological Interpretation of the Cargo Cult. PhD dissertation, University of Pittsburgh, Pennsylvania.

MacClancy, Jeremy V.
1983   Vanuatu and Kastom: A Study of Cultural Symbols in the Inception of a National State in the South Pacific. PhD dissertation, Department of Anthropology, Oxford University.

McDonell, Terry
1991   The Japanese Cargo Cult. *Esquire* 116 (4): 41.

McDowell, Nancy
1985   Past and Future: The Nature of Episodic Time in Bun. In *History and Ethnohistory in Papua New Guinea,* edited by D. Gewertz and E. Schieffelin, 26–39. Oceania Monograph no. 28. Sydney: University of Sydney.
1988   A Note on Cargo Cults and Cultural Constructions of Change. *Pacific Studies* 11:121–134.

McKee, Matthew
1989   Waiting for the Skies to Open. *Pacific Islands Monthly* 59 (15, Mar): 26–30.

McLeod, Charles
1947   News from the Field: White Sands. *Quarterly Jottings from the New Hebrides* 216 (Oct): 8.

Mair, Lucy
1948   *Australia in New Guinea.* London: Christophers.

Malik, Michael
   1989   Island Insurrection: Bougainville Rebellion May Keep Mine Closed. *Far Eastern Economic Review,* 3 August, 20–22.

Marsh, Don
   1968   The Surprising Gospels of John Frum: He Who Swept Sin Away. *Pacific Islands Monthly* 39 (10, Oct): 83–90.

Maude, H. E.
   1952   Introduction. In *Bibliography of Cargo Cults and Other Nativistic Movements in the South Pacific,* compiled by Ida Leeson, South Pacific Commission Technical Paper no. 30. Sydney: South Pacific Commission.

May, R. J.
   1990   Political Implications of the Bougainville Crisis for Papua New Guinea. In *The Bougainville Crisis,* edited by R. J. May and M. Spriggs, 55–61. Bathurst, NSW: Crawford House Press.

May, R. J., ed
   1982   *Micronationalist Movements in Papua New Guinea.* Political and Social Change Monograph no. 1. Canberra: Department of Political and Social Change, Research School of Pacific Studies, Australian National University.

Meade, Walter
   1988   The Perilous Lure: Obsessive Love. *Cosmopolitan* 205 (6): 170–173.

Meloy, J. Reid
   1989   Unrequited Love and the Wish to Kill: Diagnosis and Treatment of Borderline Erotomania. *Bulletin of the Menniger Clinic* 53 (6): 477–492.

Merton, Thomas
   1968   *The Geography of Lograire.* New York: New Directions.
   1979   *Love and Living.* New York: Farrar, Straus, Giroux.

Mettler, Ruben F.
   1980   The Cargo Cult Mentality in America. *Business Week,* 22 September, 22.

Michener, James A.
   1951   *Return to Paradise.* New York: Random House.

Modleski, Tania
1982 *Loving with a Vengeance: Mass-produced Fantasies for Women.* New York: Routledge.

Mosoro, Michael
1975 Stone Hide Our Cargo. *Papua New Guinea Writing* 18:5, 11.

Muller, Kal
1974 Tanna Awaits the Coming of John Frum. *National Geographic* 145 (5): 706–715.

Murray, J. S.
1949 Natives and Whites in New Hebrides. *Pacific Islands Monthly* 19 (8, Mar): 61.

Narokobi, Bernard M.
1974 Who Shall Take Up Peli's Challenge? A Philosophical Contribution to the Understanding of Cargo Cults. *Point* 1:93–104.

Nedjar, Louis
1974 *Peuples Oubliés des Nouvelles-Hébrides.* Montreal: Editions Héritage.

Nemours, Pierre
1974 *La Mort sur un Volcan.* Paris: Editions Fleuve Noir.

NYT, New York Times
1970 On a Pacific Island, They Wait for the G.I. Who Became a God. 19 April, 7.

Niven, Larry, and Steven Barnes
1981 *Dream Park.* San Francisco: Ace Books.

Ogan, Eugene
1972 *Business and Cargo: Socio-economic Change among the Nasioi of Bougainville.* New Guinea Research Bulletin no. 44. Port Moresby and Canberra: Institute for Applied Social and Economic Research.
1974 Cargoism and Politics in Bougainville. *Journal of Pacific History* 9:117–129.
1989 Plans to Aid PNG Favour Wealthy, Not Underdogs. *Canberra Times,* 6–12 July, 14.
1990 Perspectives on a Crisis (5). In *Bougainville: Perspectives on a Crisis,* edited by P. Polomka, 35–39. Canberra Papers on Strategy and Defence no. 66. Canberra: Strategic and Defence Studies Centre,

Research School of Pacific Studies, Australian National University.

O'Neill, Chuck
1988   Wacky Tribe Thinks Ex-prez LBJ Is a God! *Weekly World News,* 6 December, 29.

Opeba, Willington Jojoga
1987   Melanesian Cult Movements as Traditional Religious and Ritual Responses to Change. In *The Gospel Is Not Western: Black Theologies from the Southwest Pacific,* edited by G. Trompf, 49–66. Maryknoll, NY: Orbis Books.

O'Reilly, Patrick
1937   Sorcellerie et Civilisation Européenne aux Iles Salomon. In *La Sorcellerie dans les Pays de Mission,* 142–158. Section Missiologique no. 25. Paris: Desclee de Brouwer.
1949   Prophetisme aux Nouvelles-Hébrides: Le Mouvement Jonfrum à Tanna. *Le Monde Non-Chrétien* 10:192–208.

O'Reilly, Patrick, and Jean-Marie Sedes
1949   *Jaunes, Noirs et Blancs: Trois Années de Guerre aux Iles Salomon.* Paris: Editions du Monde Nouveau.

Otto, Ton
1991   The Politics of Tradition in Baluan: Social Change and the Construction of the Past in a Manus Society. PhD dissertation, Department of Anthropology, Research School of Pacific Studies, Australian National University, Canberra.

PIM, Pacific Islands Monthly
1941a   Crazy Natives: Strange Outbreak in Gulf Division of Papua. 11 (8, Mar): 18.
1941b   "Mekeo Madness": Queer Religious Hysteria in Papua. 12 (4, Nov): 50.
1948a   Alleged Anti-Exploitation Movement in Hebrides: Missionary Accuses Planters-Traders—Again! 19 (5, Dec): 92.
1948b   Restless Sepik Natives: Adherents of "Cargo Cult." 18 (7, Feb): 62.
1950   They Still Believe in Cargo Cult. 20 (10, May): 85.
1951   Another Native Messiah Goes to Gaol: Dealing with Cargo Cults in Melanesia. 22 (5, Dec): 103–104.
1955   Cargo Cult? Bainings Natives Killed by New Britain Patrol. 25 (12, July): 67.

1958   Many "Still Believe" in Cargo Cult: The Cargo Cult Won't Die Quietly in the Pacific. 28 (7, Feb): 59.
1959   Their Cargo-Cult Wasn't Anti-European. 30 (4, Nov): 136–137.
1962   Americans, Cargo Cult and the Future: Complicated Aftermath of the New Guinea Buka Troubles. 33 (5, Dec): 27–29.
1991   Minefield of Adventure Found in Vanuatu. 61 (2, Feb): 40.

Pataki-Schweizer, K. J.
1976   Meth-Drinkers and Lotus-Eaters: Some Educational Aspects of Transcultural Psychiatry in Papua New Guinea. *Australian and New Zealand Journal of Psychiatry* 10:129–131.

Poirier, Jean
1949   Les Mouvements de Libération Mythique aux Nouvelles-Hébrides. *Journal de la Société des Océanistes* 5 (5): 97–103.

Pokawin, Stephen
1984   Cargo Cults and Development. In Cargo Cults and Development in Melanesia, edited by W. Ferea, 73–82. Ms, University of Papua New Guinea, Port Moresby.

PC, Post-Courier (Papua New Guinea)
1976a   Clamp Down on Cults. 30 September, 3.
1976b   Cults Will Continue. 24 February, 8.
1976c   E.N.B. Leaders Condemn the Cargo Cults. 21 December, 7.
1977a   Projects in Danger at Pomio: Cargo Cult Must Stop . . . Or Else. 28 July, 11.
1977b   Robbery—Highlanders' Version of Cargo Cult. 18 August, 19 (by an Enga Highlander).
1978   Guise Warns on Cult Mass Killings. 18 December, 1, 4.
1980   Levi Warns of Cargo "Delusion." 27 May, 13.
1983a   "Aussies Go Home." 18 August, 3.
1983b   Editorial: Happy Event on Hanover. 19 August, 4.
1983c   Hanover Awaits Christ. 17 August, 3.
1983d   Mission Failed: Cultists Left. 25 August, 3.

Pouillet, André
1992   Une Suite à la Présence Américaine: L'Affaire John Frum. *Bulletin de la Société d'Etudes Historique de la Nouvelle Calédonie* 92:37–44.

Pouwer, J.
1958   Letter to the Editor. *Oceania* 28 (3): 247–252.

Power, Tony
1972 Ode to a New Guinea Man. *Kovave* 4 (1): 8–9.

Pratkanis, Anthony R.
1992 The Cargo-cult Science of Subliminal Persuasion. *Skeptical Inquirer* 16:261–272.

Priday, H. E. L.
1950 "Jonfrum" Is New Hebridean "Cargo Cult": Interesting History of this Native Movement on the Island of Tanna. *Pacific Islands Monthly* 20 (6, Jan): 67–70; 20 (7, Feb): 59–65.

QJNH, Quarterly Jottings from the New Hebrides
1959 Resume of Recent New Items. 263 (Oct): 4–6.

Quirk, Tom, Tim Duncan, and Richard de Lautour
1990 The Clever Country as a Cargo Cult: National Needs and Higher Education. *Quadrant* 34 (10): 45–50; 34 (11): 59–65.

Ramsey, Margaret A., and Frank W. Lutz
1975 The Cargo Cult in the Isles of Higher Education. *Journal of the College and University Personnel Association* 26 (1): 26–33.

Raspberry, William
1986 Tapping the Poor's Capacity to Produce. *Tulsa World*, 7 January, 11.

Rentoul, Alexander
1949 "John Frum": Origin of New Hebrides Movement. *Pacific Islands Monthly* 19 (6, Jan): 31.

Rice, Edward
1974 *John Frum He Come: A Polemical Work about a Black Tragedy.* Garden City, NY: Doubleday.

Richardson, David J.
1987 Roots of Unrest: Decolonialization in Vanuatu with Particular Reference to Tanna. MA thesis, Department of History, University of Hawaii, Honolulu.

Rimoldi, M. R.
1971 The Hahalis Welfare Society of Buka, New Guinea. PhD dissertation, Department of Anthropology, Australian National University, Canberra.

Robinson, Neville K.
1981 *Villagers at War: Some Papua New Guinea Experiences in World War II.* Pacific Research Monograph no. 2. Canberra: Australian National University.

Robinson, Phyllis M.
1950 Intellectual Opposition in Conditions of Culture Contact. BA thesis, Department of Anthropology, Sydney University.

Roscoe, Paul B.
1988 The Far Side of Hurun: The Management of Melanesian Millenarian Movements. *American Ethnologist* 15:515–529.

Rosenstiel, Annette
1953 An Anthropological Approach to the Mau Mau Problem. *Political Science Quarterly* 68:419–432.

Ruhen, Olaf
1957 *Land of Dahori: Tales of New Guinea.* Philadelphia: J. B. Lippincott.
1963 *Mountains in the Clouds.* Adelaide: Rigby.

Ryan, D'Arcy
1947 The Influence of the Missions on Native Culture in Melanesia. BA Honors thesis, Department of Anthropology, University of Sydney.

Ryan, Peter
1992 New Symbols for Same Old Cargo Cult. *Age,* 26 September, 2.

Ryman, Anders
1987/ John Frum: Won't You Please Come Home? *Geo: Australasia's*
1988 *Geographic Magazine* 9 (4): 78–93.

Said, Edward
1978 *Orientalism.* New York: Pantheon Books.

Salisbury, R. F.
1958 An "Indigenous" New Guinea Cult. *Kroeber Anthropological Society Papers* 18:67–78.

Scarr, Deryck
1984 *Fiji: A Short History.* Laie, HI: Institute for Polynesian Studies, Brigham Young University.

Schwartz, Theodore
1973 Cult and Context: The Paranoid Ethos in Melanesia. *Ethos* 1:153–174.

1976 The Cargo Cult: A Melanesian Type Response to Change. In *Responses to Change: Society, Culture, and Personality*, edited by George Devos, 157–206. New York: A. Van Nostrand.

Schwarz, Brian
1984 Holy Spirit Movements. In *An Introduction to Melanesian Religions*, edited by E. Mantovani, 255–278. Point Series no. 6. Goroka: The Melanesian Institute for Pastoral and Socio-Economic Service.

Schwimmer, Erik G.
1977 F. E. Williams as Ancestor and Rain Maker. In *Francis Edgar Williams: 'The Vailala Madness' and Other Essays*, edited by E. Schwimmer, 11–47. Honolulu: University Press of Hawaii.

Scott, Michael W.
1990/ Constitutions of Maasina Rule: Timothy George and the *Iora*.
1991 *Chicago Anthropology Exchange* 19:41–65.

Shadbolt, Maurice, and Olaf Ruhen
1968 *Isles of the South Pacific*. Washington, DC: National Geographic Society.

Shears, Richard
1980 *The Coconut War: The Crisis on Espiritu Santo*. Sydney: Cassell Australia.

Siikala, Jukka
1979 The Cargo Proper in Cargo Cults. *Temenos* 15:68–80.

Simpson, Colin
1979 *Pleasure Islands of the South Pacific*. Sydney: Methuen.

Sinclair, Alexander
1957 *Field and Clinical Survey Report of the Mental Health of the Indigenes of the Territory of Papua and New Guinea*. Port Moresby: Territory of Papua and New Guinea.

Skole, Joe
1986 Vanuatu—A Small Republic That's Very Big on Volcanoes. *San Francisco Examiner*, 12 October, T20–21.

Smyth, W. John
1975 Some Reflections on the Teaching of Economics and Commerce in a Developing Country. *Journal of Economic Education* 7 (1): 45–49.

Souter, Gavin
1964 *New Guinea: The Last Unknown.* London: Angus & Robertson.

Standish, Bill
1989 Bougainville: Undermining the State in Papua New Guinea. *Pacific Research* 2 (4): 3–5, 10.

Stanley, David
1989 *South Pacific Handbook.* 4th ed. Chico, CA: Moon Publications.

Stanner, W. E. H.
1958 On the Interpretation of Cargo Cults. *Oceania* 29:1–25.

Steinbauer, Friedrich
1979 *Melanesian Cargo Cults: New Salvation Movements in the South Pacific.* St. Lucia: University of Queensland Press.

Stephen, Michelle
1971 *Cargo Cult Hysteria.* Occasional Paper no. 1. Melbourne: Research Centre of Southwestern Pacific Studies, La Trobe University.

Stow, Randolph
1979 *Visitants.* London: Secker & Warburg.

Strelen, John G.
1977 *Search for Salvation: Studies in the History and Theology of Cargo Cults.* Adelaide: Lutheran Publishing House.

Suhre, Terry
1990 Locations of Desire: New Work by Phyllis Bramson, Michiko Itatani, and Vera Klement. *The Living Museum* 52 (2): 23–25.

Swatridge, Colin
1985 *Delivering the Goods: Education as Cargo in Papua New Guinea.* Manchester: Manchester University Press.

Territory of New Guinea
1935 *Report to the Council of the League of Nations on the Administration of the Territory of New Guinea, from 1st July, 1933, to 30th June, 1934.* Canberra: Australian Government Printer.

1936 *Report to the Council of the League of Nations on the Administration of the Territory of New Guinea, from 1st July 1934, to 30th June, 1935.* Canberra: Australian Government Printer.

1937 *Report to the Council of the League of Nations on the Administration of the Territory of New Guinea, from 1st July, 1935, to 30th June, 1936.* Canberra: Australian Government Printer.

1939   *Report to the Council of the League of Nations on the Administration of the Territory of New Guinea, from 1st July, 1937, to 30th June, 1938.* Canberra: Australian Government Printer.

Territory of Papua
1942   *Annual Report for the Year 1940–1941.* Canberra: Australian Government Printer.

Theroux, Paul
1992   *The Happy Isles of Oceania: Paddling the Pacific.* New York: G. P. Putnam's Sons.

Thomas, Gordon
1935   A Plea for Better Regulation of Mission Activities in New Guinea. *Pacific Islands Monthly* 6 (4, Nov): 25–26.

Thornton, Robert
1991   The End of the Future? *Anthropology Today* 7 (1): 1–2.

Thorpe, John
1972   *The Cargo Cult.* Bolinas: Big Sky Books.

Tiffin, Helen
1981   Melanesian Cargo Cults in *Tourmaline* and *Visitants. Journal of Commonwealth Literature* 16:109–125.

Toner, Stephen J.
1988   Television and the American Imagination: Notions of Romance. *Journal of Popular Culture* 22 (3): 1–13.

Torgovnick, Marianna
1990   *Gone Primitive: Savage Intellects, Modern Lives.* Chicago: University of Chicago Press.

Trompf, Garry W.
1981   Melanesian "Cargo Cults" Today. *Current Affairs Bulletin* 58 (1): 19–22.
1984   What Has Happened to Melanesian "Cargo Cults"? In *Religious Movements in Melanesia Today (3)*, edited by Wendy Flannery, 29–51. Point Series no. 4. Goroka: Melanesian Institute for Pastoral and Socio-Economic Service.
1990   The Cargo and the Millennium on Both Sides of the Pacific. In *Cargo Cults and Millenarian Movements: Transoceanic Comparisons of New Religious Movements*, edited by Garry Trompf, 35–94. Berlin: Mouton de Gruyter.
1991   *Melanesian Religion.* Cambridge: Cambridge University Press.

Trumbull, Robert
1977 *Tin Roofs and Palm Trees: A Report on the New South Seas.* Seattle: University of Washington Press.

Tucker, Frank
1988 The Relationship between Cargo Cult and Rebel Movement in Irian Jaya. *Catalyst* 18 (2): 163–186.

Vanuatu Institute of Technology
1981 *Vanuatu: Discover Our Islands.* Port Vila: Vanuatu Institute of Technology.

Villaret, Bernard
1975 *Au Vent des Iles: Deux Cent Soixante Quinze Paradis (ou Enfers) Insulaires de par le Monde.* Paris: Berger-Levrault.

Voice of Vanuatu
1981 VP Platform—A New Cargo Cult? 84 (10 July): 4.

Wagner, Roy
1979 The Talk of Koriki: A Daribi Contact Cult. *Social Research* 46:140–165.
1981 *The Invention of Culture.* Rev and exp ed. Chicago: University of Chicago Press.

Waiko, J.
n.d. Why We Do Not Receive Cargo from Our Dead Relatives. *Kovave* (pilot issue): 28–31.
1973 European-Melanesia Contact in Melanesian Tradition and Literature. In *Priorities in Melanesian Development,* edited by R. May, 417–428. Canberra: Australian National University; Port Moresby: University of Papua New Guinea.

Walker, Martin
1989 The Cult of Russia's New Rich. *Manchester Guardian Weekly,* 19 Nov, 21–22.

Wallace, Irving, David Wallechinsky, and Amy Wallace
1984 They Wanted to Buy Lyndon Johnson. *Los Angeles Times,* 22 April.

Walter, Michael A. H. B.
1983 Cargo Cults: Forerunners of Progress. In *Religious Movements in Melanesia Today (1),* edited by W. Flannery, 190–204. Point Series no. 2. Goroka: The Melanesian Institute of Pastoral and Socio-Economic Service.

Watkins, June E.
1951   Messianic Movements: A Comparative Study of Some Religious Cults among the Melanesians, Maoris, and North American Indians. MA thesis, Department of Anthropology, University of Sydney.

Webster, Paul
1992   Hi-tech Mickey—Overpriced, Over the Top, and Over Here. *Manchester Guardian Weekly* 146 (16, 19 April): 7.

Weightman, B., and H. Lini, eds
1980   *Vanuatu: Twenty-Wan Tingting long Taem Blong Independens.* Suva: Institute of Pacific Studies, University of the South Pacific.

Wetherell, David, and Charlotte Carr-Gregg
1984   Moral Re-Armament in Papua, 1931–42. *Oceania* 54:177–203.

Weymouth, Ross
1984   The Bible and Revival Movements. In *Religious Movements in Melanesia Today (3),* edited by W. Flannery, 195–208. Point Series no. 4. Goroka: The Melanesian Insitute for Pastoral and Socio-Economic Service.

White, Geoffrey M., and Lamont Lindstrom, eds
1989   *The Pacific Theater: Island Representations of World War II.* Honolulu: University of Hawaii Press.

Whiteman, Darrell
1984   The Cultural Dynamics of Religious Movements. In *Religious Movements in Melanesia Today (3),* edited by W. Flannery, 52–79. Point Series no. 4. Goroka: The Melanesian Institute for Pastoral and Socio-Economic Service.

Williams, F. E.
1923   *The Vailala Madness and the Destruction of Native Ceremonies in the Gulf Division.* Anthropology Report no. 4. Port Moresby[?]: Territory of Papua.
1934   The Vailala Madness in Retrospect. In *Essays Presented to C. G. Seligman,* edited by E. E. Evans-Pritchard et al, 369–379. London: Routledge & Kegan Paul.

Willis, Paul
1990   *Common Culture: Symbolic Work at Play in the Everyday Cultures of the Young.* Boulder, CO, and San Francisco: Westview Press.

Willis, Susan
1991   *A Primer for Daily Life.* London: Routledge.

Wilson, Bryan R.
1973   *Magic and the Millennium: A Sociological Study of Religious Movements of Protest among Tribal and Third-World Peoples.* New York: Harper & Row.

Woodcock, George
1976   *South Sea Journey.* London: Faber & Faber.

Worsley, Peter
1957   *The Trumpet Shall Sound: A Study of "Cargo" Cults in Melanesia.* London: Macgibbon & Kee.

Wright, Derek
1985   Fragments: The Cargo Connection. *Kunapipi* 7 (1): 45–58.
1986   The Mansren Myth in Randolph Stow's *Visitants. International Fiction Review* 13 (2): 82–86.

Žižek, Slavoj
1989   *The Sublime Object of Ideology.* London: Verso.

Index

ABOUT THE AUTHOR

Lamont Lindstrom is professor of anthropology at the University of Tulsa. Since 1978 he has been involved in anthropological and linguistic research projects in Melanesia, primarily in Vanuatu. He is the author of *Knowledge and Power in a South Pacific Society* and a co-author of *Kava: The Pacific Drug*.

SOUTH SEA BOOKS

Lee Boo of Belau: A Prince in London, by Daniel J. Peacock, 1987.

Nuclear Playground, by Stewart Firth, 1987.

France and the South Pacific: A Contemporary History, by Stephen Henningham, 1992.

Isle of Resilience: Conflict and Dreamspace in Tanna, by Joël Bonnemaison, forthcoming 1994.

Production Notes

Composition and paging were done on the
Quadex Composing System and typesetting
on the Compugraphic 8400 by the design
and production staff of University of
Hawaii Press.

The text and display typeface is Compugraphic
Bembo.

Offset presswork and binding were done by
The Maple-Vail Book Manufacturing Group.
Text paper is Glatfelter Offset Vellum,
basis 50.